ACCOUNTING
MADE SIMPLE

REVISED EDITION

A Made Simple Book
Broadway Books
New York

ACCOUNTING MADE SIMPLE

REVISED EDITION

Joseph Peter Simini, C.P.A., D.B.A.

Distinguished Professor Emeritus
Accounting and Information Systems
University of San Francisco

A MADE SIMPLE BOOK
DOUBLEDAY
NEW YORK LONDON TORONTO SYDNEY AUCKLAND

The Library of Congress Cataloging-in-Publication Data has cataloged the Doubleday edition as:
Simini, Joseph Peter.
   Accounting made simple.
   Includes index.
   1. Accounting. 1. Title.
HF5635.S593 1987   657   86-21786
ISBN 0-385-23280-2 (pbk.)

23 22 21 20 19 18 17 16 15 14

DEDICATED TO THE MEMORY OF MY FATHER AND MOTHER
PAUL AND IDA SIMINI

AND TO MY PATIENT WIFE
MARCELLINE

ABOUT THIS BOOK

This book has been designed to continue the study of accounting where *Bookkeeping Made Simple* ended. There is a great deal more to the subject than the simple posting of books. Accounting is a basic management tool; used properly, it helps management determine the efficiency of the organization. Of course, it measures the success or failure of business operations in terms of dollars, but more than that it points out weaknesses and indicates areas of improvement.

It is assumed that the reader of this book knows the elements of bookkeeping; if he does not, it is suggested that he first read *Bookkeeping Made Simple* in this same Made Simple series. For those readers who studied bookkeeping some time ago and who may not remember some basic bookkeeping principles and techniques *Bookkeeping Made Simple* will serve as an excellent refresher as well.

This book is organized to follow the accounting curriculum in most colleges and will, it is hoped, serve as a useful supplementary text for college use. Considerable emphasis has been placed on cost accounting—though the treatment is, necessarily, less extensive than will be found in specialized cost accounting texts. The reasons for this emphasis are made clear at the beginning of Chapters 11 and 12.

Most of the chapters are followed by sets of practice exercises. These are designed to test your understanding of the material presented in the text. It is strongly recommended that you work out all the exercises and check your answers with those given at the back of the book.

I would like to express my appreciation to New England Business Services, Pegboard Systems, Inc., and First America Title Insurance Company of San Francisco for the use of their forms; also the University of San Francisco for the use of its library. In reading the book prior to its revision I realized what a debt of gratitude I owed the editors that helped me in putting together the original edition of this book—Miss Jean Anne Vincent of Doubleday & Company, Inc., and Mr. Robert Ginsburg of Ken Publishing Company, New York. To those who wrote with corrections to the first edition, thank you. To those who at various times and in various places asked, "Are you the one who wrote *Accounting Made Simple?*" and proceeded to tell me how the book helped in their studies in college, or graduate school, or wherever, thank you.

If the reader of this book would like to find sources of forms for his accounting needs, the author will furnish the name of a suitable supplier if the reader will describe his situation in enough detail. These requests should be sent with $2.00 to cover postage and handling to the author at P.O. Box 31420, San Francisco, California 94131-0420.

Many people have a hand in any book. This one is no exception. There are the editors and production people at the publishers. There are those who encourage. And others. But the buck has to stop somewhere. Any mistakes of fact in text and illustration are mine.

To the readers—may you have a pleasant time reading this book. That's the way it was intended.

JOSEPH PETER SIMINI

San Francisco

CONTENTS

Contents

Chapter 1

FINANCIAL STATEMENTS

Owners, managers, suppliers, credit grantors, and others interested in a business enterprise are generally confronted with financial statements prepared by accountants. These include the **Balance Sheet** showing the firm's condition on the last day of the accounting period, an **operations statement** (Profit and Loss Statement) for the accounting period, and a statement that tells about changes in the equity of the owner or owners of the business. In this chapter each of these financial statements will be discussed.

BALANCE SHEET

A business is always in a condition of equality: what it owns equals what it owes to either its creditors or its owners. This can be expressed in equation form:

Assets = Liabilities + Owners' Equity

Assets are those resources that the business owns. **Liabilities** are obligations owed by the business to persons (or businesses) other than its owners. **Owners' Equity** is what the business owes the owners. The Balance Sheet shows all of these elements at the last day of an accounting period. For purposes of analysis and better use of the data presented by the accountant, further classification is considered necessary.

Current Assets. Some assets are of greater utility than others. Financial analysts recognize this greater utility, and a special category of assets, called **current assets,** has been established for inclusion in the Balance Sheet. Current assets include cash and other assets that can reasonably be expected to be converted to cash or sold or consumed in the near future through the normal operations of the business. Cash includes currency or coins and money equivalents (checks, money orders, etc.). Other assets that can reasonably be expected to be converted to cash in the current fiscal period are **accounts receivable** and **notes receivable.**

Accounts receivable are amounts due from customers for purchases of goods or services on open credit. Notes receivable are amounts due from customers for purchases of goods or services evidenced by a formal document called a **promissory note.** Notes receivable may be obtained when a business loans money to others. Assets that can reasonably be expected to be sold in the current fiscal period, in a merchandising (selling or retailing) business, are included in the category **merchandise inventory.** Other assets that can reasonably be expected to be used in the current fiscal period are called **office supplies, store supplies, delivery supplies, prepaid insurance,** and the like. For purposes of the current assets definition, the "near future" is generally defined as one year from the Balance Sheet date.

Plant Assets. Tangible assets that are relatively long-lived (more than one year), are relatively fixed (in size, shape, or form) or permanent in nature, and are used by the business in its operation are called **plant assets,** sometimes also called **fixed assets.** Examples of plant or fixed assets are land, buildings, trucks, typewriters, machinery, and the like. These assets are generally relatively expensive and will be used over long periods of time. The fact that the life of these assets extends over many fiscal periods makes it necessary for the accountant to allocate the cost of the asset to current and future operations on some rational basis. This allocation is called **depreciation accounting** and will be discussed in Chapter 5.

Other Assets. This category includes all assets that cannot be classified as current assets or plant assets. It includes **investments** (in stocks and bonds of other companies, including affiliates, in real estate, in funds for special purposes) and **intangibles** (franchises, patents, copyrights, trademarks, and good will).

Current Liabilities. Those liabilities owed to creditors that must be paid within the current fiscal period (the same time period used for current assets above) are called **current liabilities.** Current liabilities that are incurred on open credit are called **accounts payable.** Current liabilities evidenced by a formal document are called **notes payable.** When a business knows that it owes money to someone other than the owners but has no bill, or the amount is not payable for another few weeks, these liabilities are called **accrued liabilities** and include salaries and wages earned by employees but not yet paid, interest due on obligations of the business, and sales, payroll, and income taxes (where appropriate).

Long-term Liabilities. All liabilities that are not due to be paid in the current fiscal period are called **long-term liabilities.** Businesses are sometimes financed through the use of long-term credit. When the amount due is for money borrowed on a note from a bank or other lender and is not due within the current year, the liability is termed **notes payable.** When the amount due is for money borrowed from a group of investors under a bond indenture contract, the liability is called **bonds payable.** When the amount due is for money borrowed to complete purchases of property, and that property is used as security to insure payment, the liability is called **mortgages payable.** The current portion of the amount due is shown as current liabilities, and the remainder (the noncurrent portion) is shown under long-term liabilities.

Owners' (or Owner's) Equity. The third section of the Balance Sheet tells what the business owes its owners. There are three basic types of ownership—**proprietorship,** an unincorporated business owned by one person; **partnership,** an unincorporated business owned by two or more persons; and **corporation,** an incorporated business owned by one or more persons. On the Balance Sheet, the owners' equity entry shows how much the business owes its owners on the Balance Sheet date. This equity is shown in different ways, depending on the type of ownership.

Central Hardware
Balance Sheet
December 31, 19—

ASSETS

Current Assets
Cash		$ 1,000	
Accounts Receivable		3,000	
Notes Receivable		1,500	
Merchandise Inventory		40,000	
Office Supplies		200	
Store Supplies		300	
Prepaid Insurance		500	
Total Current Assets			$ 46,500

Plant Assets
Land		$ 5,000	
Buildings	$76,000		
Less Accumulated Depreciation	3,000	73,000	
Store Equipment	20,000		
Less Accumulated Depreciation	6,000	14,000	
Total Plant Assets			$ 92,000
Investments			50,000
Patents			10,000
Good Will			5,000
TOTAL ASSETS			$203,500

LIABILITIES

Current Liabilities
Accounts Payable	$15,000	
Notes Payable	5,000	
Accrued Salaries	1,000	
Accrued Taxes	2,000	
Total Current Liabilities		$ 23,000

Long-term Liabilities
Notes Payable	$20,000	
Mortgages Payable	50,000	
Total Long-term Liabilities		70,000
TOTAL LIABILITIES		$ 93,000

CAPITAL

William Jones, Capital	110,500
TOTAL LIABILITIES AND CAPITAL	$203,500

The Balance Sheet is for a proprietorship. In the capital section only one line appears, showing the ending balance of capital. If the same business was owned by two partners equally, the Balance Sheet shown on page 3 would be the same except for the capital section, which would then read:

CAPITAL

James Jefferson, Capital	$55,250	
Robert Washington, Capital	55,250	
TOTAL CAPITAL		$110,500

(It is not necessary that the partners' capital accounts be equal. A partnership equity section could read

Frank Fournier, Capital	$57,000	
John Bugatto, Capital	53,500	
TOTAL CAPITAL		$110,500

if the formula for recording equity changes in the partnership and other factors made the equities come out this way.)

If the same business was organized as a corporation the Balance Sheet would be the same except for the capital section, which would be changed to read:

CAPITAL

Common Stock $100 par value (500 shares authorized, issued, and outstanding)	$50,000	
Retained Earnings	60,500	
TOTAL CAPITAL		$110,500

Here are some important facts to remember about Balance Sheets:

1. They are prepared to reflect the financial condition of the business at a particular date.
2. The heading is always as follows:

Name of Company
Balance Sheet (or Statement of Condition)
Date

3. The assets and liabilities are classified into meaningful categories.
4. The capital section changes with type of ownership.
5. Total assets always equal total liabilities and capital.

FORMS OF PRESENTATION

The Balance Sheet shown above is called the **report form.** If the assets are shown on the left and totaled, and the liabilities and capital shown on the right and totaled, the resulting balance sheet is called the **account form.** This might be shown schematically as follows:

Central Hardware
Balance Sheet
December 31, 19—

ASSETS			LIABILITIES		
Current Assets			Current Liabilities		
Cash	XX		Accounts Payable	XX	
Etc.	XX		Etc.	XX	
		XX			XX
Plant Assets			Long-term Liabilities		
Land	XX		Notes Payable	XX	
Etc.	XX		Etc.	XX	
		XX			XX
Investments		XX	**TOTAL LIABILITIES**		$ 93,000
Patents		XX			
Good Will		XX	**CAPITAL**		
			William Jones, Capital		110,500
			TOTAL LIABILITIES AND		

Either the report form or the account form is correct. Generally, published annual reports use the report form. The liability section is occasionally shown after the capital section. In proprietorships and partnerships, we sometimes find the capital statement incorporated into the Balance Sheet, so that changes in equity can be read directly on the Balance Sheet, eliminating the use of the capital statement as a separate presentation. Sometimes the balance sheet figures for the current year-end and the past year-end are shown. This allows for an immediate comparison of the financial positions at those dates.

BALANCE SHEET ANALYSIS

There are some relationships that can be developed from Balance Sheet figures. One is the **current ratio,** which tells how many times the current liabilities could be paid with the current assets. The formula is:

$$\text{Current Ratio} = \frac{\text{Current Assets}}{\text{Current Liabilities}}$$

Another is **working capital,** which tells how much in current assets would be left over if all current liabilities were paid with the current assets. The formula is:

Working Capital
$$= \text{Current Assets} - \text{Current Liabilities}$$

Another is the **acid-test ratio,** which tells how many times the current liabilities can be paid with the so-called liquid current assets. The formula is:

$$\text{Acid-Test Ratio} = \frac{\text{Cash} + \text{Notes and Accounts Receivable} + \text{Readily Marketable Securities}}{\text{Current Liabilities}}$$

All of these relationships are measures of a business's financial strength and are used by owners, managers, lenders, and others in evaluating the company's ability to pay its obligations. The ratios that might be indications of healthy financial strength vary from one type of business to another, and can best be obtained for a particular business from the auditor, from a trade association for that industry, or from a banker or stockbroker. Working capital varies, depending on the type of business and its size. Generally, local banks will help interested persons to analyze a business.

STATEMENT OF PROPRIETORS' EQUITY

Besides knowing the condition of the business as a whole on any one particular date, we may want to know what changes have occurred in the equity since the last time a Balance Sheet had been prepared.

Investments. These are what the owners put into the business in terms of assets, less the liabilities assumed by the business. An owner can invest cash (an asset), or a building (another asset) *and* the mortgage (a liability) due on it. The investment may be made at the beginning of the business or at any time during its life. The beginning balance of any one period is the total of all undistributed equity up to that time.

Disinvestments. These are what the owners take out of the business in terms of assets, less business liabilities assumed by the owner. Usually the owners take out less than the profit the business generates. If this procedure is followed, the business will grow in size. In a proprietorship or partnership, generally, there is no restriction on how much the owners may disinvest. In a corporation there are certain restrictions on what may be given to the owners.

Profits and Losses from Operations. If a business generates a profit, the equity becomes greater and assets minus liabilities become equally greater. (Remember, assets always equal liabilities plus equity.) If a business operates at a loss, the equity becomes smaller, and the assets minus liabilities become equally smaller.

Equity Statement—Proprietorship:

Central Hardware
Statement of Proprietor's Capital
Year Ending December 31, 19—
[OR Year Ended December 31, 19—]*
[OR January 1–December 31, 19—]

Equity Balance, January 1, 19—	$ 92,500
Profit for Year 19—	70,000
Investment During Year	5,000
	$167,500
Less Withdrawals	57,000
Balance, December 31, 19—	$110,500

* Note alternative treatment.

Equity Statement—Partnership:

Central Hardware
Statement of Partners' Capital
Year Ending (Ended) December 31, 19—
OR January 1–December 31, 19—*

	Jefferson	Washington
Equity Balance, January 1, 19—	$46,250	$46,250
Profit for Year 19—	35,000	35,000
Investment During Year	2,500	2,500
	$83,750	$83,750
Less Withdrawals	28,500	28,500
Balance, December 31, 19—	$55,250	$55,250

* Note alternative treatment.

As we saw earlier, the capital section of a corporation's Balance Sheet is divided into capital stock and retained earnings. Usually, the only changes in equity involve profits or losses for the period, the distribution of retained earnings to the owners, and some other changes to the retained earnings, so a statement is not prepared for all of the equity but only for changes in retained earnings. Any change to equity other than retained earnings can be footnoted on the Balance Sheet.

Capital Section of Balance Sheet—Corporation:

Common Stock $100 par value (500 shares authorized, issued, and outstanding)*	$50,000	
Retained Earnings	60,500	
TOTAL CAPITAL		$110,500

* An additional 50 shares of common stock were sold this year.

Central Hardware Corp.
Retained Earnings Statement
OR Earned Surplus Statement*
Year Ending (Ended) December 31, 19—
OR January 1–December 31, 19—*

Retained Earnings Balance, January 1, 19—		$47,500
Profit for Year 19—		25,000
		$72,500
Less: Income Taxes on Profits	$10,000	
Dividends Declared	2,000	$12,000
Balance, December 31, 19—		$60,500

* Note alternative treatment.

OPERATIONS STATEMENT

The owners and other interested parties want to know how much profit (or loss) was generated by operations. In other words, did running a hardware store this year prove profitable or not? What were the sales and expenses? The Profit and Loss Statement (or Income and Expense Statement) for the period answers these questions.

Income and Expense. The net increase in assets due to operations (sales of goods or services) is called **income** (or **revenue**). Because a business has sold goods or rendered a service, assets in the form of cash, accounts or notes receivable, or some other asset are increased. In all businesses income is produced while at the same time the business is burdened with certain expenses. **Expenses** are the costs expired during the period related to the production of income. The concept of cost expiration is one that is best explained on the basis of its effects. One effect is that equity is reduced. When the equity of a business is reduced because it is necessary to produce income, there is expired cost. It may be the result of a single event (replacing a broken pane of glass) or a continuing event (labor performed by workers). The second effect may be that assets are reduced in value because cash has been paid out or asset utility has been decreased, or that liabilities are increased as equity is decreased.

If income is measured when cash is received, and expenses are measured when cash is spent, the business is said to be operating on a **cash basis.** If income and expenses are measured when the transactions occur (regardless of the physical or constructive flow of cash), the business is said to be operating on an **accrual basis.**

Types of Businesses. There are three basic types of businesses classified according to operations: service, merchandising, and manufacturing. A business that gives advice or service exclusively and in which there is no transfer of title to goods is a **service** business. Examples include a law, medical, or accounting practice, or a dry cleaner. A business that acquires goods for sale to its customers is a **merchandising** business, such as a department store, mail-order house, grocery store, or shoe store. A business that changes the form of goods by analysis or synthesis, or that assembles goods, is a **manufacturing** business, such as a refinery (analysis), steel mill (synthesis), or auto assembly plant.

Each type of business has its own form of operations statement, and the following are examples:

Service Business:

William Smith, M.D.
Income Statement
Year Ending (Ended) December 31, 19—
OR January 1–December 31, 19—

Fee Income		$60,000
Expenses:		
Salaries	$6,000	
Rent	4,000	
Telephone	600	
Supplies	2,000	
Car Rental	2,400	
		$15,000
PROFIT FOR YEAR		$45,000

Fee Income		$200,000
Expenses:		
Salaries	$50,000	
Rent	12,000	
Telephone	2,700	
Supplies	5,000	
Licenses	500	
Insurance	14,000	
		84,200
PROFIT FOR YEAR		$115,800

Merchandising Business:

Jones Bakery
Income Statement
Year Ending (Ended) December 31, 19—
OR January 1–December 31, 19—

Sales		$840,000
Cost of Goods Sold		
(see separate schedule)		490,000
GROSS PROFIT ON SALES		$350,000
Expenses:		
Selling	$210,000	
Administrative	60,000	270,000
NET PROFIT FROM OPERATIONS		$ 80,000

The Cost of Goods Sold is determined by pricing each sale or by means of a formula:

	Beginning Inventory
plus	Purchases
equals	Goods Available for Sale
less	Ending Inventory
equals	Cost of Goods Sold

The Cost of Goods Sold Schedule usually appears on the financial statements as an exhibit shown separately, although it can be included in the operations statement. When it is shown separately, it appears as follows:

Jones Bakery
Cost of Goods Sold Schedule
Year Ending (Ended) December 31, 19—
OR January 1–December 31, 19—

Inventory, January 1, 19—	$ 35,000
Purchases During the Year	526,000
Goods Available for Sale	$561,000
Inventory, December 31, 19—	71,000
COST OF GOODS SOLD	$490,000

Manufacturing Business:

The basic operating statement is the same for a manufacturing business as it is for a merchandising business although the titles in the Cost of Goods Sold Schedule are changed:

	Beginning Inventory
plus	Cost of Goods Manufactured
	(see separate schedule)
equals	Goods Available for Sale
less	Ending Inventory
equals	Cost of Goods Sold

Cost of Goods Manufactured is calculated as follows:

	Beginning Work-in-Process Inventory
plus	Direct Labor Used During Period
plus	Direct Materials Used During Period
plus	Overhead for Period
equals	Total Work-in-Process During Period
less	Ending Work-in-Process Inventory
equals	Cost of Goods Manufactured

Here are some important facts to remember about operations statements:

1. They are prepared to reflect the results of operations over a *period* of time, rather than at *one moment* in time, as is the Balance Sheet.
2. The heading is always

Name of Company
Income Statement (or equivalent title)
Some period of time

3. The operations statement varies with the type of business operation.
4. In more complicated types of business operations, supporting schedules can be used to make the statement more meaningful.

Operations Statement Analysis. Certain comparative figures are often given on an operations statement. One is the ratio of Cost of Goods Sold to Sales, which measures the Cost of Goods Sold as a percentage of Sales:

$$\frac{\text{Cost of Goods Sold}}{\text{Sales}} \times 100\%$$

In Jones Bakery (above) the Cost of Goods Sold to Sales Ratio is:

$$\frac{\$490,000}{\$840,000} \times 100\% = 58.33\%$$

Another is Gross Profit to Sales, which measures the percentage of Sales left after the Cost of Goods Sold is subtracted. Gross Profit to Sales tells what percentage of the sales are available for selling and administrative expenses and profits. The formula is:

$$\frac{\text{Gross Profit}}{\text{Sales}} \times 100\%$$

Again, in Jones Bakery (above) the Gross Profit to Sales Ratio is:

$$\frac{\$350,000}{\$840,000} \times 100\% = 41.67\%$$

Another is Selling Expenses to Sales, which measures the percentage of Sales spent for purposes of selling the goods (advertising, salespeople's salaries, etc.). The formula is:

$$\frac{\text{Selling Expenses}}{\text{Sales}} \times 100\%$$

Again, in Jones Bakery (above) the Selling Expense to Sales Ratio is:

$$\frac{\$210,000}{\$840,000} \times 100\% = 25.00\%$$

Another is Administrative Expenses to Sales, which measures the percentage of Sales spent for administrative purposes (officers' salaries, insurance, office equipment, etc.). The formula is:

$$\frac{\text{Administrative Expenses}}{\text{Sales}} \times 100\%$$

Again, in Jones Bakery (above) the Administrative Expense to Sales Ratio is:

$$\frac{\$60,000}{\$840,000} \times 100\% = 7.14\%$$

Another is Net Profit to Sales, which measures the percentage of the Sales that reflects profit to the business. The formula is:

$$\frac{\text{Net Profit}}{\text{Sales}} \times 100\%$$

Again, in Jones Bakery (above) the Net Profit to Sales Ratio is:

$$\frac{\$80,000}{\$840,000} \times 100\% = 9.53\%$$

There are percentages that have been developed by trade associations, banks, and other organizations that help the businessman compare his business' performance to others in the trade to determine if his is more successful or less. The businessman also wants to compare this year's results against those of previous years.

In using these percentages, it is important to compare similar businesses—not a drugstore compared to a grocery store, and it is important to compare businesses in the same locality—not a grocery store in San Francisco to one in New York. National or regional figures or percentages are sometimes employed for comparative purposes, but you should recognize that some small deviations might occur between the business under analysis and the figures or percentages used.

St. John Grocery
Income Statement
Year Ended December 31, 19—

Sales	$212,000	100.0%
Cost of Goods Sold	162,200	76.5
Gross Profit on Sales	$ 49,800	23.5
Operating Expenses:		
Selling Expenses	$20,000	9.4
Administrative Expenses	17,400	8.2
Total Operating Expenses	37,400	17.6
Net Operating Profit	$ 12,400	5.9%
Other Income	1,000	
	$ 13,400	
Other Expense	1,400	
NET INCOME	$ 12,000	

In reviewing the preceding exhibit notice that as the Cost of Goods Sold percentage decreases the Gross Profit increases. Therefore the business should devote some effort to reducing the cost paid for the merchandise to be sold. Notice also that as the Selling Expenses percentage and the Administrative Expenses percentage decrease the Net Operating Profit percentage increases. (In many statements the percentages stop at the Net Operating Profit percentage. If it would be meaningful for analysis purposes to continue, the percentages can be calculated for Other Income, Other Expense, and the remaining items on the Income Statement.)

EXERCISES

Exercise No. 1. From the following trial balance and the account "Wilkinson, Capital" prepare a Balance Sheet, Statement of Proprietor's Capital, and Profit and Loss Statement for the Golden Gate Landscaping Company.

Golden Gate Landscaping Company
Trial Balance
December 31, Year A

Cash	$ 562	
Accounts Receivable	2,116	
Garden Supplies	402	
Truck	2,100	
Accumulated Depreciation—		
Truck		$ 560
Gardening Tools	317	
Prepaid Insurance	109	
Accounts Payable		107
Contracts Payable		
(11 payments @ $60/mo.)		660
Wilkinson, Capital		4,500
Wilkinson, Drawing	3,600	
Income From Landscaping		7,350
Telephone Expense	50	
Garden Supplies Used	2,516	
Depreciation Expense—Truck	560	
Gas and Oil Expense	373	
Office Supplies Expense	27	
Insurance Expense	207	
Miscellaneous Expense	238	
	$13,177	$13,177

Wilkinson, Capital

Year A	
Jan. 1 Balance	$3,500
May 6 Investment	1,000

Exercise No. 2. Using the same data as in Exercise No. 1 show only the liabilities and owner's equity sections of the Balance Sheet when no separate Statement of Proprietor's Capital is used.

Exercise No. 3. From the following trial balance of Santini & Casey, Insurance Brokers, and the two capital accounts shown, prepare a Balance Sheet (showing a detailed equity section) and an Income Statement.

Santini & Casey, Insurance Brokers
Trial Balance
Year Ending December 31, Year A

Cash	$ 4,015	
Accounts Receivable	700	
Commissions Receivable	5,603	
Office Supplies	1,210	
Office Furniture	9,315	
Accumulated Depreciation—		
Office Furniture		$ 3,702
Automobiles	7,600	
Accumulated Depreciation—		
Automobiles		3,300
Prepaid Insurance	570	
Prepaid Rent	600	
Premiums Payable		2,950
Accounts Payable		111
M. Santini, Capital		10,000
M. Santini, Drawing	5,200	
W. Casey, Capital		10,000
W. Casey, Drawing	5,200	
Commissions Income		29,585
Wages Expense	9,050	
Rent Expense	2,400	
Telephone Expense	1,100	
Office Supplies Used	560	
Insurance Expense	210	
Automobile Expense	2,300	
Depreciation Expense—		
Office Equipment	955	
Depreciation Expense—		
Automobiles	2,010	
Miscellaneous Expense	1,050	
	$59,648	$59,648

M. Santini, Capital

	Year A		
	Jan. 1	Balance	$8,000
	March 3	Investment	2,000

W. Casey, Capital

	Year A		
	Jan. 1	Balance	$10,000

Exercise No. 4. From the data given in Exercise No. 3 prepare a separate Statement of Partners' Capital and show how the liability and equity sections of the Balance Sheet would appear.

Exercise No. 5. From the accounts below prepare the equity section of the Balance Sheet for Szalay, Inc., and the Retained Earnings Statement for Year A.

Capital Stock

	Year A		
	Jan. 1	Balance	
		5,000 shares of $10 par value authorized.	
		4,000 shares issued.	$40,000
	April 15	Issued 500 shares.	5,000

Retained Earnings

Year A				Year A		
March 31	Dividend Declared	400		Jan. 1	Balance	$17,000
June 30	Dividend Declared	450		Dec. 31	Profit for Year Before	
Sept. 30	Dividend Declared	450			Income Taxes	8,000
Dec. 31	Dividend Declared	450				
Dec. 31	Estimated Income Taxes	3,900				

Exercise No. 6. From the partial trial balance shown, prepare an Income Statement for the year ending January 31, Year B, for Lluria Importers, incorporating the Cost of Goods Sold Schedule into the statement. (The figures have been adjusted as of January 31, Year B.)

Sales		$437,103
Beginning Inventory	$ 39,060	
Ending Inventory		36,202
Merchandise Purchases	321,322	
Purchase Freight and Insurance	7,512	
Sales Salaries	29,227	
Depreciation Expense— Store Equipment	2,051	
Store Supplies Used	11,050	
Office Salaries	5,602	
Depreciation Expense— Office Equipment	527	
Communications Expense	706	
Insurance Expense	409	

Chapter 2

CASH

Cash can be defined as coins, currency, those items that can be immediately converted to coins and currency, and credits in a bank account. Cash is the most liquid of the assets. When cash flows from buyer to seller, the value of a transaction is definitely established.

INTERNAL CONTROL OF CASH TRANSACTIONS

Cash is *received* by a business from customers, lenders, owners, and from other sources. Cash is *paid* by the business for goods and services to creditors and others. It is important that all cash received by the business be recorded properly, and that cash available to the business be spent only for the purchase of necessary goods and services or for the payment of the business's obligations. The internal organization of duties and areas of responsibilities of those persons dealing with cash is called **internal control of cash transactions.** This control must extend from the time cash is received by the business until the time it is disbursed. In large organizations, there is one person responsible for cash receipts and another for cash disbursements.

Cash Receipts. When cash is received by a business, a record should be made at that time. In a supermarket, the cash register is used to ring up the sale, and a duplicate tape that remains locked in the register furnishes a check on the amount of cash received. In some businesses, a handwritten receipt is given to the person paying the company. Or one employee can list all receipts of cash before turning them over to the cashier. In some businesses, a shopping service is used to see that the clerk records the sale properly. (A shopping service is an organization that sends a person into a store to shop and act like a regular customer. The person asks questions about merchandise, records the sales clerk's responses and attitudes, and checks the general efficiency of the clerk's work.)

In other cases, a wrapper-cashier system is used in which the salesperson writes up the sale, but the wrapper-cashier wraps the purchase and collects the money. From these examples, we see that there are two ways in which cash receipts are recorded correctly: (1) by preparing a document at the time of the receipt of cash; or (2) by involving more than one person in the transaction. It is important that the one who initially receives the cash prepare a document and that this document be recorded in the books of account. Besides using locked tapes, some companies use prenumbered forms to control the original receipt document sequence. The person who prepares the initial recording should not have authority to write off or adjust any amounts owing from customers. He should not post to or prepare accounts receivable trial balances. He should not assist in the preparation or mailing of monthly statements to customers. As a further safeguard, the person who deposits each day's receipts in the bank should not be the one who reconciles the bank account.

Cash Disbursements. When cash is paid out, the person making the disbursement should satisfy himself that the business has received the goods or services for which it is paying. One method used to insure that only approved invoices will be presented for payment is the **voucher system.** This system consists of a document (voucher) that has to pass through a series of checking operations before payment can be made. At each step, the person processing the voucher examines it for validity and then signs it before it goes on to the next verification step. When the cashier is presented with a properly approved voucher, he prepares a check that is given, along with the voucher, to a person authorized to sign the check. The check-signer should deposit all checks to creditors in the mailbox to prevent anyone in the company from taking and cashing a check that may have been prepared to pay a fraudulent invoice. All undelivered checks should be returned to the signer, perhaps using a post office box only for this purpose. The signer should investigate the reason for nondelivery. This would help prevent the cashing of checks by an employee who might have access to the regular mail. The person who signs checks should not be the one approving invoices for payment. Someone other than the check-signer should reconcile the bank account.

Those who are responsible for cash should take precautions to establish good internal control over both its receipt and disbursement. Many businessmen feel that controlling receipts is all-important, and set up elaborate systems for this but leave the disbursements with relatively no control.

THE BANK ACCOUNT

In most businesses, a bank is used as a depository for cash. When this is done, the account "Cash" reflects the balance of the amount on deposit in the bank.

In opening a bank account, the business decides what bank to use on the basis of the services the bank offers, the interest of the bank officers in the business, the distance of the bank from the business, the charges made by the bank for the services rendered, and similar factors.

Signature Card. The bank requires the business to fill out a **signature card.** This establishes the responsibility of both the bank and the depositor. It specifies the name of the account, type of account (checking, savings, etc.), the type of organization (individual, partnership, corporation, or not-for-profit), the person(s) who can sign checks, and the method and frequency of delivering statements.

Deposit Ticket. When the business wants to deposit money, the **deposit ticket** (Fig. 1a) is filled out, showing the amount of coins and bills, each check, listed separately (Fig. 1b), and the total amount of the deposit. Notice that certain numbers are printed in the lower left corner of the face of the deposit ticket, as well as on the check. These show the Federal Reserve District

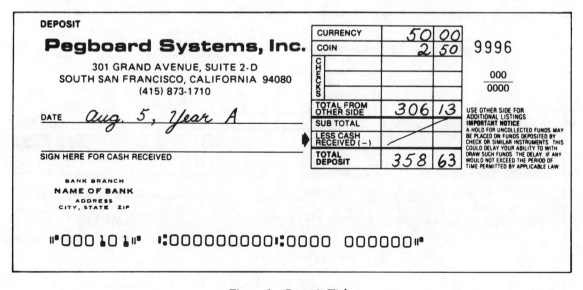

Figure 1a. Deposit Ticket.

CHECKS LIST SINGLY	DOLLARS	CENTS
1 11-35	$ 35	72
2 7-103	49	35
3 9-653	65	37
4 10-75	57	93
5 1-2	63	33
6 1-10	34	43
7		
8		
9		
10		
11		
12		
13		
14		
TOTAL	306	13

ENTER TOTAL ON THE FRONT OF THIS TICKET

Figure 1b. Deposit Ticket (Reverse Side).

routing numbers, the drawer bank's institutional number, a code checking digit, the depositor's account number, the amount of the transaction, and the check number on each check. These numbers are printed at the bottom of the check in such a way that they can be "read" by high-speed computer input mechanisms, which are almost universal in all banks.

Check. When the business wants to withdraw money, a check is prepared and given to the **payee,** the person or business named on the check. (See Fig. 2.) A check is a three-party instrument. It orders the bank **(drawee)** to pay the payee a certain sum of money in the **drawer's** account. The payee can go to the drawee bank for the money or he can deposit the check in his own bank, which will collect the check from the drawee bank.

Statement. Periodically, usually once a month, the bank delivers to the depositor a **bank statement,** shown in Fig. 3. This starts with the depositor's balance at the beginning of the period. It lists the deposits made to the account as **credits** (additions to the account) and all the checks paid by the bank as **debits** (subtractions from the account). It also lists **credit memos** (money received by the bank for the depositor's account, such as a note collection) and **debit memos** (charges for service, such as activity charge, check-imprinting charge, etc.).

Entries Involving Cash Receipts:

Cash	$500	
Accounts Rec. / OR Sales / OR some other credit		$500

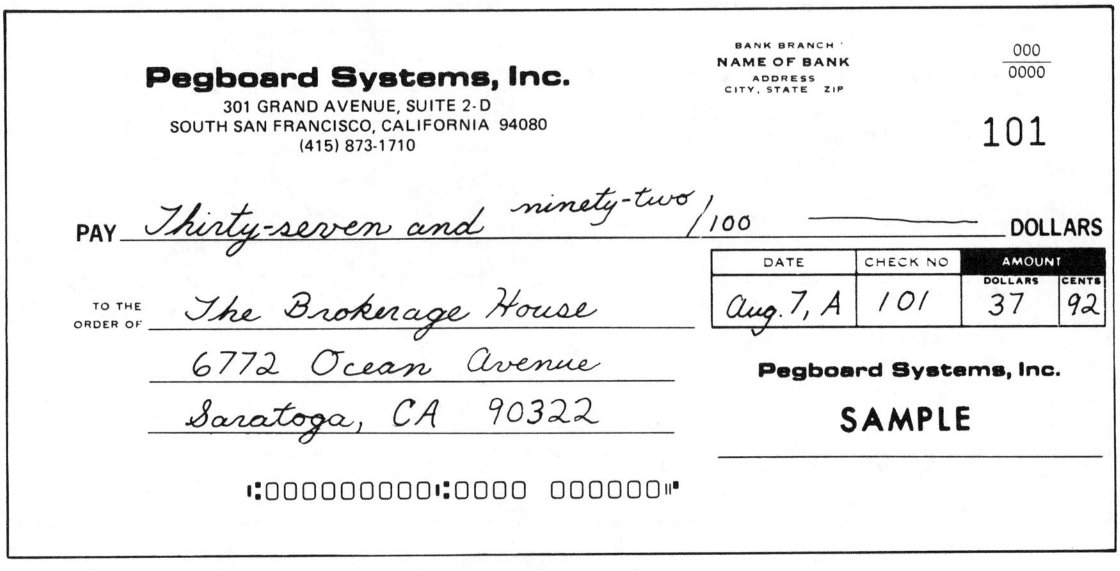
Pegboard Systems, Inc.
301 GRAND AVENUE, SUITE 2-D
SOUTH SAN FRANCISCO, CALIFORNIA 94080
(415) 873-1710

BANK BRANCH
NAME OF BANK
ADDRESS
CITY, STATE ZIP

000/0000

101

PAY Thirty-seven and ninety-two/100 DOLLARS

DATE	CHECK NO	AMOUNT DOLLARS	CENTS
Aug. 7, A	101	37	92

TO THE ORDER OF The Brokerage House
6772 Ocean Avenue
Saratoga, CA 90322

Pegboard Systems, Inc.
SAMPLE

⑆0000000000⑆0000 000000⑈

Figure 2. Check.

```
                          STATEMENT

BLANK BANK
Oakridge Branch
223 West Side
Our Town CA 94100
              CUSTOMER: Pegboard Systems, Inc.
                        301 Grand Avenue, Suite 2-D
                        South San Francisco CA 94080

          Date of this statement—August 31, Year A
```

Summary		
Previous Statement balance July 31, Year A		$ 325.33
Total of 19 deposits for		7,697.22
Total of 30 checks for		6,455.34
Total of 1 bank credit for		510.00
Total of 2 service charges for		12.00
Statement balance August 31, Year A		$2,065.21

Deposits					
08-05	358.63	08-06	467.35	08-07	487.68
08-10	392.92	08-11	494.53	08-12	420.48
08-13	489.47	08-14	429.62	08-17	480.52
08-18	403.72	08-19	361.04	08-20	422.68
08-21	319.64	08-24	303.23	08-25	334.76
08-26	435.08	08-27	336.06	08-28	376.70
08-31	383.11				
	Total of 19 deposits $7,697.22				

Checks Check Number	Date Posted	Amount of Check	Check Number	Date Posted	Amount of Check
122	08-13	480.49	138	08-17	7.85
123	08-10	20.86	139	08-13	45.85
*125	08-14	49.38	140	08-21	476.64
126	08-14	195.15	141	08-28	246.70
127	08-05	73.28	142	08-28	7.72
128	08-05	9.18	143	08-24	707.61
129	08-06	820.09	144	08-14	633.89
130	08-10	253.95	145	08-25	95.02
131	08-07	270.42	146	08-31	644.64
132	08-12	3.04	147	08-26	62.69
133	08-12	873.74	*149	08-18	81.99
134	08-18	79.18	*151	08-18	49.75
135	08-12	6.42	152	08-24	6.59
136	08-17	65.49	*154	08-26	74.76
137	08-21	50.68	155	08-28	62.29
		Total of 30 checks $6,455.34			

```
Credit Memo  08-19 Collected note from Robert Jones Co.
             Principal—$500.00;
             Interest—$10.00
             Total of 1 Credit Memo  $510.00

Debit Memos  08-06 Check imprinting—$7.00
             08-19 Note Collection Fee—$5.00
             Total of 2 Credit Memos  $12.00
```

Figure 3. Bank Statement.

Then the money is deposited and the bank makes an entry on its books:

Cash	$500
Depositor's Account	$500

Note that what you consider an asset (cash in bank) the bank considers a liability because the bank owes the money to you, the depositor.

Entries Involving Cash Payments:

Assets		
OR Expenses	}	$300
OR some other debit		
Cash		$300

Then the check is given or mailed to the payee and negotiated by him. Eventually, it returns to the business's bank, which makes an entry on its books.

Depositor's Account $300	
Cash	$300

Note that the bank recognizes that it has reduced its liability to the depositor.

Reconciling the Statement. When the bank statement, the canceled checks, and credit memos and debit memos are received by the depositor, he reconciles the ending balance in the account as shown by the bank with the balance in his Cash account. If the bank added deposits on the day the business received the money and subtracted the checks as they were written, *and* if the business added moneys received by the bank on the day the bank received them, *and* if the business subtracted charges on the day the bank made them, the ending balance on the bank statement and the balance in the business's Cash account would be equal. There are delays, however, because cash received one day is deposited the next, and checks made out one day may be subtracted by the bank some time later (because of mail delivery time and the time it takes for checks to be deposited by the payee and returned to the drawer's bank). In the case of credit memos and debit memos, there are delays caused by mail time between the bank and the depositor.

A convenient form of bank reconciliation starts with the bank balance, to which are added all receipts shown on the business's books not credited by the bank ("deposits in transit") and from which are subtracted all checks not yet cashed by the bank; these are totaled. A separate listing starts with the Cash account balance, to which all bank credit memos are added and from which are subtracted all bank debit memos; these are totaled. The two totals should be equal, and if they are, the bank statement is reconciled (Fig. 4). If the two totals are not equal, the depositor looks through the books to see if he properly recorded all items for the period and if he properly added and subtracted all items in the journals and the Cash account and the checkbook (where a stub balance is maintained). Then he rechecks the items in the bank reconciliation. When the account is reconciled, adjusting journal entries

The Bank Reconciliation:		
Balance per bank statement, August 31		$2,065.21
ADD Deposits in Transit: August 31		311.65
		$2,376.86
LESS Outstanding Checks: August 31		
#119 From prior reconciliation (still uncashed)	$201.03	
#124	2.71	
#148	1.96	
#150	40.02	
#153	7.76	
		$ 253.48
BALANCE August 31		$2,123.38
Balance of Cash Account: August 31		$1,625.38
ADD Bank Credits		
Note collected	$500.00	
Interest collected	10.00	
		$ 510.00
		$2,135.38
LESS Bank Debits		
Check Imprinting Charge	$ 7.00	
Collection fee	5.00	
		$ 12.00
		$2,123.38

Figure 4. Bank Reconciliation.

should be made to reflect the changes made to the account by the bank as shown on the credit and debit memos.

After the bank account is reconciled, adjusting entries are required to bring into the company books the changes made by the bank. For ease in illustration, one entry might be made for the bank credits, as follows:

Cash	$510	
Notes Receivable		$500
Interest Income		10

One entry might be made for the bank debits, as follows:

Bank Charges	$12	
Cash		$12

PETTY CASH

If the company deposits all cash receipts in the bank intact, then all payments must be made by check. This method is both costly and inconvenient, and so a **petty cash fund** can be established for the purpose of paying small amounts, such as reimbursement to the person who runs errands for carfare, parking meter fees, etc., or for payment of postage-due letters, delivery fees, etc., when received in the office.

Establishing the Fund. A petty cash fund should be large enough to pay the anticipated bills but not so large as to tempt anyone to misuse it. It should be replenished at periodic intervals. When management decides the type of transaction that will be paid from the fund, the size of the fund, and the replenishment cycle, the fund is established by appointing a petty cashier and drawing a check payable to him or to "Petty Cash." The petty cashier takes this check to the bank and receives coins and currency, and the fund is ready for use.

Disbursements from the Fund. When the need for a petty cash payment occurs, the petty cashier prepares a **petty cash voucher,** shown in Fig. 5, and gets a signature on the voucher (and, if appropriate, some document such as a bill or receipt) from the person to whom the money is given. These vouchers should be serially prenumbered, and documentations such as bills and receipts should be attached. The total of coins, paper currency, and the vouchers should always equal the amount for which the fund was established.

Fund Replenishments. When the petty cash fund needs more cash, the petty cashier prepares an analysis of the petty cash vouchers. This analysis, illustrated in Fig. 6, shows how much of the amounts spent should be charged to the various expense accounts, and should be accompanied by the petty cash vouchers in numerical order. The first number of the current request should be

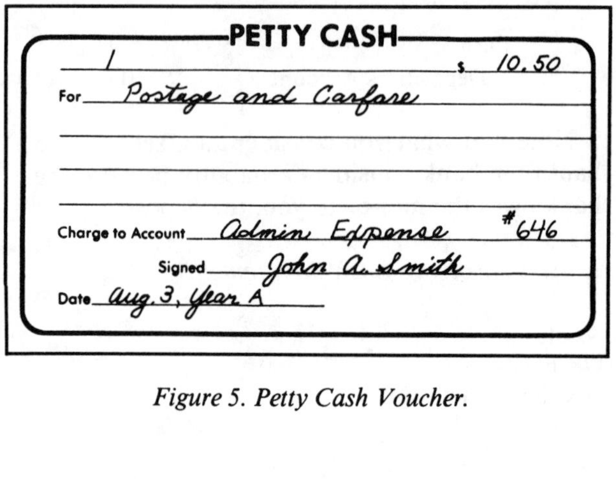
PETTY CASH
1 $ 10.50
For Postage and Carfare
Charge to Account Admin Expense #646
Signed John A. Smith
Date Aug. 3, Year A

Figure 5. Petty Cash Voucher.

OFFICE FUND VOUCHER

Voucher No. __42__

From __August 1,__ 19 _A_ to __August 31,__ 19 _A_   Paid by Check No. __133__

AUDITED BY	APPROVED BY	

DATE	RECEIPT NO.	TO WHOM PAID	FOR WHAT	ACCT. NO.	AMOUNT
Aug. 3	1	John Smith - Mailbox	Postage & Carfare	646	10 50
3	2	Frank Owen	Telegram	638	2 95
4	3	John Smith - Mailbox	Postage & Carfare	646	10 50
5	4	Bay Paper Co.	Drinking Cups	630	12 19
12	5	James Bound	Lunch with Supplier	648	6 75
14	6	John Smith - Mailbox	Postage & Carfare	646	10 50
17	7	Frank Owen	Telegram	638	3 15
19	8	Pacific Vista Grocery	Coffee Supplies	639	7 03
24	9	John Smith - Mailbox	Postage & Carfare	646	10 50
27	10	James Bound	Lunch with Supplier	648	6 65
28	11	Frank Owen	Telegram	638	3 41
			TOTAL DISBURSED		84 13
			CASH ON HAND	counted	15 87
			AMOUNT OF FUND		100 00

DISTRIBUTION

630	638	639	646	648								Recap	
12 19	2 95	7 03	10 50	6 75								a/c #	$
	3 15		10 50	6 65									
	3 41		10 50	13 40								6 30	12 19
	9 51		10 50									6 38	9 51
			42 00									6 39	7 03
												6 46	42 00
												6 48	13 40
													84 13

Figure 6. Petty Cash Analysis.

verified with the last number of the previous request to insure the continuity of number sequence. All numbers should be accounted for, from the first to the last, on each replenishment request. When the data are examined, a check is drawn payable to the petty cashier or to "Petty Cash" for the amount of money expended. The petty cashier cashes the check, receiving coins and currency, and he again has cash equal to the established amount.

Increasing or Decreasing the Fund. When the fund is to be increased, the replenishment check is made larger by the additional amount, or a separate check for the increase can be prepared. In either case, the amount is a fund increase, and the petty cashier is responsible for the larger amount.

When the fund is to be decreased, the replenishment check is made smaller by the reduction, or the petty cashier can deposit with the general cashier the amount by which the fund is to be decreased. In either case, the fund is decreased,

and the petty cashier is responsible only for the decreased amount.

Entries for Petty Cash:

Petty Cash	$100	
Cash		$100
To establish Petty Cash fund.		

The petty cashier cashes the check and has $100 in cash. Assume that he disburses $84.13 over a period of time. He prepares a replenishment request (Fig. 6) for $84.13 and counts $15.87 in cash remaining in the fund:

[Various Expenses]	$84.13	
Cash		$84.13
To replenish Petty Cash fund.		

The petty cashier cashes the check for $84.13 and with the $15.87 balance again has $100 in the fund.

EXERCISES

Exercise No. 7. A business receives cash from the following sources:

a. Cash sales of $300.

b. Payment from Jonathan Jones on credit sale of $400.

c. Investment by owner, Bill Smyth, of $200.

d. Proceeds from a $10,000 note (not discounted).

e. Proceeds of $940 from an original discount note made with the bank having a face value of $1,000.

Prepare the journal entry for each transaction.

Exercise No. 8. Checks are written as follows:

a. For the month's rent, $325.

b. For merchandise, $700 (terms: 2/10—paid in the discount period).

c. For disinvestment by the owner, Frank Corum, $500.

Prepare the journal entry for each transaction.

Exercise No. 9. Prepare the deposit ticket (Fig. 7) for the items enumerated below:

Five $20 bills; 11 $10 bills; 6 $5 bills; 47 $1 bills; 200 half dollars; 120 quarters; 112 dimes; 320 nickels; 67 pennies.

Fourth National Bank (60-132) check of $117.62; Bank of America (11-198) check of $73.15; Exchange National Bank (19-37) check of $215.00.

Exercise No. 10. The bank statement for the month of September, Year A (which follows the one for August, Year A, shown in Fig. 3) (Fig. 8), the Daily Cash Receipts Register for September, Year A (Fig. 9), the Check Register for September, Year A (Fig. 10), and the Cash account of Pegboard Systems, Inc. (Fig. 11), are shown below.

a. Prepare the bank reconciliation for September 30, Year A.

b. Prepare the necessary adjustments.

The September 14 debit of $5.00 represents a

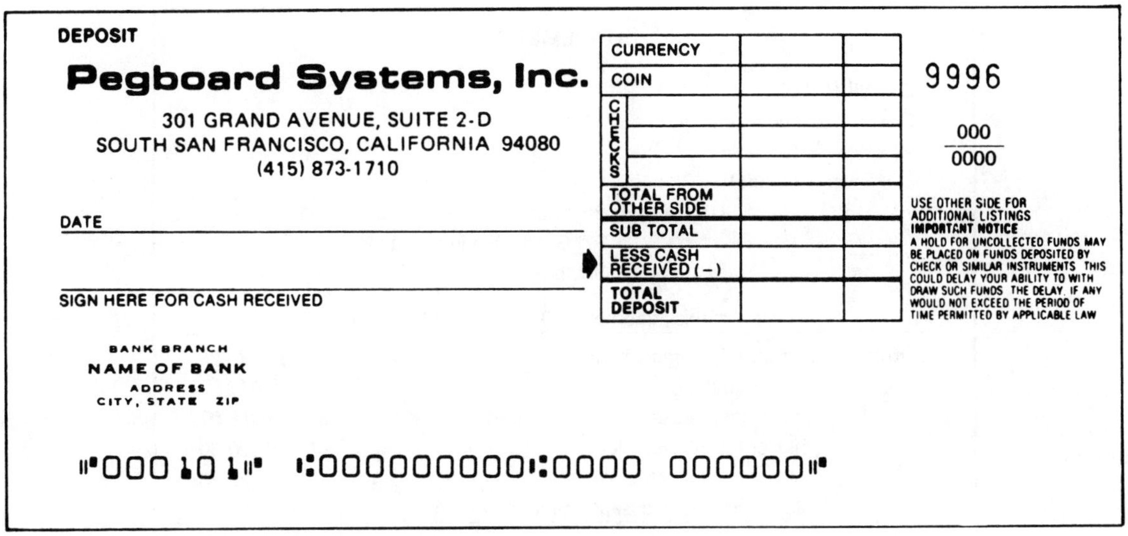
DEPOSIT

Pegboard Systems, Inc.

301 GRAND AVENUE, SUITE 2-D
SOUTH SAN FRANCISCO, CALIFORNIA 94080
(415) 873-1710

DATE

SIGN HERE FOR CASH RECEIVED

CURRENCY		
COIN		
CHECKS		
TOTAL FROM OTHER SIDE		
SUB TOTAL		
LESS CASH RECEIVED (−)		
TOTAL DEPOSIT		

9996

000
0000

USE OTHER SIDE FOR ADDITIONAL LISTINGS
IMPORTANT NOTICE
A HOLD FOR UNCOLLECTED FUNDS MAY BE PLACED ON FUNDS DEPOSITED BY CHECK OR SIMILAR INSTRUMENTS THIS COULD DELAY YOUR ABILITY TO WITH DRAW SUCH FUNDS THE DELAY, IF ANY WOULD NOT EXCEED THE PERIOD OF TIME PERMITTED BY APPLICABLE LAW

BANK BRANCH
NAME OF BANK
ADDRESS
CITY, STATE ZIP

⑈000101⑈ ⑆000000000⑆0000 000000⑈

Figure 7. Deposit Ticket for Exercise No. 9.

service charge for a customer's returned check of $10.73 (this check is uncollectible). The September 24 collection fee is for collecting the non-interest-bearing note of $200.

```
┌─────────────────────────────────────────────────────────────────────┐
│                          STATEMENT                                    │
│                                                                       │
│  BLANK BANK                                                           │
│  Oakridge Branch                                                      │
│  223 West Side                                                        │
│  Our Town CA 94099                                                    │
│               CUSTOMER: Pegboard Systems, Inc.                        │
│                         301 Grand Avenue, Suite 2-D                   │
│                         South San Francisco CA 94080                  │
└─────────────────────────────────────────────────────────────────────┘
```

Date of this statement—September 30, Year A

Summary	Previous Statement balance August 31, Year A	$2,065.21
	Total of 20 deposits for	8,012.93
	Total of 28 checks for	3,845.07
	Total of 1 bank credit for	200.00
	Total of 2 bank debits for	20.73
	Statement balance September 30, Year A	$6,412.34

Deposits

09-01	311.65	09-02	399.11	09-03	461.93
09-04	466.08	*09-08	324.65	*09-10	714.41
09-11	432.88	09-14	355.60	09-15	354.77
09-16	385.31	09-17	370.49	09-18	462.15
09-21	362.79	09-22	458.90	09-23	326.43
09-24	310.09	09-25	367.63	09-28	377.98
09-29	300.51	09-30	469.57		

Total of 20 deposits $8,012.93

Checks

Check Number	Date Posted	Amount of Check	Check Number	Date Posted	Amount of Check
124	09-01	2.71	166	09-11	365.66
148	09-03	1.96	167	09-15	1.27
150	09-21	40.02	168	09-14	47.70
153	09-10	7.76	169	09-15	6.53
156	09-15	681.26	170	09-21	1.77
157	09-03	184.13	171	09-16	39.14
158	09-10	66.19	172	09-21	64.23
159	09-03	73.18	173	09-30	1.79
160	09-04	127.84	174	09-28	431.34
161	09-08	30.11	175	09-21	80.00
162	09-14	47.70	176	09-28	645.33
163	09-15	98.68	177	09-29	2.62
164	09-22	8.73	179	09-23	25.87
165	09-17	59.89	181	09-28	701.66

Total of 28 checks for $3,845.07

Credit Memo   09-24 Collected note (no interest) $200.00
Total of 1 Credit Memo for $200.00

Debit Memos   09-14 Returned check $10.73
09-14 Service charge $5.00
09-24 Collection fee $5.00
Total of 3 Debit Memos for $20.73

* N.B. September 7 is Labor Day and, in California, September 9 is Admissions
    Day. On both these days the banks are closed.

Figure 8. Bank Statement for Exercise No. 10.

Figure 9. Cash Receipts Register for Exercise No. 10.

Daily Cash Receipts Register

September	amount
1	399 11
2	461 93
3	466 08
4	324 65
5 Saturday	
6 Sunday	
7 Labor Day	
8	328 86
9	385 55
10	432 88
11	355 60
12 Saturday	
13 Sunday	
14	354 77
15	385 31
16	370 49
17	462 15
18	362 79
19 Saturday	
20 Sunday	
21	458 90
22	326 43
23	310 09
24	367 63
25	377 98
26 Saturday	
27 Sunday	
28	300 51
29	469 57
30	398 10
	8096 38

Check Register
September

Payee	Ck. No.	Check amount	accounts Payable
The Paper House	154	206 37	206 37
One and Only Supplies	155	122 16	122 16
Johnson Supply Co.	156	681 26	681 26
Tomorrow Today	157	184 13	184 13
Western Hotel	158	66 19	66 19
Stevenson Office Supply	159	73 18	73 18
Air-Lift Airlines	160	127 84	127 84
Long Distance Phone Co	161	30 11	30 11
Chevron Oil Co.	162	47 70	47 70
Bad City Tax Collector	163	98 68	98 68
Rubber Stamp Co.	164	8 73	8 73
American Telephone	165	59 89	59 89
Africa Importing	166	365 66	365 66
Anderson Co.	167	1 27	1 27
Petty Cashier	168	47 70	47 70
Postmaster	169	6 53	ETC
Mackey Co - Freight	170	1 77	
City Water Dept.	171	39 14	
Gotham Window Service	172	64 23	
Mackey Co - Freight	173	1 79	
Bettermaid Products	174	431 34	
Interest Expense	175	80 00	
Orchard Supplies	176	645 33	
Franklin Parts Co.	177	2 62	
Danford Auto	178	197 35	
City Office Supplies	179	25 87	
Computer Services	180	92 06	
Anderson Imports	181	701 66	
		4410 56	

Figure 10. Check Register for Exercise No. 10.

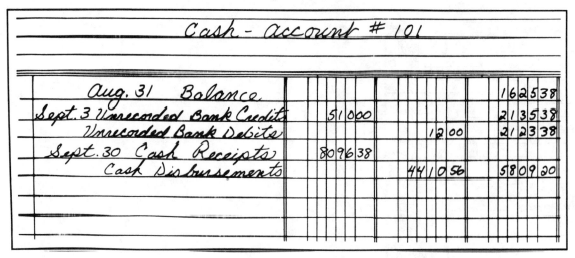

Cash - Account # 101					
Aug. 31 Balance					1625 38
Sept. 3 Unrecorded Bank Credits	510 00				2135 38
Unrecorded Bank Debits			12 00		2123 38
Sept. 30 Cash Receipts	8096 38				5809 20
Cash Disbursements			4410 56		5809 20

Figure 11. General Ledger Cash Account for Exercise No. 10.

Pegboard Systems, Inc.
301 GRAND AVENUE, SUITE 2 D
SOUTH SAN FRANCISCO, CALIFORNIA 94080
(415) 873-1710

BANK BRANCH
NAME OF BANK
ADDRESS
CITY, STATE ZIP

000
0000

101

PAY _____ **DOLLARS**

DATE	CHECK NO	AMOUNT	
		DOLLARS	CENTS

TO THE
ORDER OF _____

Pegboard Systems, Inc.

SAMPLE

⑆000000000⑆0000 000000⑈

Figure 12. Check for Exercise No. 11.

Exercise No. 11. The petty cashier gives you the petty cash expenditures shown in Fig. 6 (with the supporting documents) and requests a replenishment check. Fill in the check below (Fig. 12) to replenish the fund.

Chapter 3

SALES ON ACCOUNT

INCREASING SALES

Every business strives to increase sales. With increased sales there is generally an increase in the dollar amount of gross profit but a smaller increase in expenses, resulting in a larger net profit. To illustrate:

	Year A	Year B	Percentage Increase
Sales	$100,000	$120,000	20%
Cost of Sales (75% of Sales)	75,000	90,000	20%
Gross Profit	$ 25,000	$ 30,000	20%
Operating Expenses	15,000	16,200	8%
Net Profit	$ 10,000	$ 13,800	38%

Operating expenses generally rise so little because they include rent, taxes on property, depreciation on equipment, and other items that do not change in dollar amount as sales vary. These are the **fixed charges.** Also included in operating expenses may be salesmen's salaries, heat and light, store supplies, and other items that do vary as sales vary. The example shows that a 20% increase in sales yields a 38% increase in net profit. Although these figures are hypothetical, the principle they illustrate is quite valid.

As long as a business can increase its sales at a greater rate than it increases its operating expenses, it tries to do so because the net profit will be increasing at an even greater rate than sales income.

One of the easiest ways to increase sales is by extending **credit** to the customer. This extension of credit, however, has some drawbacks. One is a delay between the time of sale and the time of collection. The table at the bottom of this page shows the difference between a sale for cash and a sale for credit with a subsequent payment.

After the customer pays, the account balances are the same; but in the time that has elapsed between the sale and the receipt of the pay-

	Cash Sale			Credit Sale		
Date of Sale	Cash	$500		Accounts Receivable	$500	
	Sales		$500	Sales		$500
				(passage of some time period)		
Date of Collection				Cash	$500	
				Accounts Receivable		$500

ment, the business has had no use of the cash resulting from the sale. This lack of cash may have a decided effect on the success of the business.

Credit Risks. Another disadvantage of credit sales is that the customer may never pay the amount that is owed. In other words, the business has extended credit to the wrong customer. The business must decide to whom it will extend credit. The extension of credit to most business customers is largely granted on the basis of ratings compiled by such credit reference organizations as Dun & Bradstreet. The Dun & Bradstreet rating is related to the size of the company in terms of tangible net worth and a composite credit appraisal.

The extension of credit to small businesses and to individuals may be on the basis of a report from a credit-rating bureau or on the basis of such factors as the potential customer's earnings, past credit record, marital status, ownership of a home or a car, or character references. When these factors are studied, each customer is rated as to his "creditability," an estimate of the assurance that a customer granted credit will pay the amount he owes. The lower "creditability" a business is willing to accept, the more customers it may have, but the greater the possible loss from noncollection of accounts receivable. So the business must draw the line at some point. No matter where the line is drawn, there will be some persons included in the acceptable "creditability" group who will not pay if they become customers. There will also be some persons not included in the acceptable "creditability" group who would pay if they had been permitted to become customers.

There are two pressures on the credit manager or other person who determines to whom credit will be extended and to whom it will be denied. One is the sales manager, who wants an ever-expanding source of potential customers. The other is the treasurer, who wants to collect for every sale made. The successful sales manager must expand the group of potential customers without unduly increasing losses due to uncollectible accounts.

COLLECTIONS ON ACCOUNTS RECEIVABLE

In any company selling on credit, some effort should be made to establish a system for the collection of accounts receivable. The collection effort should start with a clearly defined policy that is explained to the customer when credit is granted. The customer is reminded of the policy at the time of sale by the printing of the major features of the policy on the sales invoice (usually in the form: TERMS: NET 30 or 2/30, NET 60), or by a complete explanation of the credit policy on the credit card or monthly statement. NET 30 means that the amount due is payable in full thirty days after the invoice date. 2/30, NET 60 means that a 2% discount is permitted on accounts paid within thirty days, or the entire amount must be paid within sixty days. There are numerous variations of credit terms. When the customer fails to send in a payment on the due date, some form of reminder should be sent to him. The reminders should be made often and they should be more forceful as time goes by.

An understandable credit policy, firmly administered, is a valuable resource to a business. It aids in reducing losses from noncollectibility, in creating good will, and in keeping the business financially healthy.

DIRECT WRITE-OFF OF ACCOUNTS RECEIVABLE

When a customer fails to pay what he owes and all collection efforts have been made, it is advisable to remove the account from the general ledger and the subsidiary ledger. One method of removing the account is called the **direct write-off.** In this method, an account called Bad Debt Expense is debited and the Accounts Receivable account is credited (both in the general ledger and the subsidiary ledger). The loss in asset value is taken at the time it is determined that the receivable is valueless.

Example:

Year A—There are $100,000 of sales on account, of which Jones buys $500.

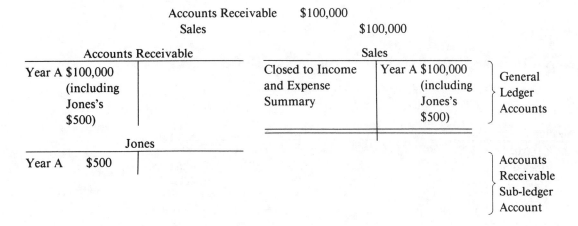

Year C—It is determined that Jones will not pay.

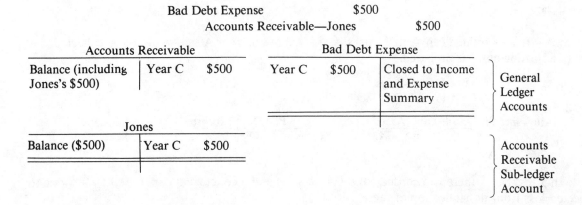

This method is the simplest for recording losses on accounts receivable. It has, however, the disadvantage of not measuring income and its related expense in the same year.

MATCHING INCOME AND BAD DEBT LOSS

As we have seen in the above example, the sale was recognized in Year A, but the expense related to the sale was recognized in Year C. This method overstates Year A net income and understates Year C net income. A method that is used to estimate losses from uncollectible accounts in the year of the sale is called the **allowance and write-off method.**

In this method an estimate is made of those accounts that will not be paid, and this amount is charged to the Bad Debt Expense account and is credited to the Allowance for Uncollectible Accounts account. This latter is an **asset valuation** account, appears in the asset section of the Balance Sheet, and normally has a credit balance. (It is sometimes called a **contra-asset** account.)

This estimated amount may be determined:

1. As a percentage of the year's credit sales.
2. As a percentage of the year's total sales (where there is a fairly constant relationship between cash and credit sales from year to year).

3. As a percentage of the year-end accounts receivable.

4. By an analysis of the year-end accounts receivable.

When the receivable is determined later to be uncollectible, the account is written off against the allowance previously established.

Example:

Year A—There are $100,000 of sales on account (of which Jones buys $500).

Accounts Receivable	$100,000	
Sales		$100,000

Accounts Receivable		
Year A $100,000 (including Jones's $500)		

General Ledger Accounts

Sales		
Closed to Income and Expense Summary	Year A $100,000 (including Jones's $500)	

Jones	
Year A $500	

Accounts Receivable Sub-ledger Account

Year A—It is estimated (on some basis) that $4,000 of the Year A sales will not be collected, and an adjusting entry is prepared.

Bad Debt Expense	$4,000	
Allowance for Uncollectible Accounts		$4,000

Allowance for Uncollectible Accounts		Bad Debt Expense	
	Year A $4,000	Year A $4,000	

General Ledger Accounts

(Note that in Year A there is recorded $100,000 of sales and a concurrent expense of $4,000 due to expected loss from noncollection of these sales.)

Year C—It is determined that Jones will not pay.

Allowance for Uncollectible Accounts	$500	
Accounts Receivable—Jones		$500

Accounts Receivable	
Balance (including Jones's $500)	Year C $500

Allowance for Uncollectible Accounts	
Year C $500	Balance (which might include some of the Year A allowance)

General Ledger Accounts

Jones	
Balance $500	Year C $500

Accounts Receivable Sub-ledger Account

The entry to write off the uncollectible account is an intra Balance Sheet entry and does not affect the income statement.

ACCOUNTS PREVIOUSLY WRITTEN OFF

Occasionally an account that has been written off will be paid by the customer. When this happens the original entry that wrote the account off is reversed, and then the regular entry for the receipt of cash on accounts receivable is made. Since the write-off entry can vary, depending on what method was used at the time the account was written off, the first entry will vary as follows:

Direct Write-off Method:

> Accounts Receivable—Jones $500
>   Bad Debt Expense $500

This, in effect, represents a reduction of the current year's expenses or, if there is no other bad debt expense, an extraordinary income.

Allowance and Write-off Method:

> Accounts Receivable—Jones $500
>   Allowance for
>   Uncollectible Accounts $500

Note that it is an intra Balance Sheet entry and does not affect the income statement.

Under either method, the entry to record the receipt of cash is:

> Cash $500
>   Accounts Receivable—Jones $500

INCOME TAX TREATMENT

Under the Tax Reform Act of 1986 the reserve method for computing deductions for bad debts on income tax returns has been repealed for all taxpayers except small banks. Later acts may well reverse this decision. Under the Tax Re-

form Act of 1986 the following cannot use the cash method of reporting income:

1. C corporations,
2. Partnerships that have one or more C corporations as partner or partners,
3. Tax shelters, and
4. Trusts that are subject to the tax on unrelated income, but only with respect to that income.

The following may use the cash method of reporting income:

1. Small businesses with average annual gross receipts of $5 million or less over the past five years,
2. Farmers, and
3. Personal service corporations.

STATEMENT PRESENTATION

The Balance Sheet:

Direct Write-off Method:

Accounts Receivable $500,000

Allowance and Write-off Method:

Accounts Receivable $500,000
Less—Allowance for
  Doubtful Accounts   7,000 $493,000

The Income and Expense (or Profit and Loss Statement) Statement:

Both methods charge Bad Debt Expense which is included in General and Administrative Expenses.

USING ACCOUNTS RECEIVABLE AS A SOURCE OF CASH

Often, a business will need cash and will have accounts receivable that will come due at some future time. The business can arrange with a financial institution to use these receivables as a source of cash. This may be done in one of three ways:

1. Pledging the receivables: Under this arrangement, the financial institution selects certain receivables as a pledge against a loan of money to the business. Usually, the business collects the accounts and applies the money collected against the loan balance.

2. Assigning the receivables: Under this arrangement the financial institution selects the receivables to be used as security for the loan of money to the business. The business may continue to collect the receivables and apply the money received against the loan balance, or the lending institution may do the collecting. When the financial institution collects the receivables, the method is called **factoring,** and the financial institution is called a **factor.** The factor usually accepts the receivables **with recourse;** that is, if the receivable is considered uncollectible the business will allow the factor to return the receivable and select another in its place. After the

loan is paid off, all uncollected receivables are returned to the business.

3. Selling the receivables: Under this arrangement, the financial institution selects receivables and pays the business for those selected. The financial institution charges a fee for this service. Some financial institutions and banks have established a credit card system. The credit application is made to the institution that approves the credit and issues the credit card. The business pays a fee to become part of the system. When the sale is made a credit slip is prepared, and the business turns a copy of this slip over to the institution for cash, receiving the amount of the sale less a predetermined service charge. Familiar examples of this system are Visa, Mastercard, American Express, Diners' Club, and Carte Blanche credit cards.

All these methods cost money to the business, but the increased sales, less service charges and loan interest, may be such that a substantial increase in net profit can result—as the example at the beginning of this chapter showed.

EXERCISES

Exercise No. 12. An abbreviated Profit and Loss Statement for REMCO, Inc., follows:

Sales	$200,000
Cost of Goods Sold	170,000
Gross Profit	30,000
Operating Expenses	12,000
Net Profit	$ 18,000

The business is contacted by a credit card company with a proposal to redeem all credit card sales slips at 6% discount. It is estimated that sales will increase by 25% but that 20% of the current business will convert to credit card sales. The gross profit percentage would remain the same but operating expenses (excluding credit card discounts) would increase by 5% of new sales.

Should REMCO, Inc., make credit card sales? Why?

Exercise No. 13. What factors might a company selling on credit in the following circumstances look at?

a. Houses.
b. Automobiles.
c. Mail order.
d. General retail goods (department store).

Exercise No. 14. The auditor for DERINI Products finds the following after an analysis of accounts receivable:

Age of Account	Amount
0–30 days	$170,000
31–60 days	80,000
61–90 days	40,000
over 90 days	30,000

On analysis of past experience it is found that the loss ratios for overdue accounts are as follows:

31–60 days	2%
61–90 days	5%
over 90 days	10%

a. What should be the balance in the Allowance for Uncollectible Accounts account?

b. If the balance in the Allowance for Uncollectible Accounts account is $2,200 prior to the calculations made in a. above, prepare the journal entry required.

Exercise No. 15. It is decided to sell the accounts receivable to our bank at a discount of 4% with no recourse. Under this plan we give $200,000 of receivables to the bank.

Prepare the required journal entry.

Exercise No. 16. Under an arrangement with Morros Plan we pledge $150,000 of accounts receivable as security for a loan of $100,000. The accounts are to be collected by us and are to be maintained at our office. At the end of each month a photostat is to be made of each account on which a collection has been made and these copies are to be forwarded to Morros Plan with a check for the amounts collected and interest on the loan balance at the beginning of the month at 5%.

a. Prepare the entry (entries) required on transfer of the accounts to Morros Plan on February 1.

b. In February $20,000 is collected. Prepare the required February 28 entry (entries).

c. In March $50,000 is collected. Prepare the required March 31 entry (entries).

d. In April $30,000 is collected. Prepare the required April 30 entry (entries).

Chapter 4

MERCHANDISE INVENTORY

In a merchandising business, one of the larger current assets is **merchandise inventory.** These are the goods owned by the company that are for sale to customers. They may include personal apparel, furniture, automobiles, beverages, kitchenware, garden supplies, and many, many more items. They may include items for sale in a store or by mail order. They may include general merchandise (such as a department store would carry) or they may be limited to only one item, such as dresses. They might include goods from all over the world or they might be specialized (Italian imports).

PHYSICAL INVENTORY METHODS

Periodic Inventory Method. In the days when most owners ran their own businesses and the size of their inventories was small, there was little need for establishing elaborate control systems for inventories because the owners "knew" their stock. Once a year (or some other time period), the inventory was counted and priced out. Each owner (or his accountant) determined the cost of goods sold by the formula:

Beginning Inventory (same as last year's ending inventory)	$ 5,962
+ Purchases during the year	37,622
= Goods available for sale	$43,584
− Ending Inventory (will be next year's beginning inventory)	7,264
= Cost of Goods Sold	$36,320

If the Cost of Goods Sold had the proper percentage relationship to Sales, an owner assumed his inventory was all right.

This type of system requires that the store be closed for inventory (although it might be taken at night or over the weekend) and affords little accounting control because the ratio of Cost of Goods Sold to Sales is not known until the end of the period, after the inventory is taken. The reliance for control is on individual alertness on the part of the owner or manager with respect to inventory size and movement.

Today there are service organizations that use reading devices that can "read" the product code on a product. All the inventory taker has to do is "read" the product code into his recorder and enter in the number of physical units of that item in inventory. The tapes in the recording devices are then put through a computer that records the number of units, the product, and (from previously entered data that relates product and unit price) the unit price; makes the extensions; and prints out an inventory list. This is quick, convenient, and less costly than the old method of inventory taking and pricing.

Perpetual Inventory Method. When business has a more extensive inventory than the owner or management can "know" intimately, a more positive control, the **perpetual inventory system,** is used (Fig. 13). Here a card for each type of item is used. (There may or may not be prices on these cards.)

As items are received, the number of units is placed in the "receipts" column, and the balance is accordingly increased. As items are sold, the number of units is placed in the "sold" column,

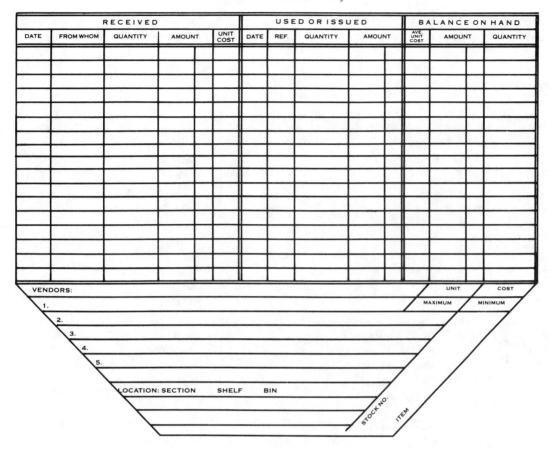

RECEIVED					USED OR ISSUED				BALANCE ON HAND		
DATE	FROM WHOM	QUANTITY	AMOUNT	UNIT COST	DATE	REF.	QUANTITY	AMOUNT	AVE. UNIT COST	AMOUNT	QUANTITY

VENDORS:

UNIT — COST

1.   MAXIMUM — MINIMUM

2.

3.

4.

5.

LOCATION: SECTION   SHELF   BIN

STOCK NO.   ITEM

Figure 13. Perpetual Inventory Card.

and the balance is reduced. In this way the owner or manager can tell how much of any item is on hand simply by checking the inventory card.

This system requires an investment in cards and card files and the services of someone to keep the card file current. It requires the processing of data when goods are received and when they are sold. But it enables management to control the relationship between Sales and Cost of Goods Sold on a current basis. It also permits a closer control of inventory through the accounting records. It permits the use of cyclic rather than year-end inventory taking.

If all sales tickets are priced out with the Cost of Goods Sold when the entry for removal of the goods is made, the relationship between Sales and Cost of Sales can be currently established. Any error in sales price can be determined immediately, and corrective action can be taken.

When acccounting control is kept over inventory by use of this system, pilferage is less likely to occur, because employees do not know when a count of the item they are taking will be made and the shortage discovered. This is in contrast to the periodic system, in which the counting time is definitely established in the future, permitting pilfering in the interim with comparative safety from detection.

When inventory is controlled under the perpetual inventory system, a count of inventory at any time can be compared with the balance shown on the card (plus adjustments on the card balance for recent receipts and sales not recorded). In this system, the inventory is "cycled" for physical counting, or a count can be made when purchase requisitions are prepared. In any event, all goods should be counted at least once a year.

When a discrepancy is noted between the physical count and the adjusted card balance, the situation should be analyzed and the reasons for the discrepancy established. Corrective action should be taken to remedy the situation, and an adjustment made on the card to reconcile it with the reality of the physical count.

Inventory Entries:

Transaction	Periodic Method		Perpetual Method	
Purchase of goods	Purchases $1,000 Cash (or Accts. 　Pay.)	$1,000	Inventory $1,000 Cash (or Accts. 　Pay.) [An entry is made on the item card(s) for the item(s) purchased.]	$1,000
Sales	Cash (or Accts. 　Rec.) 2,000 　Sales	2,000	Cash (or Accts. 　Rec.) 2,000 　Sales	2,000
Cost of Goods Sold	No entry for the cost of sales at this time. The Cost of Goods Sold is determined at year end by use of the Cost of Goods Sold formula.		Cost of Goods Sold 1,500 Inventory [An entry is made on the item card(s).]	1,500
Shortage of inventory item	Not determinable during year except by chance.		Inventory Over 　and Short 150 　Inventory	150
Overage of inventory item	Not determinable during year except by chance.		Inventory 200 　Inventory Over 　and Short	200

PRICE LEVEL CHANGES AND PRICING METHODS

First In First Out. In the years prior to World War II, when the price level rise was relatively small, prices were thought to follow the flow of goods. The oldest goods were sold first and the newest goods were retained in inventory. The oldest prices, therefore, were applied to Cost of Goods Sold, and the newest prices applied to Inventory. This system was a natural extension of the physical movement phenomenon and became known as the FIFO Inventory Method, although the more proper name would be the FIFO Cost of Goods Sold Pricing Method. The term "FIFO" comes from the initial letters of First In First Out.

Average. A closer analysis of price movements shows that prices do not remain steady or move upward or downward at a fixed rate. Rather, they move around a trend line. During periods of small fluctuations it may be better to determine the average price of a type of item on hand and use this average for pricing Cost of Goods Sold and the Ending Inventory. The average price is changed as new inventory is purchased.

Last In First Out. In periods of stable prices, or in periods of relatively small upward or downward trends in prices, the FIFO and average methods yield fairly realistic Cost of Goods Sold and Ending Inventory values. However, when America found itself preparing for and engaged in World War II, prices began an upward trend that was steeper than usual and has continued for over forty-five years. The use of the FIFO and average methods did not yield realistic Cost of Goods Sold and income-expense matching. So a method of pricing was devised that would more closely match current income and expense in an inflationary period. This method uses more recent prices for Cost of Goods Sold and leaves older prices in the inventory and is called LIFO, for **Last In First Out.**

COMPARISON OF FIFO, AVERAGE, AND LIFO

Let us assume a company has no inventory of Item X at January 1, Year A, purchases 300 units in Year A, sells 200 units in Year A, purchases 150 units in Year B, and sells 250 units in Year

		Purchases			Sales	
Year A	Jan. 2	100 @ 10¢	$10.00	Jan. 15	50 @ 20¢	$10.00
	Feb. 10	50 @ 11¢	5.50	April 20	70 @ 20¢	14.00
	May 19	150 @ 12¢	18.00	Oct. 12	80 @ 21¢	16.80
		300	$33.50		200	$40.80
Year B	April 9	75 @ 12¢	$ 9.00	May 12	100 @ 22¢	$22.00
	June 10	75 @ 11¢	8.25	July 15	150 @ 21¢	31.50
		150	$17.25		250	$53.50

	FIFO		Average		LIFO	
Year A	Sales (200)	$40.80	Sales (200)	$40.80	Sales (200)	$40.80
	Cost of Sales:		Cost of Sales:		Cost of Sales:	
	100 @ 10¢ $10.00		$\frac{\$33.50}{300} = 11\frac{1}{6}$¢ each		150 @ 12¢	$18.00
	50 @ 11¢ 5.50					
	50 @ 12¢ 6.00				50 @ 11¢	5.50
	200 $21.50		200 @ 11⅙¢ $22.33		200	$23.50
	GROSS PROFIT $19.30					
	December 31		GROSS PROFIT $18.47		GROSS PROFIT	$17.30
	Inventory		December 31		December 31	
	100 @ 12¢ $12.00		Inventory		Inventory	
			100 @ 11⅙¢ $11.17		100 @ 10¢	$10.00
Year B	Sales (250)	$53.50	Sales (250)	$53.50	Sales (250)	$53.50
	Cost of Sales:		Cost of Sales:		Cost of Sales:	
	100 @ 12¢ $12.00		100 $11.17		75 @ 11¢	$ 8.25
	75 @ 12¢ 9.00		150 17.25		75 @ 12¢	$ 9.00
	75 @ 11¢ 8.25		250 $28.42		100 @ 10¢	10.00
	250 $29.25				250	$27.25
	GROSS PROFIT $24.25		GROSS PROFIT $25.08		GROSS PROFIT	$26.25
	Gross Profit for Both Years $43.55		Gross Profit for Both Years $43.55		Gross Profit for Both Years	$43.55

B, leaving no inventory at December 31, Year B. This may be presented in tabular form, as illustrated on page 33, so that the detailed time sequence can be more clearly shown.

It can be seen that in the period of inflation (Year A in the illustration), FIFO yields higher profits than LIFO. In the period of deflation (Year B in the illustration), LIFO yields higher profits than FIFO. (Note that we are discussing pure price movement and cost pricing with no modification.) Profits using average price will generally fall between the FIFO and the LIFO profits.

Note that the profit over the extended period of time (two years) is the same for all methods because, in the illustration, all sales are the same (therefore total sales are the same), and all purchases are the same, and there is no beginning and no ending inventory. The effect of using the various pricing systems is to match income and expense more closely, or for ease in the accounting process. The effect on the records in the short run is to shift income between years; in the long run, there is no effect on income.

COST OR MARKET, WHICHEVER IS LOWER

After the inventory cost is determined, using FIFO, average, or LIFO, the inventory is compared to present market value to eliminate the excess prices of any item of inventory that can be currently replaced at a lower price. This elimination of excess prices gives the most conservative inventory value and reduces the profit of the current period by the amount the inventory is written down. This can be done in three ways.

1. Item by Item: By comparing the book cost of each item to the current market cost, taking the lower of the two costs, and multiplying that cost by the number of units on hand.
2. Group by Group: Multiplying the number of units on hand in an inventory group by the book cost and getting a total; then multiplying the same number of units on hand by the current market price and getting a total, and taking the smaller total, for each inventory group.
3. Total Inventory: Multiplying each item on hand in the inventory by its book cost and adding these, getting a total; then multiplying the

same units on hand by the current market price and adding these and getting a total; and taking the smaller total.

Examples:

Assume three classes of inventory (Groups A, B, and C).

Assume two items in each group and prices as shown:

A1 100 units—cost $10—market $11
A2 200 units—cost 55—market 50

B1 200 units—cost 14—market 12
B2 300 units—cost 15—market 17

C1 150 units—cost 22—market 21
C2 200 units—cost 21—market 22

The inventory value using the Item by Item method:

A1	100 × $10	$	1,000
A2	200 × 50		10,000
B1	200 × 12		2,400
B2	300 × 15		4,500
C1	150 × 21		3,150
C2	200 × 21		4,200
			$25,250

The inventory value using the Group by Group method:

A1 100 × $10	$ 1,000 × $11	$ 1,100	
A2 200 × 55	11,000 × 50	10,000	
	12,000	$11,100	$11,100
B1 200 × 14	$ 2,800 × 12	$ 2,400	
B2 300 × 15	4,500 × 17	5,100	
	$ 7,300	$ 7,500	7,300
C1 150 × 22	$ 3,300 × 21	$ 3,150	
C2 200 × 21	4,200 × 22	4,400	
	$ 7,500	$ 7,550	7,500
			$25,900

The inventory value using the Total Inventory method:

A1	100 × $10	$ 1,000 × $11	$ 1,100
A2	200 × 55	11,000 × 50	10,000
B1	200 × 14	2,800 × 12	2,400
B2	300 × 15	4,500 × 17	5,100
C1	150 × 22	3,300 × 21	3,150
C2	200 × 21	4,200 × 22	4,400
		$ 26,800	$26,150

In comparing the inventory values determined by these three methods we have:

Item by Item	$25,250
Group by Group	25,900
Total Inventory	26,150

The spread between the lowest (Item by Item) and highest (Total Inventory) value is less than 4%. The Item by Item method is often used because the lower cost is selected first and only one multiplication step is performed; whereas in the other two methods the multiplication is performed for both the book cost and the market cost and then the comparison is made.

The adjusting entry to reduce inventory cost from book cost to cost or market, whichever is lower, is:

Loss Due to Decline in Market Price   XXX
    Inventory   XXX

TWO OTHER PRICING METHODS

There are two additional methods that use other than invoice price to determine ending inventory value.

Retail Method. This method requires that a detailed record be kept of the difference between cost (invoice) price and the retail price. When an item is purchased, the retailer changes the price to a higher one for use in sales to his customers. This increase in price is called **markon.** The retail price can be increased further, called **markup,** or it can be decreased, called **markdown,** even below cost, if the situation suggests such action (competition, popularity of product, etc.). A pair of columns are used on a worksheet to summarize beginning inventory, purchases, and goods available for sale at both cost and retail. When the ratio of cost to retail price of goods available for sale is known, the Ending Inventory is determined by multiplying the retail price of the inventory by that ratio. To determine Cost of Goods Sold, the formula Beginning Inventory + Purchases—Ending Inventory is used.

Gross Profit Method. Another method for determining inventory without using invoice prices is the gross profit method, which is based on the assumption that if the percentage of Gross Profit to Sales is known the Cost of Goods Sold can be determined from Sales, and the Ending Inventory can be found by using the Cost of Goods Sold formula. This method should be avoided unless the inventory is determined in some other manner for purposes of comparison. The lack of control and the possibility of overlooking inventory shortages when this method is used can make the apparent savings in accounting costs very expensive indeed.

INCOME TAX TREATMENT

The Internal Revenue Service has rules concerning inventory valuation. These rules have changed over the years as economic and other factors were better reflected by the new inventory rules included in the regulations. It is wise to get the current IRS regulations so that inventory valuation will conform with the rule(s) approved at the time the income tax returns are prepared.

Presentation of Inventory on the Balance Sheet:
The merchandise inventory is a current asset and is usually shown after the Accounts and Notes Receivable in the following manner:

Merchandise Inventory (valued at
    LIFO or market, whichever is lower) $XXXXX

EXERCISES

Exercise No. 17. Concerning the periodic inventory method:

a. Mention some advantages of using this method.
b. Mention some disadvantages of using this method.

Exercise No. 18. From the following partially adjusted trial balance of the Plev Yak Co., prepare a Cost of Goods Sold Statement for the year ended March 31, Year A:

Merchandise Inventory	$ 150,000	
Merchandise Inventory	130,000	$150,000
Purchases	1,600,000	
Purchase Returns and		
Allowances		30,000
Purchase Discounts		31,000
Freight In	12,000	

Exercise No. 19. Fill out the perpetual inventory card (Fig. 7) for Item 6290, Rocker Arms.

Balance, January 1, 1965	500 pieces
Received, January 19	60 dozen
Used, February 3	125 pieces
Received, February 10	20 dozen
Returned to vendor, February 11	9 pieces
Used, February 17	75 pieces

Exercise No. 20. When the reorder point for Item 3XB is reached, the count of the items shows 150 units but the perpetual inventory card shows 140 units. The unit price is $1.25. Prepare the adjusting entry.

Exercise No. 21. A sale is made for cash (200 units costing $1.50 each are sold for $2 each). The periodic inventory method is used.

a. Prepare the Sales entry.
b. Prepare the Cost of Sales entry.

Exercise No. 22. A count is made of Item 66-329B and 297 units are counted. The perpetual inventory card shows 325 units. The unit price of the item is $1.60. Prepare the adjusting entry.

Exercise No. 23. Concerning the perpetual inventory method:

a. Mention some advantages of using this method.
b. Mention some disadvantages of using this method.

Exercise No. 24. A sale is made for cash (300 units costing $4 each are sold for $5 each). The perpetual inventory method is used.

a. Prepare the Sales entry.
b. Prepare the Cost of Sales entry.

Exercise No. 25. The following information is taken from the perpetual inventory card for Item 49-3B127:

Balance, January 1, Year A	1,000 units $5.700 each
Received, January 31	2,000 units 6.200 each
Received, February 15	2,000 units 6.400 each
Received, March 18	2,000 units 6.600 each
Sold, April 20	3,000 units 7.40 each
Sold, May 15	1,500 units 8.00 each

Complete the following table:

	LIFO	Average	FIFO
Sales	___	___	___
Cost of Goods Sold	___	___	___
Gross Profit	___	___	___
Inventory, May 31	___	___	___

Exercise No. 26. Below is a table of items showing the invoice price and current market price for each item. What is the value of the inventory using Cost or Market, whichever is lower?

		Invoice Price	Current Price
A1	100 units	$ .60	$ .67
A2	120 units	1.20	1.10
A3	600 units	2.10	2.00
A4	210 units	3.00	2.90
B1	430 units	4.00	4.10
B2	10 units	.75	.72
B3	25 units	4.50	4.30
C1	900 units	7.90	8.10
C2	42 units	5.75	5.60
C3	150 units	8.15	8.04
C4	200 units	6.15	6.27

Exercise No. 27. From the figures cost = $4 each and selling price = $5 each, what is the gross profit

a. As a percentage of the selling price?

b. As a percentage of the cost?

Chapter 5

ASSETS USED IN OPERATIONS OVER LONG PERIODS

Some businesses need equipment and other assets that will be used over long periods of time. An example of this might be a delivery truck. The entry to record the purchase of a truck for $20,000 cash would be:

Delivery Equipment	$20,000	
Cash		$20,000

Note that the debit was not made to an expense account. Although the asset will be used up by the business in its operation, the debit to expense comes at a later time with another entry.

Another example might be the purchase of ten trucks costing $20,000 each under an agreement to pay $60,000 in cash and the assumption of $140,000 in notes. The entry would be:

Delivery Equipment	$200,000	
Cash		$ 60,000
Notes Payable		140,000

Again, note that the debit was not made to an expense account.

In assets of this type, the problem of accounting is twofold: to determine the cost of the asset (not difficult in the examples above) and to allocate, on some mathematical basis, the cost of the asset to the fiscal periods of its expected economic life.

This type of asset might be defined as a tangible asset of a relatively fixed or permanent nature used in the operation of the business, or as an intangible asset used by the business in its operation.

TYPES OF ASSETS

Basically, there are five types of these assets:

1. Land: In this sense land is considered as industrial or commercial property: building site, a site for a parking lot. It does not include farmland, which is treated differently and is outside the scope of this volume.

2. Buildings: Buildings are shelters for housing operations or protecting assets: office building, factory, garage, apartment house, storage warehouse.

3. Man-made Assets: These include all tangible assets other than buildings: office equipment, factory equipment, sales furniture and fixtures, delivery equipment, automobiles.

4. Natural Assets: All assets produced by nature which man converts to his own use. There are two subtypes:

   a. Extractive resources: gold, oil, coal, etc.
   b. Regenerative resources: trees, cattle, crops.

5. Intangible Assets: These are nonphysical assets created by legal contract, statutory operation, or other such means. There are two subtypes:

   a. Limited life: franchises, patents, copyrights.
   b. Unlimited life: good will, trademarks.

These assets have certain distinguishing characteristics. Land costs are normally not charged to operations. Buildings, being so intimately tied to land, are sometimes bought with the land, creating a problem of cost allocation between land and building. Land and buildings are called **realty.** Sales of realty are generally made under conditions of great formality. Buildings have a relatively longer life as compared to other man-made assets.

Equipment assets are of varying types, are used for varying purposes, and have lives that vary greatly. In general, such equipment asset lives will be shorter than building lives, and equipment assets may have a salvage value that is a larger percentage of cost than would be the salvage value of a building.

Those businesses that extract natural assets must build physical facilities so that operations can begin or continue. The cost of the physical facilities and the cost of the natural assets must be allocated to the years of expected economic extraction, although the physical facilities may last much longer. In the regenerative natural assets, there are rules for plant assets approximating those in use with office and factory assets.

Intangible assets are written off over their contractual term, or a shorter period if the economic life of the intangible is shorter than the stated term. Those intangible assets having no term can be kept at their original cost until the economic value has shrunk.

REALTY PURCHASES

The transfer of realty is a formal type of property transfer which dates back over a thousand years. The Statute of Frauds (1677) mentions that contracts for transfers of interests in real property had to be in writing to be enforceable. This is due, in part, to the fact that every piece of property is unique—no property has the exact legal description of any other property. Sales are usually made by agent, and the transfer is handled by an escrow agent or title company and requires some passage of time for searching of title, examination of property, and other technicalities. Title is recorded in the County Clerk's office, where one can trace property ownership to the first owners (in the eastern United States, to the royal English grants; in the western United States, to the royal Spanish grants).

Industrial or Commercial Land. In this book, the discussion of land will be limited to industrial or commercial land, where the purchaser buys a place or *situs* for purposes of locating some facility. Farmland purchases may initially be similar to industrial and commercial land purchases, but when the farmland is prepared for and used in agricultural production the accounting treatment differs. What is purchased, then, in an industrial or commercial land transfer, is a place with a unique legal description which, over the years, will not change. Even if the land is leveled or a basement dug or rocks blasted out, the legal description does not change. The cost can vary, but the legal description remains the same. It is this aspect of land that makes it nondepreciable for accounting purposes—the cost of land remains on the books until it is disposed of and, generally, no attempt is made to charge operations with the cost of land.

Cost of Purchase of Land Only. The basic cost of land is developed from a document called the **purchaser's escrow statement,** shown in Fig. 14. The document is prepared by the escrow company (or similar agency) as part of the transfer process. When a contract of sale has been concluded between the buyer and seller, a copy is given to the escrow agency. Buyer and seller perform as the contract requires before the transaction is complete. The escrow agency and title company see that the contract terms are complied with. (An escrow company may only hold and pay money; a title company may search and guarantee title. In San Francisco County, for example, the title companies do both.) The escrow statement shows the purchase price, prepaid taxes, if any (or taxes in arrears), the prepaid insurance (if the purchaser does not furnish his own insurance), the title insurance charges, the escrow charges, and incidental fees related to the purchase. In the case of the example shown in Fig. 14 the land was purchased for $50,000, but the entry to record the transaction is:

Land	$50,552.00	
Prepaid Interest	400.00	
Interest Expense	85.55	
Cash		$51,033.71
Tax Expense		3.84

The tax expense will be charged to operations to reduce the amount of taxes expense from the

First American Title Company of San Francisco

MAIN OFFICE: 300 PINE STREET (94104) · P.O. BOX 3078, RINCON ANNEX · (415) 989-1300
SAN FRANCISCO, CALIFORNIA 94119

☒ BUYER'S   ☐ BORROWER'S
Order Number

ESCROW INSTRUCTIONS   Date *Jan. 15, 19 B*

To: FIRST AMERICAN TITLE COMPANY
I/We hand you herewith

$ 5,000

which you are authorized to deliver and/or record when you have received for my account the following:

DEED TO 99320 GEARY ST., SAN FRANCISCO, CALIF.

FROM JOHN SMITH AND SUSAN SMITH / JT

and when you can issue your standard coverage form policy of title insurance with a liability of $ *50,000*
on the property described as

99320 GEARY ST., SAN FRANCISCO, CALIF.

showing title vested in
HUSBAND/WIFE   *FRANK GALLAGHER AND ESTHER GALLAGHER, AS JOINT TENANTS*

Subject to:
1. Printed exceptions and conditions in said policy.
2. ☐ all   ☒ 2nd half   General and special taxes for fiscal year 19 *A* 19 *B*
3. Assessments and/or bonds not delinquent.
4. Exceptions numbered *1 to 5* as shown in your preliminary title report dated *JAN. 5, 19 B*
   issued in connection with the above order number.
5. *TRUST DEED IN FAVOR OF WELLS FARGO BANK IN THE AMOUNT OF $20,000.*

Upon consummation of this escrow, you are authorized to disburse in accordance with the following statement. Prorate as of
JAN 23, 19 *B* on the basis of a 30 day month. Taxes based on the latest available tax figures.

	Debits		Credits	
Sales Price	50,000	00		
Paid outside of Escrow to				
Deposit by *FRANK GALLAGHER AND ESTHER GALLAGHER*			5,000	00
Encumbrance of Record				
Loan Trust Fund				
Assumption Fee				
New Loan *WELLS FARGO BANK – COLUMBUS BRANCH – SF*			20,000	00
Deed of Trust ☒ 1st ☐ 2nd ☐ 3rd				
Loan Charges: Loan Fee $ *400.00* Tax Res. $				
Appsl. Fee $ Ins. Res. $				
Cred. Rept. $ FHA Prem. $				
Int. Est. @ *14* % Fr *JAN. 12* To *JAN. 23* $ *85.55*				
Total	485	55		
☐ Pay Fire Ins. Prem.				
☐ Pay Tax Service	5	00		
☐ Pay Taxes				
☐ Personal Property Tax				
☐ Pay Assessments or Bonds				
☐ Prorate Taxes Fr. *JAN. 1* To *JAN. 23* on $ *29.26 / 6 MO.*			3	84
☐ Prorate Fire Ins. Fr. To on $				
☐ Prorate Int. @ % Fr. To on $				
☐ Prorate Rent Fr. To on $				
Draw Doc. $				
Notary Fee $	10	00		
Title Prem. Std. $ *315.00* ALTA $ *60.00*	375	00		
Escrow $	142	00		
Recording $	20	00		
Balance Due ☒ To Close ☐ The Undersigned			26033	71
Totals	51,037	55	51,037	55

These instructions are effective until *FEB. 1*, 19 *B* and thereafter unless revoked by written demand and authorization satisfactory to you. Incorporated herein and made a part hereof by reference are the "General Provisions" and any additional instructions appearing on the reverse side of this page.

Received: *JAN. 4*, 19 *B*
First American Title Company

By *Annette Anderson*

Address *4262 EAST LAKE AVE. S.F. CA.*
Phone No. *(415) 001-2345*

x *Frank Gallagher*
x *Esther Gallagher*

Figure 14. Purchaser's Escrow Statement (Land Only).

actual taxes paid at the tax due date to the taxes for the period the property has been owned by the purchaser.

If a piece of property is purchased with a building on it but the building is torn down because only the land is desired, the total purchase price of the land is the cost of the parcel (modified by the items described above) plus the cost of tearing the building down and preparing the land for use. If, in the example above, land was purchased on which there was a building that was torn down at a cost of $7,500, the entry for removal would be:

Land	$7,500	
Cash or Accounts Payable		$7,500

The cost of the property would be $18,259.10.

Sometimes a piece of property is purchased with a building that is to be removed, but a wrecking company will pay to remove it. If, in the original example above, the building is to be torn down and the wrecking company pays $6,000 to salvage the building, the entry would be:

Cash	$6,000	
Land		$6,000

The cost of the property would be $4,759.10.

Proration of Cost of Land and Building. When land and building are purchased as a single unit, the problem of proration of cost between land and building arises. The proration can be done by examining the escrow document for all items that pertain to prepaid items (such as prepaid taxes and insurance) and for items of income (proration of rent income) and for liabilities (cleaning deposits and lease deposits). Of the remaining items the ones pertaining solely to land are separated, as are those pertaining solely to buildings. Then the remainder is divided between land and building.

This final proration can be made on the basis of the assessed valuation of the land and the building as shown on the tax bill; or the proration can be figured on the basis of an appraisal made at the time of sale or on some other basis. Care should be used in properly allocating the cost between land and building.

Example:

Two purchasers buy an improved piece of realty for $260,000 (both land and building). They pay $20,000 down ($5,000 when they make the offer and $15,000 on acceptance) and agree to assume the present first loan of $180,652 (and to pay an assumption fee of 1% of the present balance for that privilege). This present loan is secured by a First Deed of Trust in favor of Marin Savings and Loan Company. The seller agrees to accept a note secured by a Second Deed of Trust in the amount of $30,000. There are tenants in the building who have paid to the seller $1,925 in lease and cleaning deposits and the purchasers assume that liability. The Assessor's Tax Roll shows the assessed valuation for property tax purposes as $20,000 for the land and $80,000 for the improvements (building). No independent appraisal was made at the time of the purchase.

When the Escrow Statement (Fig. 15) is analyzed, the liabilities and income and expense items are put into the entry. The balancing figure of $263,927.12 is the cost of the total realty purchase and represents the purchase price offered and all the related charges ($260,000 + $1,806.52 + $250 + $15 + $20 + $300 + $10 + $1,124.60 + $376 + $25). The Assessor's figures are used to split the $261,820.60 into land and buildings as follows:

$$\text{Land} \quad \frac{\$20,000}{\$100,000} \times \$263,927.12 = \$52,785.42$$

$$\text{Building} \quad \frac{\$80,000}{\$100,000} \times \$263,927.12 = \$211,141.70$$

The completed entry is:

Land	$ 52,785.42	
Building	211,141.70	
Interest Expense	84.79	
Prepaid Fire Insurance	716.00	
Tax Expense	197.10	
Cash		$ 51,174.83
Mortgage Payable—		
Marin S&L Co.		180,652.00
Mortgage Payable—		
M/M Brown		30,000.00
Rent Income		1,173.18
Rental Deposits Payable		1,925.00

First American Title Company of San Francisco

MAIN OFFICE: 300 PINE STREET (94104) · P. O. BOX 3078, RINCON ANNEX   (415) 989-1300
SAN FRANCISCO, CALIFORNIA 94119

☒ BUYER'S   ☐ BORROWER'S   **ESCROW INSTRUCTIONS**   Date *FEB. 28 19 B*
Order Number
To: FIRST AMERICAN TITLE COMPANY
I We hand you herewith   *5,000.00*

which you are authorized to deliver and or record when you have received for my account the following:

DEED TO 9871 OAKLAND AVE,
SAN FRANCISCO, CALIFORNIA

and when you can issue your standard coverage form policy of title insurance with a liability of $ *260,000.00*
on the property described as

9871 OAKLAND AVE.
SAN FRANCISCO, CALIFORNIA

showing title vested in

STEVEN MANA, A MARRIED MAN,
AS HIS SEPARATE PROPERTY

Subject to:
1. Printed exceptions and conditions in said policy.
2. ☐ all ☒ 2nd half General and special taxes for fiscal year 19 *A* 19 *B*
3. Assessments and or bonds not delinquent.
4. Exceptions numbered *1 - 3*   as shown in your preliminary title report dated *FEB. 13, 19 B*
   issued in connection with the above order number.
5. *DEED OF TRUST RECORDED IN FAVOR OF SELLER # 30,000.00*

Upon consummation of this escrow, you are authorized to disburse in accordance with the following statement. Prorate as of
MAR. 14 , 19 *B* on the basis of a 30 day month. Taxes based on the latest available tax figures.

	Debits		Credits	
Sales Price	260,000	00		
Paid outside of Escrow to				
Deposit by *ABRAHAM MANA AND SARAH MANA*			5,000	00
PAID ON ACCEPTANCE BY SELLER			15,000	00
Encumbrance of Record *MARIN SAVINGS + LOAN - COLUMBUS AVE.*			180,652	00
Loan Trust Fund				
Assumption Fee *1 %*	1,806	52		
New Loan *FROM SELLER - JAMES BROWN & MADELE BROWN*				
Deed of Trust ☐ 1st ☒ 2nd ☐ 3rd			30,000	00
Loan Charges: Loan Fee $ Tax Res. $				
Appsl. Fee $ *250.00* Ins. Res. $				
Cred. Rept. $ *15.00* FHA Prem. $				
Int. Est. @ *130* % Fr *MAR. 1* To *MAR. 14* $ *84.79*				
Total	349	79		
☒ Pay Fire Ins. Prem.	716	00		
☒ Pay Tax Service	20	00		
☐ Pay Taxes				
☐ Personal Property Tax				
☐ Pay Assessments or Bonds				
BROKERAGE FEE ON NEW LOAN - 1% Due SMITH REALTY	300	00		
☐ Prorate Taxes Fr. *MAR. 1* To *JUNE 30* on $ *335.00/HA*	197	10		
☐ Prorate Fire Ins. Fr. To on $				
☐ Prorate Int. @ % Fr. To on $				
☐ Prorate Rent Fr. *MAR. 14* To *MAR. 31* on $ *2,200.00/M*			1,173	18
RENTAL DEPOSITS (PER SCHEDULE)			1,925	00
Draw Doc. $				
Notary Fee $	10	00		
Title Prem. Std. $ *955.00* ALTA $ *169.60*	1124	60		
Escrow $	376	00		
Recording $	25	00		
Balance Due ☒ To Close ☐ The Undersigned			31,174	83
Totals	264,925	01	264,925	01

These instructions are effective until   , 19   and thereafter unless revoked by written demand and authoriza-
tion satisfactory to you. Incorporated herein and made a part hereof by reference are the "General Provisions" and any additional
instructions appearing on the reverse side of this page.
Received: *March 2* , 19 *B*   *Abraham Mana*
First American Title Company   *Sarah Mana*
                                        Address *817 NORTH BEACH DR. SF. CA.*
By *Annette Anderson*   Phone No. *(415) - 001 - 3219*

Figure 15. Purchaser's Escrow Statement (Land and Buildings).

Cost of a New Building. When a building is put up on bare land, the cost of the building includes soil tests, architect's fees, excavation costs, cost of in-progress alterations, interest on the money borrowed for the building during construction, and the prorated portion of the property taxes to the time of completion. When the contractor completes the job and the owner accepts it as completed, the construction is at an end. All amounts paid and liabilities assumed up to that time are costs of construction.

Cost of a Remodeled Building. When a building is purchased with the intent to reconvert or remodel it before use, all the costs of design, reconversion or remodeling, painting and decoration, repairs to roofs and windows, etc., up to the time the building is ready for occupancy in its refurbished condition, are part of the cost.

Capital Expenditures vs. Revenue Expenditures. After the initial cost has been determined for fixed assets, expenditures will be made in connection with these fixed assets. Expenditures made to repair the asset for the purpose of maintaining its utility are revenue expenditures chargeable to income for that period. Expenditures made to change the utility character of the asset are capital expenditures and are added to fixed asset cost.

PERSONALTY PURCHASES

Purchases of all tangible assets that are not realty are called **personalty purchases** and include:

Office Equipment: typewriters, desks, chairs, filing cabinets, adding machines, calculators, computers, telephone equipment, copiers, duplicators, mailroom equipment, etc., used in general offices. (Some large companies might classify further into Accounting Office Equipment, Factory Office Equipment, Sales Office Equipment, etc.)

Store (or Sales) Equipment: sales counters, display counters, sales floor shelving, cash registers, display racks or fixtures, freezers and coolers, used in displaying and selling goods and in storing the merchandise for sale. (For purposes of control, this group of equipment

assets could be further classified into Dept. 1 Sales Equipment, Dept. 2, etc.)

Factory Equipment: lathes, drill presses, looms, pickling tanks, conveyor belts, fork-lift trucks, used to produce finished goods or used in the movement of goods around the factory. (This might be further classified into Production Equipment, Factory Transportation Equipment, Factory Storeroom Equipment, etc.)

Delivery Equipment: trucks and other vehicular equipment used to deliver the product in external transportation. The term usually refers to delivery from the store to the customer. When the equipment is used to deliver materials from a supplier to the factory, a separate category called Factory Transportation Equipment is sometimes set up.

Jigs and Fixtures: tools, fixtures, jigs, gauges, and other specially designed and accurately made devices that are used in production.

Small Tools: an inventory of stock tools that the company has on hand for use by the employees in furthering productive effort. Since this class includes hammers, wrenches, pliers, etc., that are subject to pilferage, special controls must be established to prevent loss.

Cost of Personalty. The cost of these assets includes all costs necessary to get the asset in the place wanted in the condition wanted. Therefore, if a business buys a machine F.O.B. New York for $10,000 but must spend $200 for freight and insurance during transit and $500 for installation and testing, the cost of this machine is not $10,000 but $10,700. If a truck costs $6,000 but the business orders a special color and lettering at $200 additional, the asset cost is $6,200.

DEPRECIATION ACCOUNTING

Depreciation accounting is that branch of accounting that has for its aim the allocation of fixed asset cost to present and future operations on the basis of some equitable and rational mathematical system. Although the purchase of the asset occurs at one time, the use of the asset goes on into future periods. Therefore, the asset's cost must be allocated to the periods that receive benefit from the expenditure so that the net income, in the year of purchase, is not distorted, as it would be if the total cost was charged to expense in that one period. The distribution should be equitable so that each period receives its fair share during the lifetime of the asset. The allocation should be based on some rational mathematical system which is determined at the beginning of use so that varying personal judgments over the years of the asset's life will not affect the charging procedure.

Factors Involved in Depreciation. To determine what use might be had from an asset we must examine those factors that would make the asset less useful. These factors fall into two classes, physical and functional. Physical factors include:

1. Wear and tear: the lessening in utility that comes from normal use of the asset.
2. Decay: the lessening in utility by the effect of nature.
3. Destruction: the lessening of utility due to the asset's physical destruction.

Functional factors include:

1. Obsolescence: the reduction of utility that results from the development of a better machine or process.
2. Inadequacy: the reduction in utility that comes about because more production is needed than this asset or combination of assets can give. (Such a situation may force an earlier retirement of this asset or combination of assets than was originally contemplated.)

When we determine the economic utility of a fixed asset so that the concepts of depreciation accounting can be applied, all of the factors listed above should be taken into consideration. They are generally reduced to a statement expressing utility for a definite number of years or for the production of a definite number of units.

Depreciation Formulas. After the utility statement is expressed, the question of how much to charge the present period, and each succeeding period, has to be resolved. The amount to be charged is the cost less the estimated salvage value that the property will bring after its utility has been dissipated. Various mathematical methods have been devised for the allocation; the ones currently in use are discussed below.

1. Straight-line: This method is based on the proposition that each time period should be charged an equal amount as any other similar time period. It is the easiest method to use from a record-keeping and computational standpoint. The formula used is:

$$\frac{\text{Cost less estimated salvage value}}{\text{Expected number of terms of utility}} = \frac{\text{Depreciation expense per term}}{}$$

"Terms of utility" can be expressed as months or years, depending upon the nature of the asset.

2. Hourly: This method is based on the same proposition as the straight-line method—that is, each time period should have an equal charge. But the time period is an hour, rather than years or months as in the straight-line method. This requires that a record be kept of the number of hours of use of the asset in each fiscal period. When the rate per hour is multiplied by the number of hours of use in a fiscal period, the resultant figure is the depreciation expense for that particular fiscal period. The formulas used are:

$$\frac{\text{Cost less estimated salvage value}}{\text{Estimated number of hours of utility}} = \frac{\text{Depreciation expense per hour}}{}$$

Then:

Depreciation expense per hour times actual hours of use in the fiscal period equals depreciation expense for the fiscal period. In this method, the depreciation expense for the fiscal period varies as the usage of the fixed asset varies.

3. Output: This method is based on the proposition that each unit of output should bear an equal share of the allocated cost. It requires that a record be kept of the output in the fiscal period. When the rate per unit of output is multiplied by the number of units produced, the resultant figure is the depreciation expense for the fiscal period. The formulas used are:

$$\frac{\text{Cost less estimated salvage value}}{\text{Estimated number of units of output}} = \frac{\text{Depreciation expense per unit of output}}{}$$

Then:

Depreciation expense per unit of output times actual units produced in the fiscal period equals depreciation expense for the fiscal period. In this method, the depreciation expense for the fiscal period varies as production from the usage of the fixed asset varies.

At this point it might be well to show the accounting entries used to record the depreciation expense, to show the related accounts involved, and to discuss a few other concepts before returning to depreciation formulas.

The Accounting Entry. The depreciation expense is recorded on the books by means of a journal entry at the end of each fiscal period. The entry is:

Depreciation Expense—Asset	$XXX	
Allowance for Depreciation—Asset		$XXX

(Where the word "Asset" appears above, the account title will be Office Equipment, Store Equipment, Delivery Equipment, etc., as appropriate.)

When a fixed asset is acquired during the year or disposed of during the year, the depreciation expense must be prorated when the straight-line method and the methods discussed below are used. (The proration is not needed for the hourly or output methods.) The proration statement can be modified so that anything purchased in a fiscal period will (or will not) be depreciated for the entire fiscal period, which might be a month, a quarter, or a year. A similar statement would be established for disposition. The rule is a matter of company policy, not accounting principle.

The General Ledger Accounts. The cost is recorded as shown previously and is posted to the general ledger account:

Office Equipment (or Store Equipment, etc.)	
Date of purchase Cost	
Date of improvement Cost	

The account remains at original cost until a capital expenditure is made, at which time the amount of this expenditure is added to cost. No other entry is made to this account in relation to a specific asset until that asset is disposed of in some fashion. The two accounts affected by the depreciation expense entry are Allowance for Depreciation—Asset (Office Equipment, Store Equipment, etc., as appropriate) and Depreciation Expense—Asset:

Allowance for Depreciation—Asset		
	12/31/Year A	$AXX
	12/31/Year B	$BXX

As the entry is made each year, the credit is posted to the Allowance for Depreciation account, which is a contra-asset or asset valuation account. The balance keeps getting larger, ultimately equaling cost less estimated salvage value (except when an asset is disposed of before the end of its full expected life). This account balance tells how much of the cost of particular assets has been charged to operations.

Depreciation Expense—Asset	
12/31/Year A $AXX	Closed to P&L Summary
12/31/Year B $BXX	Closed to P&L Summary

Note that this account operates in the same manner as any other expense account. It is closed to the Profit and Loss Summary so that no balance is carried over from one year to the next.

Another account that can be used in connection with fixed assets is Repairs and Maintenance. When revenue expenditures are made for fixed assets the entry is:

Repairs and Maintenance Expense	$XXX	
Cash or Accounts Payable		$XXX

The posting is made to the Repairs and Maintenance Expense account as follows:

Repairs and Maintenance Expense	
Year A charges	Closed to P&L Summary
Year B charges	Closed to P&L Summary

Note that this account also operates in the same manner as any other expense account. It is closed to the Profit and Loss Summary each year so that no balance is carried over from one year to the next.

Book Value. On the Balance Sheet assets are shown at cost less accumulated depreciation. One method used to show this is:

Plant Assets:		
Land		$ 50,000
Building	$350,000	
Less Accumulated		
Depreciation	69,000	281,000
Office Equipment	$ 25,000	
Less Accumulated		
Depreciation	6,000	19,000
TOTAL PLANT ASSETS		$350,000

Another method is:

Plant Assets	Cost	Accumulated Depreciation	Book Value
Land	$ 50,000	—	$ 50,000
Building	350,000	$69,000	281,000
Office Equipment	25,000	6,000	19,000
	$425,000	$75,000	$350,000

Note that Land has no accumulated depreciation because it is not subject to depreciation accounting, as we saw earlier.

Book value is a term that is used to indicate how much of the cost of fixed assets has not yet been depreciated. In this sense it is strictly an accounting term, not to be confused with "book value" as used in relation to corporate stock (which will be explained later).

The question of book value of fixed assets has been the subject of much discussion in professional accounting circles in the past few years. The normal accounting procedure is to report fixed assets at cost less accumulated depreciation, the latter determined by some rational mathematical system. However, since fixed assets are relatively long-lived, changes in price level generally affect the market value of the asset. Under the principle of conservatism, accountants will reduce the value of the asset from book value to current market value in periods of declining prices. This reduction in value is taken as an extraordinary loss in the period in which it occurs.

In periods of rising prices, however, conservative practice leaves the fixed asset book value at cost less accumulated depreciation. But this might not reflect current market value and, in fact, may be lower by thousands of dollars. At present, accountants are aware of the fact that this practice distorts the financial statements, but they have reached no generally accepted method of showing this on the financial statements. The reader of financial statements, therefore, should be aware that discrepancies between the present realistic values of fixed assets and those recorded on the books do sometimes exist, and that they tend to show fixed asset values at a price lower than the realistic price.

Accelerated Depreciation Formulas. During World War II the government was in need of various war materials, much of them requiring large investments of capital for plant facilities. Because these facilities were for special purposes that would have no use in civilian production without extensive revamping, the government allowed a method for depreciating them over a period of not less than sixty months.

As a result of this concept of charging the cost of fixed assets over a much shorter time than previously considered acceptable under good accounting principles (and for other reasons), there were written into the Internal Revenue Act of 1954 two other methods—the Declining Balance Method and the Sum-of-the-Years-Digits Method.

4. Declining Balance Method: In using this method, a constant factor is applied to the reducing book value of the asset (the declining balance). The formula used in obtaining the ratio is:

$$\frac{100\%}{\text{Expected number of periods of use}} \times 2 = \begin{array}{c}\text{Rate to be applied} \\ \text{to the declining balance} \\ \text{(book value)}\end{array}$$

Assume an asset costing $20,000 having an expected economic life of five years; the rate to be applied would be: $\frac{100\%}{5} \times 2 = 40\%$. This factor is then applied to the reducing book value, giving a successively smaller depreciation charge each year.

Applying the 40% factor to the figures given above, we have:

	Depreciation Expense for the Year	Cost	Accumulated Depreciation	Book Value
Purchase		$20,000		$20,000
1st year's depreciation (40% × $20,000)	$ 8,000		$ 8,000	12,000
2nd year's depreciation (40% × $12,000)	4,800		12,800	7,200
3rd year's depreciation (40% × $7,200)	2,880		15,680	4,320
4th year's depreciation (40% × $4,320)	1,728		17,408	2,592
5th year's depreciation (40% × $2,592)	1,037		18,445	1,555
	$18,445			

No salvage value is used in this method because there is always a remainder which might be considered salvage value.

5. Sum-of-the-Years-Digits Method: This method applies a reducing fraction to the original cost minus salvage value. The formula for finding the fraction is: Let n be the number of periods of expected economic life. The denominator of the fraction is the sum of $n + (n - 1) + (n - 2) + \ldots + 1$. The numerator for the first year is n; the second year, $n - 1$; ... ; the last year, 1. Therefore, each year the fraction becomes smaller but the total of all the fractions equals 1.

Assume an asset costing $20,000 having an expected economic life of five years and a salvage value of $2,000:

Denominator = 5 + 4 + 3 + 2 + 1 = 15.
Fractions are ⁵⁄₁₅, ⁴⁄₁₅, ³⁄₁₅, ²⁄₁₅, and ¹⁄₁₅.

Cost minus salvage value	$20,000 − $2,000 =	$18,000
1st year's depreciation:	18,000 × ⁵⁄₁₅ =	6,000
2nd year's depreciation:	18,000 × ⁴⁄₁₅ =	4,800
3rd year's depreciation:	18,000 × ³⁄₁₅ =	3,600
4th year's depreciation:	18,000 × ²⁄₁₅ =	2,400
5th year's depreciation:	18,000 × ¹⁄₁₅ =	1,200
		$18,000

You can see from the illustration of these last two methods that they have the effect of bringing into the earlier years of the useful life of an asset a greater proportional amount of depreciation expense than would be the case under the straight-line method.

SUBSIDIARY LEDGERS

For purposes of control, to help prevent theft, to aid in the location of assets, and for purposes of insurance claims processing, among other reasons, many companies keep a detailed card file or a detailed listing (sometimes called a **register**) of all assets in a group. If this card file or register is totaled to equal the control account in the general ledger, the detailed records can constitute a subsidiary ledger. In some companies, the data are expanded to include the accumulated depreciation for each asset item. See Fig. 16.

SELLING AND DISCARDING ASSETS

When fixed asset items are sold or discarded, the accountant must be careful to depreciate the asset to the time of disposition (on some rule similar to the one discussed earlier when a fixed asset is purchased in the middle of a fiscal period). The current book value can then be determined. The amount received compared with the current book value of the asset measures the gain or loss on disposition of the fixed asset. This gain or loss is an extraordinary item and appears on

EQUIPMENT RECORD

NAME OF ASSET *BULL DOG LATHE*

SUB. ACCT. NO. *-07*   ACCT. NO. *403*

DEPARTMENT	LOCATION	ASSET NO.
DESCRIPTION *AMERICAN MACHINE TOOL CO.*		

MANUFACTURER'S SERIAL NO. *A-73564* YEAR TYPE MODEL *TH*

SIZE *6'* *10.* H.P.

FLOOR SPACE OCCUPIED *3' X 7'* AMOUNT OF INSURANCE CARRIED $ RATE $

BLDG. 1 - DEPT. 3

APPRAISED BY WHEN APPRAISED 19 APPRAISED VALUE $ SALVAGE OR SCRAP VALUE $ *300.00*

DATE ACQUIRED	DATE INSTALLED	NO. OF UNITS	DETAILS OF PURCHASE AND ASSEMBLY	POSTING REF.	ORIGINAL COST	ADDITIONAL CHARGES	CREDITS	BALANCE
2 7 A		1	PURCHASE	FJ-2-16	15500 00			15500 00
			DEPRECIATION - 1 Yr. - YEAR A	GJ-42			1520 00	13980 00
			DEPRECIATION - 1 Yr. - YEAR B	GJ-43			1520 00	12460 00
			DEPRECIATION - 1 Yr. YEAR C	GJ-40			1520 00	10940 00
			DEPRECIATION - 1 Yr. YEAR D	GJ-40			1520 00	9420 00
			DEPRECIATION - 1 Yr. YEAR E	GJ-41			1520 00	7900 00

DEPRECIATION YEAR	19 A	19 B	19 C	19 D	19 E	19 F	19	19	19	19	19
REMAINING LIFE (YRS.)	10 Yrs.										
DETERMINED BY	PLANT DEPT.										
DATE DETERMINED											
NEW DEPRE. RATE											
AMOUNT FORWARD		1520 00	3040 00	4560 00	6080 00	7600 00					
TOTAL FOR YEAR	1520 00	1520 00	1520 00	1520 00	1520 00						
AMOUNT FORWARD	1520 00	3040 00	4560 00	6080 00	7600 00						

Figure 16. Equipment Record.

the Income Statement below Net Operating Income.

Assume a factory machine costing $12,500 having an economic life of ten years and a salvage value of $500. The asset is depreciated on the straight-line basis. On January 1, Year A, the accumulated depreciation is $10,200. The asset is sold on April 1, Year A, for $1,300 cash. The depreciation per year is $\frac{\$12,500 - \$500}{10}$, or $1,200. For the period January 1, Year A, to April 1, Year A (three months), the depreciation is $300. The entry to record this is:

Depreciation Expense—
  Factory Equipment $300
  Allowance for Depreciation—
    Factory Equipment $300

The allowance for depreciation is now $10,500 and the book value is $2,000. The loss from disposition is $700. The entry to record this is:

Allowance for Depreciation—
  Factory Equipment $ 10,500
Cash   1,300
Loss on Disposition of Fixed Assets   700
  Factory Equipment $12,500

The depreciation expense entry is prepared first; then the entry is prepared debiting the assets received, debiting the corrected accumulated depreciation, debiting the loss on disposition, if any, crediting the asset at cost, and crediting the gain on disposition, if any.

If the asset is discarded and there is no asset received in return, the loss on disposition is the current book value of the asset.

ASSETS FULLY DEPRECIATED STILL USED IN PRODUCTION

When fixed assets are fully depreciated down to salvage value and are still used by the business in its operation, the current period has income but no matching depreciation expense, thereby increasing net income. Some accountants suggest that fixed assets fully depreciated still used in production be so noted on the Balance Sheet. It should be pointed out to the statement reader that the income was produced with fully depreciated assets if their amount is significant.

TRADING ASSETS

In many cases in which assets are traded for newer assets, the dealer offers a trade-in allowance for the old piece of equipment. Trade-in is a sales device and should not be recognized on the books of the company trading the old asset. Rather, the accounting records should reflect the true cost of the new asset acquired, which is the current book value of the old asset plus the cash or assets paid and the liabilities assumed. This method is called the "income tax method" and is the only one recognized by the Internal Revenue Service.

Assume a truck costing $15,600 has an estimated salvage value of $1,200 and an economic life of six years (straight-line basis is used). The balance in the Accumulated Depreciation—Truck account on January 1, Year A, is $10,400. On June 1, Year A, the truck is traded in for a new one with a list price of $16,000. A trade-in allowance of $5,000 is given by the dealer; the remainder is paid in cash.

To bring the allowance up to date:

$$\frac{\$15,600 - \$1,200}{6 \times 12} = \$200 \text{ depreciation per}$$

month. January 1 to June 1 = 5 months or $1,000 depreciation.

Depreciation Expense—Truck	$1,000	
Allowance for Depreciation—		
Truck		$1,000

(Balance in the Accumulated Depreciation—Truck account is now $11,400.)

To record the purchase of the new truck:

Truck (new)	$15,200	
Allowance for Depreciation—		
Truck	11,400	
Truck (old)		$15,600
Cash ($16,000 − $5,000)		11,000

The value for the new truck is determined by the amount of debit needed to establish debit-credit equality in the purchase entry. This is called the "adjusted basis" and is the cost that will be depreciated over the economic life of the new asset after subtracting salvage value.

OBSOLESCENCE AND INADEQUACY

When a fixed asset loses its economic value prior to the time it is depreciated down to salvage value, because of obsolescence or inadequacy, there is a **write-down** of the asset to salvage in the fiscal period in which this change in asset utility occurs. **Obsolescence** is the condition of having the utility of an asset lost as a result of the discovery or development of a better asset that has made the present one less useful. An example would be a propeller airplane being replaced by a jet airplane for long-distance flights. When the jet airplane was developed for commercial use, the economic life of the propeller airplane was shortened. The airlines had to purchase jet airplanes prior to the time the propeller planes would be depreciated to salvage value in order to compete with airlines equipped with jets. The depreciation schedules had to be revised to reflect this fact.

Inadequacy is the condition of possessing an asset that cannot adequately handle anticipated production, with the result that a new asset must be acquired to meet production needs. An example would be a situation in which a company has a machine that was purchased to produce 100,000 units per year in normal operation. With overtime, production can be increased to 125,000 units. But sales acceptance is such that future production requirements are 200,000 units per year. The old facility is inadequate and must be replaced if the company wants to take advantage of the market potential.

Management must always be aware of the

state of development in facilities in its industry and must be aware of changing market potentials. This requires that owners and managers have a communication system efficient enough to enable them to recognize these factors. Sales literature from manufacturers, salesmen from manufacturers, trade periodicals, business magazines and newspapers, trade conventions, courses established by manufacturers, business groups, or schools of business administration all are sources of information which management must consider. Sales analyses, modern projection techniques, budgeting and forecasting, salesmen's reports, and other market information must be continually used to assess market potential. The results of this information-gathering and -evaluation system must be communicated internally to the policy-makers if the company is to improve its position in the future.

INSURANCE—COVERAGE AND LOSS RECOVERIES

The ownership of fixed assets carries with it a number of risks. People can be injured by or on your property; loss from fire or theft can occur; and so on. Collision insurance for motor vehicles, public liability for buildings, business interruptions, and other risks as well as the risk against the physical loss of the facility must all be considered. Every business should make use of the services of a competent insurance agent or broker. The broker's income comes from two major sources—commissions on premiums and fees for risk analyses. Many agents sell insurance that the business orders without a thorough analysis of risk exposure. The business should know its risk exposure and buy the insurance it needs, assuming the remainder of the risk itself. Not knowing of the risk does not eliminate it. This means that a company should have its risks analyzed on a regular basis because conditions and values change. A book could be written (and indeed many books have been) on the topic of insurance risks and policies. It is not the purpose of this work to discuss all risks and the solution of the risk problem. Rather, this discussion will concern itself with the accounting treatment of the loss of physical facilities.

Most fire insurance policies include a **co-insurance clause.** This means that the policyholder assumes part of the loss under certain conditions. The figure often used for co-insurance is 80%. Assume a business bought a building (exclusive of land) for $100,000 ten years ago, buying a fire insurance policy of $80,000 having an 80% co-insurance clause. Examination of the policy reveals that the insurance company agrees to pay in the case of a fire one of three amounts, as follows:

a. The face amount of the policy ($80,000); or
b. Its share of the loss computed by a formula:

$$\frac{\text{face of the policy}}{\text{present value of the property} \times 80\%} \times \text{loss; or}$$

c. The amount of the loss; whichever is lowest.

Examples—Case 1. Assume a building valued currently at $200,000 insured under a $160,000 policy with an 80% co-insurance clause. The building burns and the loss totals $180,000. The amount paid to the insured will be computed:

a. Face amount of policy = $160,000.
b. Loss formula:

$$\frac{\$160,000}{\$200,000 \times 80\%} \times \$180,000 = \$180,000$$

c. Amount of the loss = $180,000.

The amount computed under a., $160,000, is the lowest. Therefore, when the full amount of the required insurance is purchased and a loss occurs *greater* than the face amount of the policy, the insurance company bears the loss up to the face amount of the policy, and the insurance bears the remainder (the purchaser is the co-insurer for the upper limit uninsured portion).

Case 2. Assume a building valued currently at $150,000 insured under a $120,000 policy with an 80% co-insurance clause. The building burns and the loss totals $100,000. The amount paid to the insured will be computed:

a. Face amount of policy = $120,000.
b. Loss formula:

$$\frac{\$120,000}{\$150,000 \times 80\%} \times \$100,000 = \$100,000.$$

c. Amount of the loss = $100,000.

The lowest is $100,000. Therefore, when the full amount of the required insurance is purchased and a loss occurs *less* than the face amount of the policy, the insurance company bears the loss completely and the insured bears no loss.

Case 3. Assume a building currently valued at $200,000 insured under a $120,000 policy with an 80% co-insurance clause. The building burns and the loss totals $170,000. The amount paid to the insured will be computed:

a. Face amount of policy = $120,000.
b. Loss formula:

$$\frac{\$120,000}{\$200,000 \times 80\%} \times \$170,000 = \$127,500.$$

c. Amount of loss = $170,000.

The lowest is $120,000. Therefore, when the full amount of the required insurance is *not* purchased and a loss occurs *greater* than the face amount of the policy, the insurance company pays the face amount of the policy and the insured bears the remainder.

Case 4. Assume a building currently valued at $150,000 insured under a $100,000 policy with an 80% co-insurance clause. The building burns and the loss totals $60,000. The amount paid to the insured will be computed:

a. Face amount of policy = $100,000.
b. Loss formula:

$$\frac{\$100,000}{\$150,000 \times 80\%} \times \$60,000 = \$50,000.$$

c. Amount of the loss = $60,000.

The lowest is $50,000. Therefore, when the full amount of the required insurance is *not* purchased and a loss occurs *less* than the face amount of the policy, the insurance company pays a percentage of the loss, as determined by the loss formula, and the insured bears the remainder.

From the standpoint of the insured, the co-insurance clause reduces insurance premiums by making him a co-insurer with the insurance company. The insurance company will pay all losses sustained up to the face amount of the policy if the policy is maintained at the stated percentage of current value. Thus, in Cases 3 and 4

above, the insurance coverage was not up to the proper percentage when the fire occurred, and the insured bore a larger loss than he otherwise would have borne. It is imperative that the business review the present value of the assets covered by insurance so as to take full advantage of the coverage purchased. From the standpoint of the insurance company, this continual upward revision of the value increases premium income in inflationary periods but protects the insured in the event of loss by reducing his risk. (Many insurance companies now either include clauses increasing the amount of insurance on renewal or regularly appraise the property to reflect higher values.)

What happens when a fixed asset is destroyed by a catastrophe covered by insurance? Up to the time of the catastrophe, the facility is being used in production and is subject to depreciation accounting. The book value is written off to a Gain or Loss from Catastrophe account when the unexpected happens. The amount of recovery from the insurance company is credited to the Gain or Loss from Catastrophe account.

Assume a building purchased on July 1, Year A, costing $660,000, having an economic life of 25 years with an estimated salvage value of $60,000, depreciated on a straight-line basis.

The yearly depreciation is $24,000.

On January 1, Year F, the accounts appear:

Building	
July 1, Year A $660,000	

Allowance for Depreciation—Building	
Dec. 31, Year A	
(½ year)	$ 12,000
Dec. 31, Year B	24,000
	36,000
Dec. 31, Year C	24,000
	60,000
Dec. 31, Year D	24,000
	84,000
Dec. 31, Year E	24,000
	108,000

The building is insured for various risks including flood damage. On October 1, Year F, a flood occurs and the building is a total loss.

Depreciation to October 1, Year F (9 months) is $18,000. The entry to record this is:

Depreciation Expense—Building	$18,000	
Allowance for Depreciation—Building		$18,000

The corrected balance in the Allowance for Depreciation—Building account now is $126,000 and the book value is $534,000. The building is written off, and the entry to do this is:

Allowance for Depreciation—Building	$126,000	
Gain or Loss Due to Flood	534,000	
Building		$660,000

The insurance company computes its loss at $570,000 because values have increased since the building was purchased and the policy amount was increased accordingly, and sends a check to the insured. The entry to record this situation is:

Cash	$570,000	
Gain or Loss Due to Flood		$570,000

It would appear that the company received a benefit of $36,000 as a result of the flood. But there is a loss of usefulness of the facility and an unrecorded property value increase that has not been accounted for. If the facility is not replaced, the $36,000 becomes a "gain" for accounting purposes. If the facility is replaced, the "gain" is applied to the new facility's cost to reduce it.

Assume a new building is built at a cost of $730,000 to replace the one damaged by the flood. It will be financed by a $580,000 mortgage. The entry is:

Building	$730,000	
Cash		$150,000
Mortgage Payable		580,000

The cost would then be reduced by the "gain" with the entry:

Gain or Loss Due to Flood	$36,000	
Building		$36,000

(Note: The fire insurance proceeds may or may not be invested in total in the new building.)

If only a partial loss occurs, then the amount given by the insurance company is credited to the Repairs Due to Catastrophe account, and the balance in that account is an adjustment to the depreciation basis of the asset.

Assume a fire loss that required $50,000 of remodeling to restore the asset to its condition prior to the fire. The insurance company under the co-insurance policy pays only $42,000. The true fire loss is $8,000.

The entry to record restoration is:

Loss Due to Repair of Fire Damage	$50,000	
Cash		$50,000

The entry to record the receipt of insurance proceeds is:

Cash	$42,000	
Loss Due to Repair of Fire Damage		$42,000

The balance in the Loss Due to Fire Damage account is closed to the Profit and Loss Summary account.

NATURAL ASSETS AND DEPLETION

Natural assets are those assets produced by nature which man converts to his own use. There are two subtypes: extractive resources and regenerative resources.

The extractive industries (oil, coal, gold, etc.) must locate the natural deposits, determine the value of the deposit, and determine the cost of building and operating physical facilities. The total cost to be expended must be less than the sale value of the resource extracted if the company is to make a profit. Once all the resource is extracted, the physical facility built to extract it becomes useless (except for items that can be moved or sold for scrap value). The rules of fixed asset cost allocation discussed above are modified so that the allocation is made during the time of extraction. In many cases, the Internal Revenue Code allows the deductions from income to exceed cost. This is a tremendous advantage for the business that extracts natural assets. However, if the business drills a well and gets no oil, there is a disadvantage.

The whole question of the extractive industries is a specialized field of accounting and is mentioned only because large capital investments are made in physical facilities, and many rules of accounting parallel rules of depreciation accounting in concept. These principles form what is known as **depletion accounting.**

The industries that deal in regenerative natural assets include crop farming, tree farming, fishing, poultry, and the like. In these industries, physical facilities are treated as they are in industrial situations. The problem of land preparation arises for crop farming, but again this is a specialized field of accounting and is mentioned here only because many rules of accounting in these industries parallel rules of depreciation accounting in concept.

INTANGIBLE ASSETS AND AMORTIZATION

Intangible assets are nonphysical assets that are created by legal contract, statutory operation, or other such concepts. These intangible assets are valuable rights for the business and are enforceable in law (except perhaps for good will, which is a special intangible asset). Included in intangible assets are two subtypes: limited life (franchises, patents, copyrights), and unlimited life (trademarks, good will).

The limited life intangibles may be purchased (such as a franchise) or may be developed (a patent or copyright). Where they are purchased, usually one charge is made to the intangible account. Thus, if a company pays $10,000 for a franchise to operate a taxicab company for ten years in a town, the entry is:

Franchise	$10,000	
Cash		$10,000

Each year, franchise amortization expense is charged, and the franchise account is credited with a portion of the cost:

$$\frac{\$10,000}{10 \text{ yrs.}} = \$1,000/\text{yr.}$$

Franchise Amortization Expense	$1,000	
Franchise		$1,000

When the intangible is developed, there may be a series of charges that will eventually result in the cost of the intangible (as for instance, patent development costs). If the patent is secured, the cost is allocated over the term of the patent or its economic life, whichever is shorter. The entries are the same as those shown above except that "patent" would be used rather than "franchise."

Where the intangible is for an unlimited life the asset is charged with the cost, but there is no charge to operations on a regular basis. Sometimes, in the interest of accounting conservatism, the asset is written down to a nominal value of $1.

APPRAISALS

One of the major problems in accounting today is determining how to change accounting principles so that assets purchased in years gone by, which have been recorded at cost and have been depreciated under the concepts described in this chapter, can be shown at nearer their present value rather than at book value. There is no current requirement, in generally accepted accounting principles, that the present value must be shown. However, when cost less accumulated depreciation only is shown, there can be a great disparity between book value and present value.

Assume that 25 years ago a company purchased a building (exclusive of land) for $200,000, paying $50,000 down and taking out a mortgage for $150,000 (now paid off). The building has been depreciated on a straight-line basis to $20,000 book value; the recording has all been done on a cost basis. If the company decides to remortgage the building (for whatever reason), it would want to show more than $20,000, especially if the building is now worth $300,000. So on the financial statement the book value is shown as $20,000, but the company would want the bank to know that the building is actually worth $300,000 today.

There are ways to tell what present values are. One is just knowing that the property is worth so much today—really a hunch or an unscientific sampling of local information. Another is getting an appraisal from a real estate agent or a professional appraisal company. The latter is perhaps the most accurate because the appraiser's fee is based upon the time spent on the assignment. He is a professional person who follows an established set of procedures to determine value, prepares a written report of his calculations and findings, and is most objective. Those who are, or might be, interested parties, such as real estate agents, quite often bring into the appraisal situation their personal biases of property values.

Once some realistic value is decided upon, the unrecorded excess of appraised value over book value can be recorded in the following manner:

Proprietorship:

Excess of Present Value		
over Book Value	$280,000	
Jones, Capital		$280,000

Partnership:

Excess of Present Value		
over Book Value	$280,000	
Brown, Capital		$140,000
Smith, Capital		140,000

(or whatever proportion the partnership agreement dictates).

Corporation:

Excess of Present Value over		
Book Value	$280,000	
Appraisal Surplus (Capital)		$280,000

In this manner the statements more nearly reflect the facts of present value, yet the statement reader is put on notice that there are some values that have not been arrived at in the generally accepted method of sale or value transfer.

Statement Presentation:

Balance Sheet:

Land			$50,000
Buildings		$472,000	
Less Accumulated			
Depreciation		185,000	287,000
Factory Machinery		500,000	
Less Accumulated			
Depreciation		200,000	300,000
Small Tools			55,000
Store Equipment		100,000	
Less Accumulated			
Depreciation		60,000	40,000
Office Equipment		75,000	
Less Accumulated			
Depreciation		15,000	60,000
TOTAL PLANT ASSETS			$792,00

Natural Assets:		
Wasting Asset (Coal Deposit)	$100,000	
Less Accumulated Depletion	25,000	75,000

Intangible Assets:		
Franchise	$20,000	
Patent	15,000	35,000

Another method for showing the plant assets on the Balance Sheet might be:

Plant Assets:

	Cost	Accumulated Depreciation	Book Value
Land	$ 50,000	—	$ 50,000
Buildings	472,000	$185,000	287,000
Factory Machinery	500,000	200,000	300,000
Small Tools	55,000	—	55,000
Store Equipment	100,000	60,000	40,000
Office Equipment	75,000	15,000	60,000
TOTAL PLANT ASSETS	$1,252,000	$460,000	$792,000

Profit and Loss Statement:

Factory Machinery Depreciation Expense	$35,000	
Patent Amortization Expense	7,000	
Franchise Amortization Expense	3,000	
Small Tools Expense	12,000	
Sales Equipment Depreciation Expense	5,000	
Office Equipment Depreciation Expense	2,000	
Loss from Disposal of Depreciable Assets	15,000	
Gain from Disposal of Depreciable Assets		$5,000
Loss from Natural Calamity (Fire, etc.)	12,000	
Gain from Natural Calamity (Fire, etc.)		6,000

EXERCISES

Exercise No. 28. From the Escrow Statement (Fig. 17), prepare the journal entry to be recorded on the books of Franklin Sullivan, Inc., to reflect the purchase of the empty lot at 329 Weston Road, San Francisco, Calif.

Exercise No. 29. The Smith Products Company bought realty consisting of a lot and an old building. The entry to record the purchase of the realty was:

Land	$51,300	
Prepaid Taxes	200	
Cash		$51,500

No proration of cost between land and building was made because the building is to be removed to make room for a warehouse. The company investigated the removal of the building and two methods were suggested and bids secured. The best bids under the two methods were as follows:

a. Chicago Wrecking Company will remove the building in two months, salvaging lumber, piping, fixtures, etc., will remove all debris so that the land is level, and will pay Smith Products Company $5,200.

b. Ajax Destruction Company will demolish the building in seven working days and will remove all debris so that the land is level. This will cost Smith Products $3,700.

Disregarding decisions of time involved in the

First American Title Company of San Francisco

MAIN OFFICE: 300 PINE STREET (94104) · P.O. BOX 3078, RINCON ANNEX · (415) 989-1300
SAN FRANCISCO, CALIFORNIA 94119

☒ BUYER'S   ☐ BORROWER'S   **ESCROW INSTRUCTIONS**   Date *APRIL 1, YEAR B*

Order Number
To: FIRST AMERICAN TITLE COMPANY
I/We hand you herewith

$ *10,000.00*

which you are authorized to deliver and/or record when you have received for my account the following:

DEED TO 329 WESTON ROAD, SAN FRANCISCO, CALIF.

FROM WILLIAM ALAMEDA AND FRANCES ESCOBAR

TENANTS-IN-COMMON

and when you can issue your standard coverage form policy of title insurance with a liability of $ *47,000*
on the property described as   *329 WESTON ROAD, SAN FRANCISCO, CALIF.*

showing title vested in   *FRANKLIN SULLIVAN, INC.*

9975 74th AVE.

Subject to: *SAN FRANCISCO, CALIF.*
1. Printed exceptions and conditions in said policy.
2. ☐ all ☒ 2nd half General and special taxes for fiscal year 19 *A* - 19 *B*
3. Assessments and/or bonds not delinquent.
4. Exceptions numbered *1-3*   as shown in your preliminary title report dated *MARCH 3* 19 *B*
   issued in connection with the above order number.

Upon consummation of this escrow, you are authorized to disburse in accordance with the following statement. Prorate as of
APRIL 17 , 19 *B* on the basis of a 30 day month. Taxes based on the latest available tax figures.

	Debits		Credits	
Sales Price	47,000	00		
Paid outside of Escrow to				
Deposit by *FRANKLIN-SULLIVAN, INC.*			10,000	00
Encumbrance of Record				
Loan Trust Fund				
Assumption Fee				
New Loan				
Deed of Trust ☐ 1st ☐ 2nd ☐ 3rd				
Loan Charges: Loan Fee $ Tax Res. $				
Appsl. Fee $ Ins. Res. $				
Cred. Rept. $ FHA Prem. $				
Int. Est. @ % Fr. To $				
Total				
☐ Pay Fire Ins. Prem.				
☐ Pay Tax Service	27	00		
☐ Pay Taxes				
☐ Personal Property Tax				
☐ Pay Assessments or Bonds				
☐ Prorate Taxes Fr. *APRIL 17* To *JUNE 30* on $ *68.00/6 MO.*	27	95		
☐ Prorate Fire Ins. Fr. To on $				
☐ Prorate Int. @ % Fr. To on $				
☐ Prorate Rent Fr. To on $				
Draw Doc. $				
Notary Fee $	10	00		
Title Prem. Std. $ *303.00* ALTA $	303	00		
Escrow $	142	00		
Recording $	25	00		
Balance Due ☐ To Close ☐ The Undersigned			37,534	95
Totals	47,534	95	47,534	95

These instructions are effective until *APRIL 26* , 19 *B* and thereafter unless revoked by written demand and authorization satisfactory to you. Incorporated herein and made a part hereof by reference are the "General Provisions" and any additional instructions appearing on the reverse side of this page.

Received: *APRIL 1* , 19 *B*
First American Title Company

By *Samantha Ellison*

Address   *Franklin Sullivan, Inc.*
Jasper Peters Secretary
9975 74th AVE.- SAN FRANCISCO, CA
Phone No. *(415) 002- 3795*

Figure 17. Escrow Statement for Exercise No. 28.

proposals above, prepare a journal entry to reflect the signing of a contract with:

a. Chicago Wrecking Company.
b. Ajax Destruction Company.

Exercise No. 30. Simott Properties bought an apartment building as an investment. The purchase price was $480,000. There were to be two loans taken for the purchase: the first from the First National Banking Co. of Singapore of California, Ltd., for $360,000; the second from Frank Galli (a private investor) for $40,000. The transaction is summarized on an Escrow Statement Order (Fig. 18.).

When Simott Properties was considering the purchase of the property, they had it appraised by a professional real estate appraising firm. The report showed:

Land	$125,000
Building	375,000
Total	$500,000

The assessment roll for the city shows the following:

Land	$10,000
Building	60,000
Total	$70,000

Prepare the entry on Simott Properties' books using:

a. The appraisal valuation for the proration of cost.
b. The assessment valuation for the proration of cost.

Exercise No. 31. Western Aero-Space, Inc., needed office space near its rocket-testing laboratories in the San Lazzaro Mountains and purchased an office building in the town of Devil's Slide. The cost of the realty was charged as follows:

Land	$ 18,972
Building	113,832

Before moving, management decides that certain repairs and improvements should be made. The cost of these repairs and improvements are as follows:

Architect's fees	$ 1,000
Construction costs	20,000
Repaint exterior	900
Fire escapes	2,500
Repair roof	1,000
Replace broken windows	200

a. Prepare the entry for the above. (Credit Accounts Payable.)
b. What is the total cost of the building?

Exercise No. 32. Five years later (see Exercise No. 31) Western Aero-Space, Inc., remodels the second floor and repaints the exterior of the building. The costs are as follows:

Architect's fees	$ 1,000
Construction costs	15,000
Repaint exterior	2,600

a. Prepare the entry for the above. (Credit Accounts Payable.)
b. Is there any difference in the treatment between the journal entry in Exercise No. 31 and this one? If so, explain.

Exercise No. 33. A machine costing $5,000 is purchased and shipped to the San Antonio plant of Penexco. The freight charges are $105, insurance while the machine is in transit is $75, and installation charges are $200. What is the total cost of the machine?

Exercise No. 34. A machine costs $10,600 installed and ready to use. Bay Machine Co. pays $2,000 down and agrees to assume contract obligations to pay $400 per month for 24 months. Prepare the journal entry for this transaction.

Exercise No. 35. A machine costing $9,800 is installed on January 2, 1965. It is intended to be used for eight years and will have a salvage value of $200. What is the yearly amount of depreciation charge using the straight-line method?

Exercise No. 36. A machine costing $15,000 is installed on January 2, Year A, and is used for special jobs on an intermittent basis. It will have

First American Title Company of San Francisco

MAIN OFFICE: 300 PINE STREET (94104) · P.O. BOX 3078, RINCON ANNEX · (415) 989-1300
SAN FRANCISCO, CALIFORNIA 94119

☒ BUYER'S ☐ BORROWER'S
Order Number

ESCROW INSTRUCTIONS

Date *August 5, 19 A*

To: FIRST AMERICAN TITLE COMPANY
I/We hand you herewith

TWENTY-FIVE THOUSAND & NO/100 DOLLARS
(25,000.00)

which you are authorized to deliver and/or record when you have received for my account the following:

GRANT DEED TO PROPERTY KNOWN AS
6259 GEARY DRIVE
SAN FRANCISCO, CALIF.

and when you can issue your standard coverage form policy of title insurance with a liability of $ *480,000*
on the property described as

AS ABOVE

showing title vested in

SIMOTT PROPERTIES, a limited partnership

Subject to:
1. Printed exceptions and conditions in said policy.
2. ☐ all ☐ 2nd half General and special taxes for fiscal year 19 *A* 19 *B* *(FIRST HALF)*
3. Assessments and/or bonds not delinquent.
4. Exceptions numbered *1-6*   as shown in your preliminary title report dated *JULY 22, 19 A*
   issued in connection with the above order number.

Upon consummation of this escrow, you are authorized to disburse in accordance with the following statement. Prorate as of
AUG. 15   , 19 *A* on the basis of a 30 day month. Taxes based on the latest available tax figures.

	Debits		Credits	
Sales Price	480,000	00		
Paid outside of Escrow to				
Deposit by *SIMOTT PROPERTIES*			25,000	00
Encumbrance of Record				
Loan Trust Fund				
Assumption Fee				
New Loan *FIRST NATIONAL BANKING CO. OF SINGAPORE OF CALIF. LTD*			360,000	00
Deed of Trust ☒ 1st ☐ 2nd ☐ 3rd				
Loan Charges: Loan Fee *1* % $ *3,600.00* Tax Res. $				
Appsl. Fee $ *300.00* Ins. Res. $				
Cred. Rept. $ *75.00* FHA Prem. $				
Int. Est. @ % Fr To $				
Total *3975.00*	3975	00		
☐ Pay Fire Ins. Prem.				
☐ Pay Tax Service				
☐ Pay Taxes				
☐ Personal Property Tax				
☐ Pay Assessments or Bonds				
RENTAL DEPOSITS			3742	00
☐ Prorate Taxes Fr. *JULY 1* To *AUG. 15* on $ *8,766.00/6 MO.*			730	50
☐ Prorate Fire Ins. Fr. To on $				
☐ Prorate Int. @ *12*% Fr. *AUG. 10* To *AUG. 15* on $ *360,000.00*	1,800	00		
☐ Prorate Rent Fr. *AUG 15* To *AUG. 30* on $ *4217.00/MO.*			2108	50
SECOND DEED OF TRUST - FRANK GALLI (PRIVATE)			40,000	00
15% - MONEY ON DATE OF CLOSE				
Draw Doc. $				
Notary Fee $	30	00		
Title Prem. Std. $ *1310.00* ALTA $ *360.00*	1,670	00		
Escrow $	583	00		
Recording $	50	00		
Balance Due ☐ To Close ☐ The Undersigned			56,527	00
Totals	488,108	00	488,108	00

These instructions are effective until *AUG. 15* , 19 *A* and thereafter unless revoked by written demand and authorization satisfactory to you. Incorporated herein and made a part hereof by reference are the "General Provisions" and any additional
instructions appearing on the reverse side of this page.
Received: *AUG. 5* , 19 *A*
First American Title Company   *Samuel Simott, general partner*

By *Adeline Delphi*   Address *6333 DELAWARE AVE. SAN FRANCISCO, CA.*
                                     Phone No. *(415) 001-6222*

Figure 18. Escrow Statement Order for Exercise No. 30.

an estimated salvage value of $1,000 after 2,000 hours of use. Time records of machine usage are kept as follows:

Year A	175 hours
Year B	62 hours

a. What is the hourly depreciation rate?

b. What amounts should be charged to depreciation expense in the calendar years A and B?

Exercise No. 37. A die is manufactured that will be used to produce a part for a machine that the Zetal Corp. sells. The projected sales of the machine are 20,000 units. The die costs $14,300 and is estimated to have a salvage value of $300. What is the depreciation expense per unit produced?

Exercise No. 38. With respect to the machine described in Exercise No. 37, how much depreciation expense would there be in the following years?

Year A production—7,000 units
Year B production—5,000 units
Year C production—6,500 units
Year D production—3,000 units

Exercise No. 39. With respect to the machine described in Exercise No. 37, 18,500 units are produced and the model is closed out. The depreciation expense charged to operations has been $12,950. The die is sold for $200 cash. The two accounts involved are:

Dies and Tools	
Year A	$14,300

Allowance for Depreciation—Dies and Tools	
Year A	$ 4,900
Year B	3,500
	8,400
Year C	4,550
	$12,950

What entry (entries) are made to reflect the sale of the die?

Exercise No. 40. A machine costing $20,000 is purchased on January 2, Year A, and is estimated to have a life of ten years. Complete the following schedule using the declining balance method of depreciation (200% of straight-line rate).

Explanation	Depreciation Expense for the Year	Accumulated Depreciation Dec. 31, 19—	Book Value
Purchase			$20,000
1st Year			
2nd Year			
3rd Year			
4th Year			
5th Year			
6th Year			
7th Year			
8th Year			
9th Year			
10th Year			

EQUIPMENT RECORD

NAME OF ASSET *PLANT MACHINERY*   SUB. ACCT. NO. *-05*   ACCT. NO. *402*

DEPARTMENT   LOCATION   ASSET NO. *9-136*

DESCRIPTION *Farragut Tool Machines*

MANUFACTURER'S SERIAL NO. *K-13259*   YEAR *A*   TYPE   MODEL *XKB 332*

SIZE   H.P.

FLOOR SPACE OCCUPIED *Planer Shop - Main Floor*   AMOUNT OF INSURANCE CARRIED $ RATE $

APPRAISED BY *Amer. Appraisal Co.*   WHEN APPRAISED *May 12* 19 *C*   APPRAISED VALUE $ *6,600.00* 5/12*C*   SALVAGE OR SCRAP VALUE $ *300.00*

DATE ACQUIRED	DATE INSTALLED	NO. OF UNITS	DETAILS OF PURCHASE AND ASSEMBLY	POSTING REF.	ORIGINAL COST	ADDITIONAL CHARGES	CREDITS	BALANCE
7 1 A	7 5 A	1		PJ-14	7500 00			7500 00
			DEPRECIATION 1/2 Yr. YEAR A	GJ-19			600 00	6900 00
			DEPRECIATION 1 Yr. YEAR B	GJ-18			1200 00	5700 00
			DEPRECIATION 1 Yr. YEAR C	GJ-19			1200 00	4500 00

DEPRECIATION YEAR	19 A	19 B	19 C	19 D	19	19	19	19	19	19	19
REMAINING LIFE (YRS.)	6 1/2	5 1/2	4 1/2	3 1/2							
DETERMINED BY											
DATE DETERMINED											
NEW DEPRE. RATE											
AMOUNT FORWARD		600—	1800—	3000—							
TOTAL FOR YEAR	600—	1200—	1200—								
AMOUNT FORWARD	600—	1800—	3000—								

Figure 19. Subsidiary Ledger Card for Exercise No. 42.

Exercise No. 41. Ayjay Company buys a machine costing $40,000 on January 2, Year A. It has an expected life of eight years. Assuming a salvage value of $400, determine the yearly depreciation expense using the Sum-of-the-Years-Digits Method.

Exercise No. 42. A company has a machine listed in the Plant Machinery account at a cost of $7,500. The subsidiary ledger card (Fig. 19) shows data relative to the asset.

   a. On October 1, Year E, the machine is sold for $4,000 cash. Prepare the entry (entries).

   b. On October 1, Year E, the machine is sold for $3,000 cash. Prepare the entry (entries).

Exercise No. 43. A business purchased a truck in Year A for $20,600. The estimated salvage value was $2,600. Accumulated depreciation is $17,000 up to the date the truck is traded in for a new one. The dealer agrees to give a trade-in allowance of $2,540 on a new truck costing $23,400. Prepare the entry to reflect the purchase of the new truck using the old one as a trade-in.

Exercise No. 44. On July 1, Year A, a business buys a machine costing $25,200 having an estimated life of ten years and a salvage value of $1,200. Management depreciates the machine on a straight-line basis. The accumulated depreciation at December 31, Year H, was $18,000. On October 1, Year I, the company trades the asset on a new and larger machine of the same type. This asset costs $30,000 and the dealer agrees to allow a trade-in of $1,800 on the old machine if it is used as a down payment on a new one. Management decides to depreciate the new asset on the Sum-of-the Years-Digits Method, assuming a salvage value of $1,100 and an estimated life of ten years.

a. Prepare the entry to record the depreciation of the machine on October 1, Year I.

b. Prepare the entry to record the purchase of the new machine on October 1, Year I, using the income tax method.

c. Prepare the entry to record the depreciation expense of the new machine to December 31, Year I, using the straight-line method. Assume a salvage value of $1,600 and an eight-year life.

Exercise No. 45. A machine cost $18,300 on July 1, Year A, and had an estimated economic life of ten years. On December 31, Year F, the corrected accumulated depreciation, computed on a straight-line basis, was $9,900. The asset was insured and is shown in the insurance policy schedule to have a value of $12,000. The current value of the asset is $15,000. The insurance policy has a 75% co-insurance clause. On April 1, Year H, a fire occurs and the asset is completely destroyed. The company makes the entry for depreciation expense of $450 as follows:

Machinery Depreciation Expense	$450	
Accumulated Depreciation—		
Machinery		$450

a. What is the amount that the company will receive from the insurance company?

b. Prepare the entry (entries) to close out the asset account and the Accumulated Depreciation account.

c. Prepare the entry for the receipt of cash from the insurance company.

d. Show the Loss Due to Fire account reflecting the entries required in b. and c. above.

e. Prepare the entry to close out the Loss Due to Fire account.

f. Where is the Loss Due to Fire amount shown on the Income Statement?

Exercise No. 46. A building cost $320,000 and has a current value of $500,000. It is insured against fire for $400,000. The policy has an 80% co-insurance clause. How much will be received by the owner if there is a fire and the loss is $360,000? (The corrected accumulated depreciation to the date of the fire is $120,000.)

Exercise No. 47. Assume the same facts as in Exercise No. 46 but the loss is $440,000.

Exercise No. 48. A building cost $300,000, has a current value of $600,000, and is insured against fire loss of $450,000. The policy has an 80% co-insurance clause. How much will be received from the insurance company if there is a fire and the loss is $480,000?

Exercise No. 49. Assume the same facts as in Exercise No. 48 but the loss is $96,000.

Exercise No. 50. A merchant purchases, for $10,000, an exclusive franchise to operate a service business in Fresno County. The franchise states that if the merchant generates $20,000 of business a year for five years the franchise will become permanent. What entries are necessary in the first five years of the franchise?

Exercise No. 51. Mr. Overstreet, the owner of an apartment house that cost $150,000 and has now been depreciated to a book value of $64,000, wants to present a statement to the bank to secure credit. The building has a current value of $250,000 and is insured for $180,000 under a policy having an 80% co-insurance clause. The balance owing on the mortgage is $120,000. Land has increased in value from $25,000 to $80,000. What entry is made to present the facts of current value to the bank?

Chapter 6

CURRENT LIABILITIES

Most businesses use credit to purchase inventories, supplies, goods and services, and fixed assets. The business or persons to whom moneys are owed are called **creditors** and the amounts owed are called **liabilities.** The creditors are not owners of the business and do not share in its profits; they expect to get paid only for the goods and services rendered.

There are two types of liabilities:

1. Current Liabilities: Those liabilities that, by their credit terms, are due to be paid during the next fiscal period (usually defined as one year from the Balance Sheet date).

2. Long-Term Liabilities: Those liabilities that, by their credit terms, are not due to be paid until after the end of the next fiscal period.

It does not matter when the business *plans* to pay a liability that determines its classification as current or long-term; the governing factor is the obligation's *due date*. In this chapter various types of current liabilities will be discussed. Long-term liabilities will be discussed in the following chapter.

ACCOUNTS PAYABLE

When a business wants to purchase on open credit, it makes arrangements with a supplier who extends the credit after assuring, to the best of his knowledge, that the business asking for credit is a good risk. After the credit relationship is established, the business asks the supplier to furnish goods or services with payment to be made at some future date according to the credit terms. The supplier may require that the buyer sign some form of receipt, and the supplier will later send an invoice to the purchaser. But the arrangement of credit is such that the purchaser is to pay for all purchases in any amount, not just one particular invoice.

When open credit is used to purchase goods or services, the entry is:

```
Assets
Inventories          ⎫
Expenses             ⎬ XXX
Other appropriate account ⎭
   Accounts Payable              XXX
```

Internal Control of Accounts Payable Transactions. To insure that the company will only order goods and services needed, and that the amounts owing will be paid only once, two internal control mechanisms are used. The first is **a purchasing procedure,** which can be described as follows:

1. The person needing goods or services prepares a **purchase requisition** (Fig. 20), which is given to the Purchasing Agent after proper approval. This requisition should state clearly what is requested—it should include type of material, drawings, delivery schedules, quantity schedules, and any other data that will assist the Purchasing Agent in locating vendors who can supply the material.

2. The Purchasing Agent shops the market for a vendor (in some cases he may take bids on the items required) and after selecting a vendor who can deliver the goods as stated issues a **purchase order** (Fig. 21) to the vendor. Copies of the pur-

REQUISITION ON PURCHASING DEPARTMENT
(NOT A PURCHASE ORDER)

8905

To	Purchasing Agent	Date	1/2	19 A
Deliver To	Southfield Plant	For	J.O. 675	
Address	847 Suffolk Dr., Oxnard, CA	Date Required	1/15/A	
Suggested Supplier	Adamson - Brown, NY			

	QUANTITY	PLEASE ORDER ITEMS LISTED BELOW	PRICE	AMOUNT
1	20 gr.	Cat # 6295 Reflector Clips		
2	100	Cat # 809 Shelf Brackets		
3	10 doz	Cat # 627 EZ Nuts		
4	400	Cat # A 522 B Model 3 - Converters		
5				

BUDGET CONTROL

Allowance For Period		Ordered By
	Balance Available $ 2,700	J Mitchell
$ 3200.00	Amt. This Purchase $ 1,050	Approved By
	Remaining Balance $ 1,650	Anderson Jones

Figure 20. Purchase Requisition.

YOUR FIRM NAME HERE
123 Main Street
YOUR TOWN, STATE and ZIP

Phone 123-4567

PURCHASE ORDER
1016

Show this Purchase Order Number
on all correspondence, invoices,
shipping papers and packages.

TO
ADMONSON-BROWN COMPANY
8296 West 753rd Street
New York City, NY 10037

DATE	REQUISITION NO
1/3/A	
SHIP TO	
Addressee	

REQUISITIONED BY	WHEN SHIP	SHIP VIA NYC	F.O.B. POINT	TERMS 2/10; Net 30			
QTY. ORDERED	QTY. RECEIVED	STOCK NO./DESCRIPTION		UNIT PRICE		TOTAL	
20 gr.		Cat No 6295		2	10	504	00
1,500 ea		Cat No 329 A		50	00	75	00
100 ea		Cat No 809		6	00	6	00
10 dz		Cat No A-522B Model 3		5	00	2000	00
4		Cat No 1635		37	00	148	00
						2893	00

1. Please send _____ copies of your invoice.
2. Order is to be entered in accordance with prices, delivery and specifications shown above.
3. Notify us immediately if you are unable to ship as specified.

Tim P. Jones
AUTHORIZED BY

Figure 21. Purchase Order.

chase order can be made for distribution as follows:

Receiving Department: to give the receiving clerk an idea of what is coming in and when the goods are to arrive, and so that sufficient space is available to take delivery from the carrier. The quantities of the materials ordered can be masked out; this requires the receiving clerk actually to count the material and not simply assume that what has been ordered matches what is received.

Inspection Department: to enable the department to schedule testing of materials received, if required.

Accounting Department: to assure that the cash required for payment of the invoice is available by the date of projected payment.

The Purchasing Agent keeps a copy of the purchase order for purposes of follow-up if materials are not delivered on time.

3. As the goods flow from the vendor to the purchaser, they are accompanied by a packing slip or similar document. The goods are received, counted, examined, and forwarded to the inspection department or storage areas for ultimate use or sale.

The receiving clerk prepares a receiving report that is sent to the Purchasing Agent for the purpose of comparing the actual shipment received with the original purchase order. (If the goods go to the inspection department, they are examined for quality and an inspection report is completed and forwarded to the Purchasing Agent, and then the goods go to the storage areas.)

4. After receiving each document from the vendor, the receiving department, and the inspection department (if appropriate), the Purchasing Agent checks them against the original purchase order to see if all conditions as stated in the purchase order have been complied with by the vendor, and that the goods were received as called for in the purchase order.

5. The Purchasing Agent notifies the accounting department that the vendor's invoice (which he has received directly from the vendor or indirectly through the accounting department) is a proper liability for the company.

The second internal control mechanism is the **voucher system procedure,** which can be described as follows:

1. When an invoice is approved by proper authority as a company liability, the accounting department prepares a voucher (Fig. 22). This is a standardized company form on which is transcribed all pertinent data from the approved invoices. The voucher clerk is generally familiar with the location of the necessary information on the different invoices that come into the business, and he places the information on the voucher form so that a specific item found on an invoice, such as price, will always be found in the same location on the voucher. The voucher clerk also shows the accounts to be debited, and the total amount of the invoice is credited to Accounts Payable. This distribution is generally approved by the voucher clerk's supervisor, who also approves the voucher for propriety.

2. After the approval, the voucher is entered into the Voucher Register (a form of Purchase Journal) which shows credits to Accounts Payable and the appropriate debits. At the end of the month the register is footed and cross-footed, and the entry shown above is made. (Sometimes the general ledger is posted directly from the register.)

An example of the headings of a Voucher Register might be:

Date	Voucher Number	Vendor	Amount	Merchandise Inventory	Various Accounts	General	
						Acct. No.	Amount

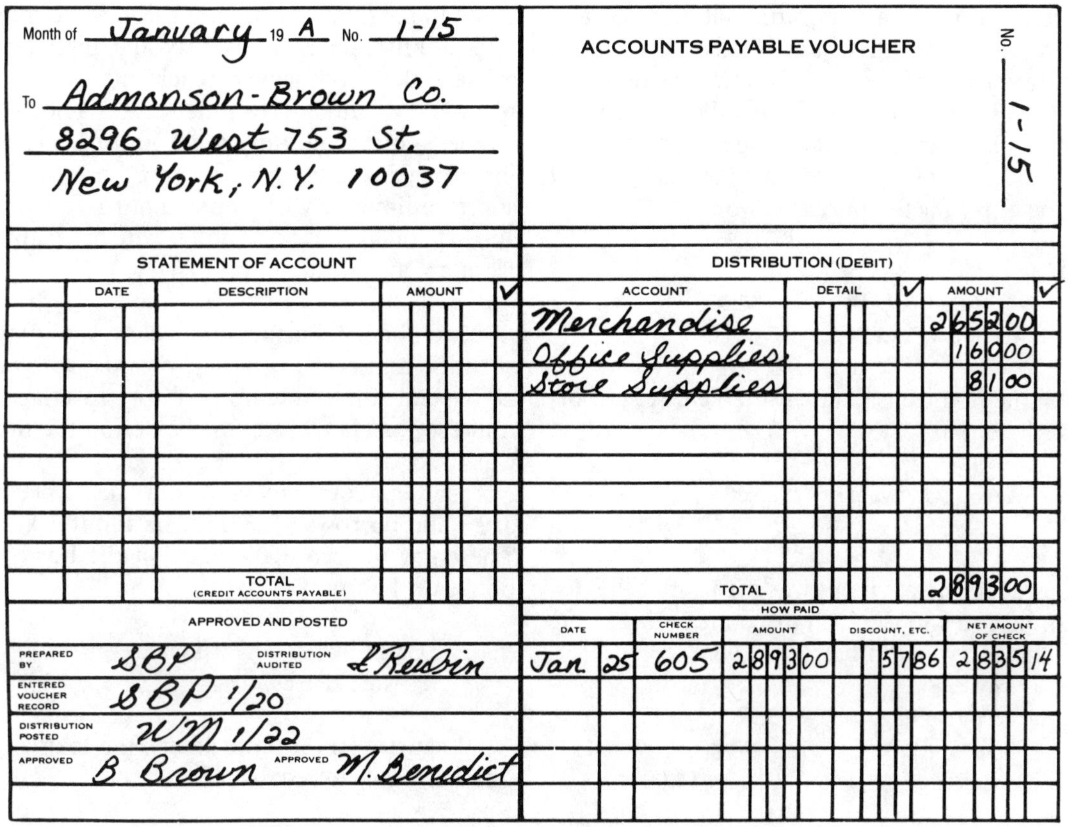

Month of January 19 A No. 1-15

ACCOUNTS PAYABLE VOUCHER

No. 1-15

To Admonson-Brown Co.
8296 West 753 St.
New York, N.Y. 10037

STATEMENT OF ACCOUNT

DATE	DESCRIPTION	AMOUNT	✓
	TOTAL (CREDIT ACCOUNTS PAYABLE)		

DISTRIBUTION (DEBIT)

ACCOUNT	DETAIL	✓	AMOUNT	✓
Merchandise			2652 00	
Office Supplies			160 00	
Store Supplies			81 00	
TOTAL			2893 00	

APPROVED AND POSTED

PREPARED BY SBP — DISTRIBUTION AUDITED L Reubin
ENTERED VOUCHER RECORD SBP 1/20
DISTRIBUTION POSTED WM 1/22
APPROVED B Brown — APPROVED M. Benedict

HOW PAID

DATE	CHECK NUMBER	AMOUNT	DISCOUNT, ETC.	NET AMOUNT OF CHECK
Jan. 25	605	2893 00	57 86	2835 14

Figure 22. Voucher.

3. When time for payment arrives, the voucher is approved for payment and is given to the treasurer's office where a check is prepared. The voucher and the check are presented to the treasurer for review of propriety of the charge and for signature on the check. The voucher and the invoice are then marked "Paid." There are two possible entries:

a. Invoice paid net (no discount):

Accounts Payable	$5,000	
Cash		$5,000

b. Invoice paid net of discount (i.e., 2%):

Accounts Payable	$5,000	
Cash		$4,900
Purchase Discount		100

CONTROLLING PURCHASE DISCOUNTS

When an invoice is billed with discount terms (2/30; net 60 or similar terms), it is important that discounts should not be missed. After the voucher is entered, a notation is made (perhaps on a calendar or in a tickler file) of the day on which the invoice must be paid. On that day the invoice is located and paid, taking the discount allowed. The entries using this procedure are the ones shown above. The Purchase Discount account might be shown on the Income Statement as a reduction of purchases or as Other Income below the Operating Income figure.

This practice is common in many firms but has the disadvantage of not showing when a discount has been missed. Another system, employing the **exception principle,** records invoices net of discount on the assumption that all discounts will be taken. If a discount is missed, then the total invoice must be paid, and the discount not taken will show in an account called Discounts Lost. If the company made a purchase of merchandise of $4,000 on credit with terms 2/30; net 60, the entry for the purchase would be:

Merchandise Purchases		
($4,000 − $80)	$3,920	
Accounts Payable		$3,920

When the invoice is paid within the discount period, the entry is:

Accounts Payable	$3,920	
Cash		$3,920

If, however, the payment was made after the discount period and the cash discount savings were lost, the entry would be:

Accounts Payable	$3,920	
Discount Lost	80	
Cash		$4,000

Management could analyze the Discounts Lost account to ascertain why the discount was not taken and could then take corrective action to insure that discounts were not missed in the future.

The Discounts Lost item is shown on the Income Statement as an addition to purchases or as Other Expense under the Operating Profit.

NOTES PAYABLE

Another type of liability is a **note payable,** defined as a written promise to pay a certain sum of money at a fixed or determinable future time. The wording is important. "Written promise" is opposed to "oral promise" and includes writing, typing, or printing on paper, cloth, or some other substance. Signatures may be written or made by proper machine impression or printing. "Certain sum of money" means that a definite quantity of money is stated. "At a fixed ... future time" means that a future date is specified, such as on October 26, 1989. "Determinable future time" means that the time can be calculated from a stated time, such as three years from today or thirty days from today because these dates will

come to pass, but it does not mean three months after John reaches his twenty-first birthday because John may never reach his twenty-first birthday. Whether a document is or is not a note is a legal question, not an accounting one. (The foregoing discussion was for purposes of showing some rudimentary concepts about notes. In the subsequent discussion, notes will be examined from an accounting point of view.)

Term Note. A business may go to a lending institution and borrow money, promising to pay it all back at some time in the future together with interest at a stated rate for the period the money was used.

Assume a company goes to a bank on February 2 and borrows $5,000 for six months at 12%. The entry to record the loan on the borrower's books on February 2 is:

Cash	$5,000	
Notes Payable		$5,000

On August 2 (six months later), the loan is paid off. The entry to record this is:

Notes Payable	$5,000	
Interest Expense	300	
($5,000 × 12% × ½)		
Cash		$5,300

The transaction above was completed within a fiscal period (assuming a calendar-year company). Let us see what happens when the money is borrowed in one year and paid back in the next year.

Assume a company goes to a bank on September 1, Year A, and borrows $5,000 for six months at 12%. The entry to record this on the borrower's books is:

Cash	$5,000	
Notes Payable		$5,000

But on December 31, Year A, four months of interest has accrued and this must be shown by an entry on December 31, Year A, as follows:

Interest Expense	$200	
Accrued Interest Payable		$200

(This entry may be reversed on January 1, Year

B.) When the note is paid on March 1, Year B, the entry may be:

a. If the reversing entry has been made:

Notes Payable	$5,000	
Interest Expense	300	
Cash		$5,300

The balance in the Interest Expense account is a $100 debit representing two months' interest ($300 debit less $200 credit).

b. If the reversing entry has not been made:

Notes Payable	$5,000	
Accrued Interest Payable	200	
Interest Expense	100	
Cash		$5,300

The balance in the Interest Expense in either case is $100.

Declining-Balance Note. A business may go to a lending institution and borrow money, promising to pay a certain amount in each of a number of periods. A portion of each payment is to be applied to the interest that has accrued since the last payment date; the balance is to be applied to the loan principal. These notes can be written in one of two fashions:

1. Equal monthly payment. In this type of loan, the installments are equal. The portion applied to the interest is less from one payment to the next, and the portion applied to the principal increases by a like amount.

2. Payment of the interest to date plus a set payment on the principal balance.

The entry for the receipt of cash is the same as in the term note above:

Cash	$5,000	
Notes Payable		$5,000

The entry for payment is:

1. Equal monthly payment of $200:

Notes Payable	$X	
Interest Expense	Y	
Cash		$200

(The debit amounts are per a schedule furnished by the lender. X increases each month and Y decreases the same amount each month.)

2. Interest to date plus equal monthly payment of $200:

Notes Payable	$200	
Interest Expense	YY	
Cash		$Z

(The interest is computed from the last payment using the simple interest formula and is added to the payment).

At the fiscal year end, an adjustment is made for the interest from the date of the last payment until the year end as follows:

Interest Expense	$XXX	
Accrued Interest Payable		$XXX

This entry can then be reversed in the following year, or a compound entry can be made as explained in the section on term notes.

Discounted Note. A business may go to a lending institution and borrow money, promising to pay it all back at one time, but the bank deducts the interest at the time the note is made, giving the borrower the net proceeds (face amount of the note less the interest deducted).

Assume a company goes to a bank on March 1 and borrows $5,000 for six months at 12% on a discounted note. The bank computes the discount at $300 and gives the company the balance ($4,700). The entry to record the receipt of cash is:

Cash	$4,700	
Interest Expense		
(or Prepaid Interest)	300	
Notes Payable		$5,000

On September 1, when the note is paid, the entry is:

Notes Payable	$5,000	
Cash		$5,000

This transaction was completed within a fiscal period (assuming a calendar-year company). But suppose that the money is borrowed in one year and paid back in the next.

Assume a company goes to a bank on November 1, Year A, and borrows $6,000 for six months for 12% on a discounted note. The bank computes the discount at $360 and gives the company the balance. The entry to record the receipt of cash is:

Cash	$5,640	
Prepaid Interest	360	
Notes Payable		$6,000

But on December 31, Year A, two months of interest has been used, and this must be shown by an entry on December 31, Year A, as follows:

Interest Expense	$120	
Prepaid Interest		$120

(This entry is not reversed on January 1, Year B.) When the note is paid on May 1, Year B, the entries are:

Notes Payable	$6,000	
Cash		$6,000

and

Interest Expense	$240	
Prepaid Interest		$240

Reducing-Balance Discount Note. An individual may go to a lending institution and borrow money. The bank prepares a contract in which the interest is deducted, fees may be added, and a repayment schedule is established. The note is prepared setting forth these terms, and the individual signs an installment note. The length of the contract is generally one year or longer. A loan of this kind is generally used for personal purposes, although smaller companies use such notes to finance vehicles or equipment.

Assume an individual owner on July 1, Year A, borrows $7,000 at 15% for the business, using his credit at the bank. The bank agrees to a one-year repayment schedule and computes the interest to be $525 ($7,000 × ½ × 15%) and adds a $47 service charge, giving the borrower $7,000. He signs a note for $7,572 to be repaid at the rate of $631 per month. The entry to record the receipt of cash is:

Cash	$7,000	
Prepaid Interest	572	
Notes Payable		$7,572

On December 31, Year A, an adjusting entry is made to record the interest expense for the six months in Year A as follows:

Interest Expense	$286	
Prepaid Interest		$286

Or the interest expense could be computed on the outstanding balance, putting a larger share of interest expense in Year A than in Year B.

Effective Interest Rate on a Note and a Discounted Note. In analyzing the charges on a note and a discounted note (both paid in full at the end of the term), it is interesting to see that although both types of notes are computed at the same rate the discounted note has a higher *effective* rate of interest.

Assume two borrowers go to the bank on January 2 to borrow approximately $1,000 to be repaid on December 31, in a lump sum. The first borrower obtains the money signing a note at 12% *interest;* the second obtains the money signing a discounted note at 12% *discount.* The proceeds of the first note are $1,000, and the borrower repays $1,120 on December 31. The second borrower receives $880 [$1,000 − ($1,000 × 12%)], and he repays $1,000 on December 31.

To determine the effective rate of interest we start with the interest formula (Interest = Principal × Rate × Time) and rewrite it as:

$$\text{Rate of Interest} = \frac{\text{Interest}}{\text{Principal} \times \text{Time}}$$

Now let us substitute figures to determine the effective interest rate:

First Borrower: $\dfrac{\$120}{\$1,000 \times 1 \text{ year}} = 12\%$ per annum

Second Borrower: $\dfrac{\$120}{\$880 \times 1 \text{ year}} = 13.6\%$ per annum

This difference of effective rate is caused by the second borrower paying the same amount in interest but having less money to use during the term.

Therefore, a borrower should try to establish the best contract and should compute the effective rate of interest under the various alternatives offered him to secure the cheapest cost of money.

ACCRUED LIABILITIES

At the close of the fiscal period there are often liabilities that have not been entered on the books because the time for computation of the liability has not arrived (payroll) or the supplier has not yet billed for the goods or services delivered (gasoline credit purchases or long-distance telephone charges).

Accrued Payroll. If the payroll is computed on a weekly basis on Friday and the fiscal period ends on a Wednesday, the company must accrue the amount earned by the employees for work done on Monday, Tuesday, and Wednesday. An analysis of the time charges for the three days may be made (or an estimate based on the full week's payroll is made, if this is more practical), and an adjusting entry is made as follows:

Sales Salaries Expense	$1,000	
Office Salaries Expense	800	
Factory Salaries Expense	7,100	
(or other appropriate salary expense accounts)		
Accrued Salaries or Accrued Salaries Payable or Salaries Payable		$8,900

and the entry is reversed in the following period.

When the next payroll is prepared, the total distribution will be made to the proper accounts as debits, the reversing entry will have credited the accounts, and the balance in the account will be the salary expense for the new period only.

Accrued Liabilities for Goods. If goods are billed on a monthly basis (as in gasoline credit card purchases) and the monthly statement received in December was dated December 15,

then all credit card purchases that do not appear on the statement should be accrued as of December 31 with an adjusting entry as follows:

Auto (or Truck) Expense	$50	
(or other appropriate expense)		
Accrued Liabilities		$50

This entry is reversed in the following period.

If goods are received prior to the end of the fiscal period but no invoice has been received, the amount owed must be accrued. If a $500 shipment of goods is received December 29 but the invoice is received January 5 of the following year, an adjusting entry is made as follows:

Merchandise Inventory	$500	
(or other appropriate account)		
Accrued Liabilities		$500

[After January 1 a reversing entry is made as follows:

Accrued Liabilities	$500	
Merchandise Inventory		$500
(or other appropriate account)]		

If a $300 shipment of goods is received on January 6 but the invoice was received on December 28 and recorded on that date, an adjusting entry must be made to remove the liability in the year the invoice was received. The entry is as follows:

Accounts Payable	$300	
Merchandise Inventory		$300
(or other appropriate account)		

and in the following year, an entry is made as follows:

Merchandise Inventory	$300	
(or other appropriate account)		
Accounts Payable		$300

ESTIMATED LIABILITIES

Some companies may have an obligation to customers under a guarantee or under an agreement to redeem coupons. The liability is certain, but the amount is not. An estimate must be made of the amount and the proper liability balance must be established. After reviewing the facts, the business will make an entry as follows:

Guarantee Expense	$3,000	
Estimated Guarantee Liability		$3,000

or

Coupon Redemption Expense	$5,000	
Estimated Coupon Redemption Liability		$5,000

When, in later periods, the liability is paid by rendering service (for a guarantee), the entry is:

Estimated Guarantee Liability	$100	
Labor Summary		$100

When, in later periods, the liability is paid by rendering cash (for a guarantee or coupon redemption), the entry is:

Estimated Guarantee Liability	$300	
Estimated Coupon Liability		
Cash		$300

Note that the expense is recorded when the liability is established, even though the amount of liability is estimated. At each year end, the estimated liability account is reviewed and adjusted upward (if there are new guarantees or coupons issued) or downward (for those guarantees or coupons that have expired).

UNEARNED INCOME

In some businesses, customers may pay for goods or services before their receipt. Examples of this type of transaction would be magazine subscriptions, taxi scrip book purchases, and traveler's checks.

When a magazine subscription is received, an entry is made as follows:

Cash (or Subscriptions Receivable)	$15	
Prepaid Subscriptions		$15

This recording is made for all subscriptions which, let us assume, total $5,000 for the year.

Upon analysis of the Prepaid Subscription account at the year-end, it is determined that $2,200 of the subscription contracts have been earned. The entry to record the conversion of liability to income is:

Prepaid Subscriptions	$2,200	
Subscriptions Income		$2,200

When a book of taxi scrip is sold, the entry is:

Cash	$10	
Scrip Liability		$10

This recording is made for all scrip sold; let us say $3,000 for the year. Here, however, the earning of the income is not a function of time, as it is in the case of the magazines. Taxi fare income arises when the rider uses scrip in payment of a fare. The entry to record the receipt of scrip in payment of the fare is:

Scrip Liability	$1	
Taxi Fare Income		$1

(Such an entry would not be made for each scrip coupon received but would be summarized for a month or similar period.)

When traveler's checks are sold, the following entry is made:

Cash	$1,010	
Traveler's Check Liability		$1,000
Traveler's Check Sales Income		10

When the checks are presented to the issuer for payment, the following entry is made:

Traveler's Check Liability	$100	
Cash		$100

(Again these would be summarized monthly.)

Because scrip and traveler's checks may be lost by the purchaser and never used in the payment of fares, an adjustment can be made in the Scrip Liability account to reduce the scrip liability to the amount expected to be used in payment of fares. This adjustment will require the analysis of sales and redemption of scrip on a detailed basis.

These are only three examples of the type of transaction in which payment is made before goods or services are received. There are others, and it might be a good idea for management to review the operations of any business to see if perhaps some system of prepayment might not be used to good advantage.

CONTINGENT LIABILITIES

In some businesses, situations arise in which there is the possibility that a liability will come about because of some circumstance that has not been provided for by insurance. One example might be the loss of a lawsuit. When the action is brought against the business, there is the possibility that the business may not be able to defend itself successfully—the liability is possible but not certain. From a review by the business's lawyers there can be some basis for assessing chances of success in the case and the amount of the award to the plaintiff.

Preparing an entry before the decision is rendered is premature because the decision might be in favor of the business. But to ignore the possibility of loss may mislead the reader of the financial statements. Therefore, two solutions to this problem are possible:

1. A footnote can be added to the equity section stating the circumstances and what would happen in the event of loss.
2. In a corporation, an entry such as this can be prepared:

Retained Earnings	$XXX	
Reserve for Contingency		$XXX

INCOME TAX ALLOCATION

The accountant's principles for measurement of income and expenses may differ from principles of measurement as set forth in the tax codes. The question is not which form of measurement is correct—each is correct but designed for a different purpose. The principles used by income tax authorities result from studies by congressional committees as to what shall be taxed and how. As a result of this difference between generally accepted accounting principles and principles of income taxation, there may arise a situation in which the income determined by the accountant for statement purposes is greater than the income determined by the accountant for tax purposes, or vice versa.

In the case in which the income on the financial statements is greater than that determined for tax purposes, there is a possibility that the difference in income is nontaxable, is partly taxable, or that the incidence of taxation is deferred. The accountant reviews the difference between the items included in the statement income and those included in tax income to determine which are nontaxable (for example, interest received from state and municipal bonds) and which are taxable in future years (such as a lesser amount of depreciation taken for statement purposes than is taken for tax purposes). The accountant then computes the amount of tax on the income that is deferred and records the liability resulting from such tax deferment. If the taxability of the item is changed in the future or if the rate of taxation is changed, of course the amount will be changed.

Assume a company uses the straight-line method of depreciation for statements, and an IRS-approved method for tax purposes, and the income is $10,000 less under the IRS method. If the tax rate for the corporation is 34%, then the tax deferred is $3,400 and the entry is:

Retained Earnings	$3,400	
Income Tax Deferred		$3,400

The deferred tax will be paid later when the IRS-approved method produces a greater income than the straight-line method.

In a case in which the income on the financial statements is *less* than that determined for tax purposes, the accountant reviews the difference between the items included in statement income and those included in tax income to determine the deferred income tax now due.

Assume the company above now has a lower income using the IRS-approved method than that generated by the straight-line method, and the difference is $4,000. (In the example above, $10,000 was the income on which the tax had been deferred; in the present example $4,000 has become taxable.) The amount of income tax now due at the 34% rate is $1,360 and the entry is:

Income Tax Deferred	$1,360	
Income Tax Payable		$1,360

An analysis of the Income Tax Deferred account at the end of each fiscal period will assist the accountant in determining how much of the deferred tax has come due in the current year and whether any adjustment to the account is necessary owing to changes in tax rates or the taxability of items of income or expense.

EXERCISES

Exercise No. 52. A business purchases merchandise on account. The amount of the invoice is $7,000. Terms are 2/10; net 30. The company records the invoices gross.

a. Prepare the entry for the purchase. (Debit Merchandise Purchases.)

b. Prepare the entry for payment made during the discount period.

c. Prepare the entry for payment made after the discount period.

Exercise No. 53. A business buys merchandise on account. The amount of the invoice is $6,000. Terms are 2/30; net 60. The company records its invoices net of discount.

a. Prepare the entry for the purchase. (Debit Merchandise Purchases.)

b. Prepare the entry for payment made during the discount period.

c. Prepare the entry for payment made after the discount period.

Exercise No. 54. A company receives $7,000 from the bank, signing a 60-day note for $7,000 at 12% interest. On the due date the note is paid. Both transactions occurred in the same fiscal period.

a. Prepare the entry to reflect the borrowing.

b. Prepare the entry to reflect the repayment.

Exercise No. 55. A company receives $8,000 from the bank on September 15, Year A, signing a 90-day note at 13% interest. The fiscal year-end for the borrower is October 31. The note is paid on the due date.

a. Prepare the entry to reflect the borrowing.

b. Prepare the entry for the accrued interest.

c. Assuming that in the next fiscal year a reversing entry is prepared:

1. Prepare the reversing entry.

2. Prepare the entry to reflect repayment.

d. Assuming that in the next fiscal period no reversing entry had been made, prepare the entry to reflect the repayment.

Exercise No. 56. A business arranges with the bank to borrow money. It signs a note for $13,600 for 36 months and receives $10,000 in cash. Prepare the entry to reflect the borrowing transaction.

Exercise No. 57. Ay Company borrowed $1,000 from the bank, giving a note with 13% interest. Bee Company borrowed $1,000, giving a note discounted at 13%. Both companies borrowed the money for one year.

a. How much money does each borrower get?

b. How much, in dollars, does each borrower pay for the use of the money received?

c. What is the effective rate of interest for each borrower?

Exercise No. 58. The normal payroll entry for one Monday-to-Friday week is:

Sales Salaries Expense	$5,000	
Office Salaries Expense	2,000	
F.I.C.A. Taxes Payable		$ 210
Withholding Taxes Payable		1,450
Salaries Payable		5,340

The last day of the fiscal year is Wednesday. Sales salaries are estimated to be 10% above normal and office salaries 5% above normal. Prepare the year-end adjusting entry.

Exercise No. 59. In reviewing shipments of merchandise and the invoices covering these shipments, the following are found:

a. Goods shipped F.O.B. shipping point on December 28, Year A, arrive on January 5, Year

	Number of Subscriptions			Prepaid Subscriptions— Year A		
Month	1-year	2-year	5-year	1-year	2-year	5-year
January	100	175	130	900	2,975	4,420
February	75	162	205	675	2,754	6,970
March	83	181	197	747	3,077	6,698
April	97	135	188	873	2,295	6,392
May	105	166	142	945	2,822	4,828
June	82	175	155	738	2,975	5,270
July	56	185	187	504	3,145	6,358
August	71	119	193	639	2,023	6,562
September	89	122	167	801	2,074	5,678
October	43	163	152	387	2,771	5,168
November	52	180	193	468	3,060	6,562
December	60	205	215	540	3,485	7,310
TOTAL	913	1,968	2,124	8,217	33,456	72,216

B. The invoice for $8,200 is received on January 6, Year B, and recorded at that time.

b. Goods shipped F.O.B. destination on December 29, Year A, arrive on January 3, Year B. The invoice for $3,500 is received on January 7, Year B, and is recorded on that date.

Prepare any entry (entries) required in Year A.

Exercise No. 60. *Better Living Review* has subscription rates of one year for $9.00, two years for $17, and five years for $34. An analysis of the Prepaid Subscription Received in Year A account is shown above:

a. How much of the subscriptions were earned in Year A?

b. How much of the subscriptions were unearned at December 31, Year A?

c. What is the adjusting entry needed at December 31, Year A?

d. How much of the subscriptions will be earned in Year B?

Chapter 7

LONG-TERM LIABILITIES

In the previous chapter we defined long-term liabilities as those liabilities that do not become due in the next fiscal period (usually defined as a year). This definition does not mean we cannot pay long-term liabilities in the next fiscal period—it means that we are not *required* to pay them in the next fiscal period. Long-term liabilities may be of the type that require periodic reduction of the amount due by some form of installment payments or they may be of the type that require one payment at a fixed future time to liquidate the amount owed. Borrowings of large sums of moneys may be made for three general purposes:

1. Purchase of real property;
2. Increase of working capital;
3. Purchase of personal property.

REALTY FINANCING AND MORTGAGES

In Chapter 5 we discussed the purchase of real property and saw in both examples that part of the purchase was advanced by a bank. We prepared an entry of which one credit was Mortgage Payable. This liability and the methods of repayment will be discussed here.

When a lending institution agrees to lend money, accepting a deed of trust on the real property as security, it must follow certain rules established by the governmental agency that regulates it (state and federal banking authorities, etc.). The lending institution appraises the prop-

erty and then lends only up to a maximum percentage of the appraisal figure. The lending percentage varies, depending upon the type of property and the policy of the lending institution. The interest rate and the charge for placing the loan may also vary among lending institutions. Lenders may offer different periods for repayment, thereby increasing or reducing the periodic payments. An additional liability may arise if the loan is repaid too rapidly. This is called the "prepayment penalty" and represents an amount added to the balance of the loan if it is repaid prior to the time set forth in the agreement between borrower and lender.

Because of the reasons above, the buyer of realty should investigate as many lending institutions as possible to secure the best mix of the:

1. size of loan,
2. interest rate,
3. length of repayment period,
4. loan placement charge,
5. prepayment penalties.

Each buyer must decide for himself what the best loan is for the purposes he is trying to achieve.

It might be interesting to look at a few situations to see how interest rate, length of loan, and placement fee affect the monthly payment.

1. Assume a loan of $250,000 is needed to purchase a parcel of real property. Two lenders agree to place a loan for 1% of the amount lent at an interest rate of 12%. However, one lender agrees to a repayment term of 24 years and the other agrees to a repayment term of 25 years.

Interest Rate	Amount of Loan	Term	Monthly Payment	Total Amount Paid
12%	$250,000	24 yrs. (288 mos.)	$2,650.96	$763,476.48
12%	$250,000	25 yrs. (300 mos.)	$2,633.06	$789,918.00
		The difference in the total amount paid is		$ 26,441.52

2. Assume that a loan of $250,000 is needed to purchase a parcel of real property. Both lenders agree to a 25-year loan at 12%. However, one agrees to a placement fee of 1%, the other to a placement fee of 2%. Both lenders will add the fee to the loan.

Interest Rate	Amount of Loan	Term	Monthly Payment	Total Amount Paid
12%	$252,500	25 yrs. (300 mos.)	$2,659.40	$797,820.00
12%	$255,000	25 yrs. (300 mos.)	$2,685.73	$805,719.00
		The difference in the total amount paid is		$ 7,899.00

3. Assume that a loan of $250,000 is needed to purchase a parcel of real property. Both lenders agree to place the loan for 1% of the amount lent with a 25-year term. However, one agrees to an interest rate of 12.7% and the other agrees to 12.5%.

Interest Rate	Amount of Loan	Term	Monthly Payment	Total Amount Paid
12.7%	$252,500	25 yrs. (300 mos.)	$2,790.90	$837,270.00
12.5%	$252,500	25 yrs. (300 mos.)	$2,753.15	$825,945.00
		The difference in the total amount paid is		$ 11,325.00

A borrower must consider more than interest rate, number of payments, and amount of the monthly payments. There are alternative uses of money that can be made, such as purchases of inventory, machinery and other business equipment, securities, etc. It may be to the borrower's benefit to accept a higher interest rate to secure a longer pay-out schedule or to extend the life of the loan to secure smaller monthly payments. Each borrower must analyze his need for money and the alternative uses of the money available to him so that he obtains the most effective use of the money borrowed.

The above examples were for repayment of an equal amount each month for the life of the loan. But another type of loan that may be written requires an equal monthly payment determined by the formula:

$$\frac{\text{Original amount of load}}{\text{Number of months in the term}}$$

to which is added one month's interest to the unpaid balance, resulting in a reducing monthly payment.

To show the amount owing on the mortgage on the Balance Sheet date, the accountant shows the amount due on the loan in the next fiscal period as current and the remainder as long-term as follows:

Current Liabilities:
Current Portion of Mortgage
Payable $ 2,026.80

Long-term Liabilities:
Mortgage Payable $20,436.90
Less current
portion above   2,026.80   18,410.10

DEBENTURES AND UNSECURED CREDIT

When larger businesses need money for working capital they sometimes obtain it on unsecured credit by issuing **debenture bonds,** securities issued against the company's general credit. The bond holders are creditors of the corporation, not owners. The business contacts an investment banker, who secures information from the company, its attorneys, and its certified public accountants. Without discussing the legal requirements of filing with the stock exchanges or the Securities and Exchange Commission, we can say that the investment banker will prepare the prospectus of the issue to be given to prospective buyers. He will determine what interest rate should be offered on the bond and he will discuss with the company the best time to place the bonds on the market. The contract between the company and the future borrowers is drawn up and signed. The bonds are printed with the date of the issue, the rate of interest, and other pertinent terms. The investment banker (or a syndicate of investment bankers) agrees to buy the issue at some value less than face value—the difference being the sales earnings of the seller, if the bonds are sold at their face value. The value of the bond is called the **face amount** and is usually in multiples of $1,000.

Example 1: Assume that the investment banker agrees to sell a 20-year $1,000,000 issue of 12% bonds and agrees to give the company $960,000. (The banker is receiving 4% for his services.) The sale is made on the issue date. The entry is:

Cash $960,000
Deferred Bond Charges $ 40,000
    Bonds Payable $1,000,000

The Deferred Bond Charges will be deferred over the life of the bond so that ultimately the $40,000 will go to Bond Interest Expense. This would make the effective rate of interest for the company 12.7%.

Example 2: Assume that the investment banker agrees to sell a $1,000,000 issue of 20-year 12% bonds for an agreed price of $40,000. However, on the date the bonds are to be sold, the market rate for bonds for the same quality (credit rating) as those of this company is 12.4%. The original contract includes a clause that in the event the interest changes the investment banker will compute the price at which to sell the bonds and will notify the company. The investment banker computes this price to be paid by the investor so that an effective rate of 12.4% interest is obtained. The formula is:

$$\text{Interest} = \text{Principal} \times \text{Rate} \times \text{Time}$$
$$\text{Principal} = \frac{\text{Interest}}{\text{Rate} \times \text{Time}}$$
$$\text{Principal} = \frac{1,000 \times 12\%}{12.4\% \times 1 \text{ year}} = \$967.75$$

That is, if an investor would pay $967.75 for a $1,000 bond, the effective rate of interest to him would be 12.4 %. The investment banker still receives a $40,000 commission, and the entry is:

Cash $927,750
Deferred Bond Charges   72,250
    Bonds Payable $1,000,000

In this example, the Deferred Bond Charges account includes both commissions ($40,000) and a discount on bonds of $32,250. (It is assumed that the company has agreed to continue with the financing at these terms.) Both are costs of obtaining the money and may be included in one account to be amortized over the life of the bond issue. Both will be added to Bond Interest Expense. This would make the effective rate of interest for the company 13.3%.

Example 3: Assume that the investment banker agrees to sell a 20-year $1,000,000 issue of 12% bonds and agrees to give the company $960,000. However, on the day the bonds are to be sold, the market will absorb 11.7% bonds from companies with similar credit rating. The original contract may have included a clause allowing the investment banker to sell the bonds at a higher price if market interest rates decline, and we will assume that such a clause is in effect. The investment banker computes the price to be paid by the purchaser so that an effective rate of 11.7% interest is obtained. The formula is:

$$\text{Principal} = \frac{\text{Interest}}{\text{Rate} \times \text{Time}}$$

$$= \frac{1,000 \times 12\%}{11.7\% \times 1 \text{ year}} = \$1,025.74$$

That is, if an investor would pay $1,025.74 for a $1,000, 12% bond, the effective rate of interest to him would be 11.7%. The investment banker would still receive $40,000 sales commission and the entry is:

Cash	$985,640	
Deferred Bond Charges	14,360	
Bonds Payable		$1,000,000

In this example, the Deferred Bond Charges account includes commissions ($40,000) offset against the premium on bonds ($25,640). The commission is a cost of obtaining money while the premium is a prepayment of interest by the buyer to the company to lower the effective interest rate. The Deferred Bond Charges account will be amortized over the life of the bond issue and will be offset against Bond Interest Expense. This would make the effective rate of interest for the company 12.9%.

It is possible that the premium may be even larger than the fee paid the investment banker. The entry in this case would be:

Cash	$XX	
Bonds Payable		$YY
Bond Premium		ZZ

This net premium would be amortized over the life of the bond issue into the Bond Interest Expense account.

Example 4: In some instances, the bonds may not be sold on the issue date but at some later time. However, the interest to be paid the investor is computed from the issue date. In this example, assume that the investment banker agrees to sell a 20-year 12% bond issue of $1,000,000, having an issue date of March 1, Year A, and

agrees to give the company $960,000. Because of a change in short-range plans, the company does not need the money until June 1, Year A, and has agreed withe the investment banker that the bonds will then be sold *at par* ($1,000,000) plus accrued interest. The accrued interest is computed as follows:

$$\begin{aligned} \text{Interest} &= \text{Principal} \times \text{Rate} \times \text{Time} \\ &= \$1,000,000 \times 12\%/A \times 3 \text{ months} \\ &= \$30,000 \end{aligned}$$

The bonds are sold, and their proceeds plus accrued interest less the commission are remitted to the company, whereupon this entry is made:

Cash	$990,000	
Deferred Bond Charges	40,000	
Bonds Payable		$1,000,000
Accrued Interest Payable		30,000
(or Interest Expense)		

If the bond interest is paid semiannually, there would be an entry to pay the interest on September 1, Year A, as follows:

Bond Interest Expense	$60,000	
Cash		$60,000

At the end of each year, the amount in the Accrued Interest Payable account should reflect the interest earned by the bondholders but as yet unpaid by the company. In this example, it would be four months' interest of $40,000. An adjustment to this account would be made to the Bond Interest Expense account. (When the bonds are not sold on the issue date, they could also be sold at a discount or at a premium necessitating entry components that would represent the net discount or premium.)

Term Bonds Payable. If the bonds are all to be paid at one time some years after the issue date they are called **term bonds.** The liability is long-term until the Balance Sheet date immediately preceding the payment date, and at that time the whole issue becomes current.

Serial Bonds Payable. If the bonds are to be paid back in installments after the issue date they are called **serial bonds.** The liability is long-term for all the bonds payable except those that will be paid within one year of the Balance Sheet date; those are current liabilities. This can be shown on the Balance Sheet as follows:

Current Liabilities		
Portion of Bonds Payable Due	$100,000	
Long-term Liabilities		
Serial Bonds Payable—Issue		
of November 1, Year A:		
Amount outstanding	$900,000	
Less current portion above	100,000	800,000

Convertible Bonds. Some corporations use a bond that is convertible into stock at some time in the future. When the bonds are originally sold the entry is the same as for any other bond. It is only at the time of election by the bondholder to take stock in lieu of cash that the entry is different. At that time the company makes the following entry:

Bonds Payable	$200,000	
Capital Stock		$200,000

(There may be other debits or credits to the entry depending on the terms of convertibility as expressed in the original bond agreement.) This type of bond gives the security of a liability to the bondholder at first, but also gives him the privilege of conversion to ownership if the business venture is successful.

CHATTEL MORTGAGES

Most companies have, at one time or another, financed purchases of trucks, delivery equipment, autos, or other equipment using credit in which the lender takes title to the personalty until the purchaser pays off the loan. When the loan is paid off, the lender transfers title to the buyer. Although legal title is in the name of the lender, the purchaser records the entry as if he had title.

If a company purchased a machine for $50,000, making a down payment of $10,000 and securing a chattel mortgage loan from a bank for $40,000, the entry would be:

Equipment	$50,000	
Cash		$10,000
Mortgage Loan Payable		40,000

As payments are made, the purchaser has to distinguish between the portion applicable to interest expense and the portion applicable to the principal.

In this type of financing the lender may require certain insurance or safety precautions so that the chattel is protected in the event of an unforeseen catastrophe. In most instances the chattel mortgage is recorded in the County Clerk's office so that anyone may be notified of the lien by the lender.

TRUSTEE ARRANGEMENTS

The trustee type of financing is similar to a chattel mortgage. It involves a seller of goods, a buyer of goods, and a lender. The amounts are relatively large and may involve a bond issue. Assume that a railroad wants some equipment, say ten freight cars. It arranges with the manufacturer to produce them and with a bank to finance them. The bank agrees to finance the purchase (or an investment banker may agree to sell a bond issue to finance the purchase) when the cars are completed, and a trustee is named to take title to the cars, collect the payments from the company, and pay interest and principal installments as required for the term of the loan. A plaque is frequently affixed to the equipment, stating the name of the trustee, the manufacturer, and the purchaser. When the payments are completed, the trustee transfers title to the railroad and the plaques are removed from the equipment.

EXERCISES

Exercise No. 61. Using a loan book at a bank, savings and loan institution, or your local library, calculate the total amount paid back under each of the following loan terms:

a. $25,000 borrowed at 12% for 25 years.
b. $25,000 borrowed at 12% for 24 years.
c. $25,000 borrowed at 11.75% for 25 years.
d. $25,000 borrowed at 12.4% for 24 years.

All are paid in equal monthly installments. Which loan is best?

Exercise No. 62. An investment banker agrees to sell $500,000 of a company's bonds, and gives the company $490,000. The bonds are sold on the issue date. Prepare the necessary entry.

Exercise No. 63. Alpha Company agrees with an investment banker to have the banker underwrite a $1,000,000 issue of 12% debenture bonds. On the issue date similarly rated bonds are bringing 12.2% interest. At what price must the bonds be sold so that the yield to the investor is 12.2%? (Ignore commissions to the investment banker.)

Exercise No. 64. Bonds of Xerxes Company are dated March 1, Year A. The investment banker agrees to pay 97.5 for the $400,000 issue on the issue date. Prepare the entry when the investment banker buys the bonds. (In the bond market, price is stated in terms of 100 as par; therefore, 97.5 means that the bonds are sold at 97.5% of par value.)

Exercise No. 65. Bonds of the Scatena Company are dated April 1, Year A. The issue is for $600,000 and the interest rate is 12.5%. On June 1, Year A, the entire issue is sold at par. The commission to the investment broker is $18,000. Prepare the necessary entry (entries) upon sales of the bonds.

Chapter 8

BUDGETING AND FINANCIAL PLANNING

The importance of planning ahead has been recognized by man since the times of antiquity—Alexander the Great planned his campaigns; the Crusades were planned movements of men and materials across a continent; Columbus planned his trip to India (discovering America in the process); the Allies planned the invasion of Europe. In our daily lives we plan. And like the generals and other strategists we compare progress to plan. Planning is a simple concept—so simple that only very few persons are unaware of it, at least in its rudimentary form and use. But when the word "plan" is changed to "budget" and the word "financial" is placed before it, panic ensues.

Let us look, then, at a budget and see what it is. A budget is a plan of future action measured in terms of quantifiable units—dollars, labor hours, tons, years, days, etc. Financial planning is nothing more than planning the financial facet of the business—sources of future income, future expenditures, future obligations, etc.

GOVERNMENTAL BUDGETING

Budgets have been used for many decades in governmental organizations, and it may be well to look at the mechanics of a budget in the government. At some prescribed time the budget must be prepared and sent to the legislative body (Congress, state legislature, board of supervisors, etc.). In advance of the date, the chief executive of the governmental unit (President, governor, mayor, etc.) must have prepared the budget for the operating departments. He reviews the budget with the department heads and submits it to the legislative body. This body, through its committee system, reviews the budget and then adopts it. The legislative body also enacts methods of taxation and rates of taxation for the various methods.

After the budget is adopted, the operating department heads are informed of the amounts they have to spend and for what purposes they can be spent. The word used to describe the amount available for particular use is **appropriation.** As moneys are spent, they are classified as to categories of expense—labor, material, supplies, etc.—called **objects** and **sub-objects.** To illustrate these terms we might take a city budget passed by the City Council authorizing the street department to spend $500,000 for snow removal—the $500,000 is the appropriation and is the maximum that is authorized to be spent for snow removal at this time. As the money is spent, the account charged is Snow Removal—Salaries or Snow Removal—Supplies. These are the account and object classifications. Usually to simplify the accounting, objects and sub-objects are given numbers: salaries may be the 100 series; salaries of supervisors may be 101; secretaries, 102, etc.

If more money than was appropriated has to be spent for any reason (say a more severe winter than had been anticipated), the operating department would go to the chief executive, who might have an emergency appropriation that could be used, or the chief executive would request an additional appropriation from the legislature. If less money than was appropriated is spent for any reason (say a milder winter than had been anticipated), the unused portion of the appropriation at the end of the fiscal period would become a surplus to the governmental unit. To facilitate operations, the department head might be given authority to shift funds between objects and sub-objects.

The appropriations that comprise the budget in a governmental unit are prepared into accounting entries, as are the estimated revenues, so that the accounting records show expected revenues and expected expenses. These entries are:

Estimated Revenues	$1,000,000	
Surplus		$1,000,000
To record the estimated revenues. (The classification of revenue types is generally made.)		

Surplus	$ 990,000	
Appropriations		$ 990,000
To record the appropriations. (The classification of appropriations is generally made.)		

As revenue is billed (in the case of real property taxes, for example) and cash is received the entries are:

Property Tax Receivable	$750,000	
Property Tax Income		$750,000
To record the tax roll billing.		

Cash	$740,000	
Property Tax Receivable		$740,000
To record the receipt of real property taxes.		

In the case of sales tax, for example, where no prior bill is sent, the entry is:

Cash	$220,000	
Sales Tax Income		$220,000
To record sales tax receipts.		

As bills are received for goods and services, and moneys are spent to pay those bills, the entries are:

Snow Removal—Supplies	$5,000	
Vouchers Payable		$5,000
To record purchase of supplies on account.		

Vouchers Payable	$5,000	
Cash		$5,000
To record payment of voucher.		

With this very formal system there is tight control over receipts and expenditures. At all times the operating department can see what is available for spending and how much has been spent.

Business does not, in most cases, operate with this rigid a system. Although many businesses prepare budgets, the budgets are not entered in the books of accounts but are collateral records used as control devices and measures of performance.

BUDGET PREPARATION

The preparation of the budget is the first step in preparing a plan of control. The budget may be prepared at the level of the chief executive, or it may be prepared at the level of the operating departments. When it is prepared at the level of the operating departments, it must be reviewed at the top and coordinated with the budgets of other departments. The sales budget, as prepared by the sales department, is based on past performance and a consideration of expected future conditions. But the sales department may tend to underestimate sales so that the actual performance exceeds the budget, thereby making the department "look good." The production budget, on the other hand, also based on past performance and a consideration of expected future conditions, may tend to overestimate production costs so that the actual performance is less than the budget, thereby making the production department "look good." The reviewing group (budget committee or similar group) has the task of making the budget as realistic as possible in light of expected future conditions.

The sales budget may start with last year's sales in units, adjusted for style and model changes and priced at expected sales prices. The production budget may start with the adjusted unit sales budget and from it may be prepared a materials budget, showing quantity of materials, dollars, and, perhaps, delivery dates; a labor budget, showing the types of skills needed, with wage rates; a factory overhead budget, showing all costs in the factory other than direct labor and direct material; and a capital budget, showing what must be spent for factory rearrangement or new equipment. From this it can be seen that various departments within the company are involved in budgeting—sales, production, production engineering, purchasing, personnel, and others. It is these various budgets that are then reviewed and coordinated by the budget committee. When a company-wide budget is established, the treasurer's office may prepare a cash budget showing expected income by source, expected expenditures by object, and loan requirements, if any.

Example:

It is decided to prepare a budget for the following year based on past experience. Last year the figures developed from accounting and collateral records were as above:

It is estimated that units sales of Items A, B, and C will increase by 15%, 20%, and 10% respectively while sales prices per unit advance 5%, 11%, and 9% respectively. The labor force in the factory will receive pay increases of 5%; direct materials will advance 7%, 8%, and 10% respectively in price; factory overhead will increase 6%. Selling expenses will advance 5% while administrative costs will rise 7%.

Item A

Sales: 100,000 × 1.15		115,000 units
Income:	$300,000 × 1.15 × 1.05	$362,250.00
Direct Labor:	$125,000 × 1.15 × 1.05	$150,937.50
Direct Material:	$ 75,000 × 1.15 × 1.07	92,287.50
Factory Overhead:	$ 50,000 × 1.15 × 1.06	60,950.00
		$304,175.00
Gross Profit on Sales		$ 58,075.00

Item B

Sales: 200,000 × 1.20		240,000 units
Income:	$200,000 × 1.20 × 1.11	$266,400.00
Direct Labor:	$100,000 × 1.20 × 1.05	$126,000.00
Direct Material:	$ 45,000 × 1.20 × 1.08	58,320.00
Factory Overhead:	$ 30,000 × 1.20 × 1.06	38,160.00
		$222,480.00
Gross Profit on Sales		$ 43,920.00

Item C

Sales: 150,000 × 1.10		165,000 units
Income:	$300,000 × 1.10 × 1.09	$359,700.00
Direct Labor:	$160,000 × 1.10 × 1.05	$184,800.000
Direct Material:	$ 60,000 × 1.10 × 1.10	72,600.00
Factory Overhead:	$ 40,000 × 1.10 × 1.06	46,640.00
		$304,040.00
Gross Profit on Sales		$ 55,660.00

Putting this data in statement form:

	Unit A	Unit B	Unit C	Total
Sales: Units	115,000	240,000	165,000	
Income	$362,250.00	$266,400.00	$359,700.00	$988,350.00
Cost of Sales:				
Direct Labor	$150,937.50	$126,000.00	$184,800.00	$461,737.50
Direct Material	92,287.50	58,320.00	72,600.00	223,207.50
Factory Overhead	60,950.00	38,160.00	46,640.00	147,750.00
	$304,175.00	$222,480.00	$304,040.00	$832,695.00
Gross Profit on Sales	$ 58,075.00	$ 43,920.00	$ 55,660.00	$155,655.00
Gross Profit (%)	16.0	16.5	15.5	
Selling Expenses	($20,000 × 1.05)			$ 21,000.00
Administrative Expenses	($25,000 × 1.07)			26,750.00
				47,750.00
Net Operating Income				$107,905.00

A detailed analysis of all costs may give more accurate estimates but it is more expensive. As in every control situation, the additional profit benefits must be measured against added costs to ascertain if an increase in net profit results. An advantage of detailed analysis that is often overlooked is the discovery of situations in which improvements in methods may result in savings.

COLLECTING PERFORMANCE DATA

In planning the budget, it is important that performance information be collected so that it can be compared against the budget figures. This specific collection may mean that there should be changes in the methods of collecting accounting data to fit the budget plan. The definitions used for budget purposes should be the same as those used for the collection of accounting data. If they are not, comparisons between budget and performance cannot be readily made, or if made without correction, may even be misleading.

The redesigning of account classifications to match the budget classifications may require some thought as well as the redesign of forms, but in the long run it should give better control. Where in the past sales were collected in total dollars, the use of a budget may require an analysis by units and dollars for each product sold as well as total dollars. The classification of expense accounts may be divided into controllable and noncontrollable expenses for purposes of corrective action.

The use of specific definitions for budgeting is not incompatible with good accounting technique; rather it is a logical extension of the accounting system. Records must be kept for historical purposes and if they can be used for control purposes as well the additional cost of record-keeping should be more than compensated for by additional profits that result from increased knowledge of the business and its operation.

COMPARISONS AND CORRECTIVE ACTION

After the budget is prepared and the accounting collection system is made compatible with it, the actual performance of the company should be compared to the estimated performance and the differences noted and analyzed. A budget by itself will not solve many problems, although additional knowledge of the operation is always useful. But the analysis and study of differences can awaken an awareness in management that efforts can be made to increase efficiency, reduce costs, and increase income. The problem areas of a business are more clearly shown and can be studied.

After the study has been made, it is management's responsibility to initiate corrective action. Without this action the company loses most of the value of the budgetary effort. Why are sales lower than expected? What can we do to increase them? Why are sales higher than expected? What can we do to sustain this additional volume? Can techniques for selling one product be extended to other product lines? Why are costs higher than expected? How can we decrease them? Why are costs lower than expected? What can we do to continue these lower costs? Can cost reductions in one area be applied to other areas? The answers to these and similar questions should bring forth corrective action that will benefit the company. The company moves from a relatively unplanned organization to one that has some form of guide to future action as related to present performance. The company has added a powerful tool of control to its inventory of management techniques. It is almost sure to improve because of the depth of analysis that has been made in the initial preparation of the budget and because of the analytic study of the differences between budgeted and actual performance.

AMENDING AND EXTENDING THE BUDGET

Once the budget is prepared there should be some mechanism for its revision to reflect changing conditions. If sales increase, what effect does this have on per-unit cost? Does this increase in sales result in higher overtime costs, quantity discounts, additional storeroom requirements, etc.? The revision of the budget should be made in some formal fashion so that the total effect of change can be determined.

In recent years there has been a tendency to realize the shortcomings of an annual budget. Assume a budget prepared in November, Year A, for the calendar year B. On January 1, Year B, the next twelve months are budgeted. As each month goes by, the budget applies to shortening periods of future time until on November 1, Year B, only two months of future time are budgeted. As soon as the calendar-year budget for C is prepared in November, Year B, there are thirteen months of budgeted future time.

This deficiency in budgets has been met in part by use of a budget that is revised periodically (monthly or quarterly). In this way the amount of future budgeted time remains approximately the same, and any current changes are reflected over the extended budget time. Here again the value of the control and what it can mean to the company in terms of additional profits must be measured in costs.

Planning is not a new concept to managers; they all plan. But budgeting—the formal recording of planning—may be a new idea to many. How many backs of envelopes and scraps of paper have been covered with plans and "budgets" only to be thrown away? Wouldn't it be more efficient to formalize these plans and budgets and then use them for purposes of control?

EXERCISES

Exercise No. 66. The following are the revenues of a municipality, South City:

Real Property Taxes	$3,572,862
Personal Property Taxes	385,140
Sales Taxes	468,438
Business Licenses	111,386
Fines	91,851

Prepare the entry to record the estimated revenue.

Exercise No. 67. The following are the estimated departmental expenses of South City:

Administration	$330,180
Legislation	86,082
Judicial	869,635
Education Department	379,784
Health Department	171,656
Police Department	198,018
Fire Department	125,344
Correction Department	169,274
Welfare Department	834,791
Street Department	594,467
Recreation Department	433,558
Office and Building Repairs	33,094
Elections	134,534
Publications, Advertising, etc.	159,399

Prepare an entry to record the estimated expenses.

Exercise No. 68. The real property assessment for South City is $41,935,000 and the tax rate is $8.52 per $100 of assessed valuation. The tax bills for real property are sent out. Prepare an entry to record the tax bills.

Exercise No. 69. Money is received by South City as follows:

Real Property Taxes	$3,368,518
Personal Property Taxes	383,273
Sales Taxes	485,683
Business Licenses	109,776
Fines	92,925

Prepare an entry to record cash receipts.

Exercise No. 70. During the year the following vouchers were processed:

Administration	$329,110
Legislative	85,877
Judicial	806,906
Education Department	379,653
Health Department	170,356
Police Department	197,172
Fire Department	122,882
Correction Department	168,940
Welfare Department	834,615
Street Department	581,687
Recreation Department	377,432
Office and Building Repairs	30,444
Elections	133,482
Publications, Advertising, etc.	158,775

Prepare the entry.

Exercise No. 71. The vouchers (see Exercise No. 70) are paid. Prepare the necessary entry.

Exercise No. 72. The Income Statement for Year A of the Progressive Company is shown below:

Sales		$200,000
Cost of Goods Sold		
Labor	$80,000	
Material	46,000	
Overhead	14,000	140,000
Gross Profit		$ 60,000
Selling Expenses	$25,000	
Administrative Expenses	20,000	45,000
Net Profit		$ 15,000

Prepare a budget for Year B, assuming:

a. sales increase 20%
b. labor increases 15%
c. material increases 20%
d. selling expenses increase 15%
e. administrative expenses increase 10%
f. overhead maintains the same ratio to sales.

Chapter 9

DEPARTMENTAL ACCOUNTING (AND DIVISIONAL ACCOUNTING NOTES)

For purposes of control, in a company that handles different lines of merchandise, it may be helpful for management to know about sales and expenses of each line to analyze better the results of business operations. From illustrations in previous chapters we have seen that the Income Statement for a merchandising business, with statistical analysis, is presented as follows:

Sales		$500,000	100%
Beginning Inventory	$ 30,000		
Purchases	260,000		
	$290,000		
Ending Inventory	50,000		
Cost of Goods Sold		240,000	48%
Gross Profit on Sales		$260,000	52%
Operating Expenses			
Selling Expenses	$140,000		
Administrative Expenses	75,000	215,000	43%
Net Operating Profit		$ 45,000	9%

If there is a variation in percentages of profit and the cost of sales in each line of goods the operating statement as presented above may be almost useless to management as a control tool.

Let us suppose that there are two departments and that sales and cost of sales are analyzed; then we might obtain a statement like this:

	Dept. 1		Dept. 2		Total	
Gross Sales	$200,000	100%	$300,000	100%	$500,000	100%
Beginning Inventory	20,000		10,000		30,000	
Purchases	75,000		185,000		260,000	
	95,000		195,000		290,000	
Ending Inventory	35,000		15,000		50,000	
Cost of Goods Sold	60,000	30%	180,000	60%	240,000	48%
Gross Profit on Sales	$140,000	70%	$120,000	40%	$260,000	52%
Selling Expenses	80,000	40%	60,000	20%	140,000	28%
Departmental Income	$ 60,000	30%	$ 60,000	20%	$120,000	24%
Administrative Expense					75,000	15%
Net Operating Profit					$ 45,000	9%

From this type of analysis we can readily see that each dollar increase in sales in Department 1 makes a greater contribution to net operating profit than each dollar increase in sales in Department 2. If industry profit figures for gross profit in each line were available, we might be able to see which line is better or worse than the industry averages. We could analyze the selling expenses by department and compare them to industry figures for each line.

SALES ANALYSIS

In preparing to make studies of income components it is important that we properly enter all items sold into one of the income classifications. An example everyone is familiar with would be the supermarket. In this type of business there are different markup percentages for different types of goods. Upon looking at the cash register keys we might find the following:

1. Groceries (canned goods, shelf goods, edibles, etc.)
2. Taxable (mops, soaps, hardware, clothes lines, etc.)
3. Drugs (aspirin, shampoo, toothpaste, peroxide, etc.)
4. Meats (meat, fish, poultry)
5. Produce (fruits, vegetables, fresh bottled fruit juices)
6. Liquors (wine, beer, spirits, mixes, snacks)

When the item is rung up, the proper key is pressed or the product code is machine-read and the sale is analyzed at the check-out counter. All items must fit one of the described classification categories. At the end of the day the register is read and a total is obtained for each category as well as the total of all sales.

This type of analysis permits a day-to-day comparison of the sale components as well as a percentage daily analysis. Assume it was anticipated that sales on Thursday were to be:

Groceries	$1,700.00	45.0%
Taxable	570.00	15.0
Drugs	190.00	5.0
Meats	475.00	12.5
Produce	285.00	7.5
Liquor	570.00	15.0
TOTAL	$3,800.00	100.0%

Assume that the case register read-out at the end of the day shows:

Groceries	$1,969.00	49.2%
Taxable	500.00	12.5
Drugs	200.00	5.0
Meats	450.00	11.3
Produce	300.00	7.5
Liquor	581.00	14.5
TOTAL	$4,000.00	100.05

An examination of these results shows that the sales were greater than expected in groceries and in total; they were less than expected in taxable, meats, and liquors; they were as expected in drugs and produce. Management can analyze the reasons for the differences and may be able to find some method of making more efficient use of the company's resources.

Sales classification can be used for purposes of preparing sales-tax returns and reports to licensing agencies, trade associations, and other interested parties. A reader might very well be interested in a sales analysis for purposes of comparing current sales data against past sales data or for reviewing progress of a new line.

In some types of businesses it might be better to departmentalize the physical space—similar to what is done in a department store. Each department has its own area and its own registers, so figures can be accumulated for each department. Generally we find that sales figures in each department are broken down by salesmen for purposes of paying commissions and measuring the performance of the personnel in the department.

EXPENSE ANALYSIS

As in income analysis it is necessary to study the components of expense and to classify them properly. Here, however, the problem is a bit more complex. In a supermarket, the effort of the clerks is spread over all lines and the lines are intermixed on the display floor. It would be hard to classify the wages of the check-out clerk to groceries, meats etc., because he handles all items in one register. The same can be said of the stock clerk who fills the shelves. However, in a department store, wages can be classified because a salesperson is assigned to a specific department.

Expenses other than wages can also be classified by department. Equipment can be classified by location, and other items can follow departmental classification, such as bags, string, tape, etc., charged to a department according to storeroom requisition. Where possible, expenses should always be charged to a department directly, so that a more accurate distribution of costs can be obtained.

There are some selling expenses that are more difficult to assign to individual departments because all departments use the facility and only a single price is paid for the total facility. An example would be rent (or taxes) for a seven-story department store. All floors have the same area but some floors are more desirable. Should all floors be allocated the same rent factor per square foot or should it vary from floor to floor? If the rent factor varies from floor to floor, should it depend upon location on the floor? What about heat for the building? How do we allocate elevator and escalator depreciation and maintenance? We might begin by saying that no allocation system will please everyone in the company. If a department is charged $500 per month rent, the department manager will think the rent charge is too high while other department managers will think it is too low.

Top management must realize that in these situations there are two kinds of departmental expenses:

1. Direct—those that can be controlled by the departmental manager.
2. Allocated—those that cannot be controlled by the departmental manager.

Where the difference is realized, the operating statement can be changed to show the controllable apart from the noncontrollable. In this way responsibility can be assigned to the department manager for those expenses over which he can exercise control, and management must assume responsibility for those over which only they can exercise control.

DEPARTMENTAL PROFIT OR LOSS

When the Income Statement is presented in departmental form, copies of the departmental results can be sent to the manager with comparisons: this year with last year same period; total to date with last year same period; actual performances with budgeted performances, etc. Each manager can see the results of his department's performance and can initiate actions that will increase his department's contribution to the total company profit. Along with the statement, management may send an evaluation of the departmental results with commendations for good performance (rarely done—but so essential to good employee morale) and recommendations for improving performance.

In some businesses there may be departments that operate at a loss. Management should know what the loss for the department is and review the advisability of maintaining the operation of that department. One such department may be a restaurant that serves both customers and employees. What might the total profit be if the restaurant was discontinued? Would the employees take more time for lunch and coffee breaks? Where would a shopper meet her friend if a meeting place is not provided? Management has to answer these questions but might not even be aware of a problem if departmental statements are not prepared.

Divisional Accounting

When a company becomes successful and diversifies its product lines, or decentralizes its operations for whatever reasons, there is a real possibility of lack of control. Then these various operations may be organized as divisions, each of which may well be set up to be a quasi-separate business. When such a situation occurs, the corporate officers want to know what is happening in the *total* company, as well as the results of the division.

These divisions may supply each other with parts or material. The supplier will "sell" to the other divisions as if they were separate companies. Yet the "profit" generated is not real until the product is finally sold outside the company. This raises the question of "transfer pricing." At what price should the product be transferred to another unit in the company? The manager of the transferring company wants the price to be what it would be if it were sold outside the company so that the operating results for his division will show "good" results. The receiving division wants the price of the transferred goods to be at the same price it might pay for those goods from its own operations or outside suppliers. This question is usually resolved by charging the product at one of three prices as determined by company policy. When statements for the whole company are prepared, any "profit" can be eliminated. These three prices are:

1. Full cost—the actual cost of the product.
2. Standard cost—what the product would cost under certain given conditions.
3. Marginal cost—the incremental cost of producing the additional volume for sale to the other division.

EXTERNAL REPORTING REQUIREMENTS

Although each division reports the results of its operation in a manner that may be readily useful to corporate management, the information may not be presented in the proper form for the ordinary users (shareowners and financial analysts) of external reports. For reporting to shareowners and financial analysts, therefore, the Financial Standards Board issues guidelines to assist the preparer and the public accountant in presenting data in ways that are more meaningful to these readers. In addition, the SEC (Securities and Exchange Commission) and the IRS (Internal Revenue Service) have established particular requirements for reporting to them.

The company may be reporting to other governmental agencies, trade associations, state and local taxing authorities, and others, each of which may issue its own set of requirements.

The simple exposition of departmental accounting shown at the beginning of this chapter can become fairly complex when applied to those large organizations. It is beyond the scope of this book to discuss this area of accounting in more detail but the reader should be aware of the existence of this area and the attempts of the accounting profession and others to solve the problems of presenting meaningful information for the diverse readership of corporate financial statements.

EXERCISES

Exercise No. 73. The total sales of the Departmentalized Stores, Inc. for the fiscal year ended March 31, Year A, are $360,000 from the following sources:

Dept. 1	$ 85,000
Dept. 2	72,000
Dept. 3	93,000
Dept. 4	110,000

The beginning inventory in each department is:

Dept. 1	$ 7,000
Dept. 2	6,000
Dept. 3	7,000
Dept. 4	11,000

The net purchases in each department are:

Dept. 1	$74,000
Dept. 2	68,000
Dept. 3	81,000
Dept. 4	99,000

The ending inventory in each department is:

Dept. 1	$ 6,000
Dept. 2	7,000
Dept. 3	8,000
Dept. 4	10,000

The selling expenses in each department are:

Dept. 1	$7,000
Dept. 2	4,000
Dept. 3	6,000
Dept. 4	4,000

The total administrative expense is $8,000. Prepare a departmentalized Income Statement with percentages, similar to the one shown at the beginning of this chapter.

Exercise No. 74. The percentage analysis of expected sales for Thursday in the Bigger Basket Supermarket is shown in the discussion on page 87. The cash register read-out at the end of the day is as follows:

Groceries	$1,960.24
Taxable	482.16
Drugs	203.84
Meats	454.72
Produce	301.84
Liquor	517.44

Compute the total sales, percentages of sales, and difference between expected and actual sales by category.

Chapter 10

INSTALLMENT SALES

There are situations in which the buyer of merchandise does not pay the total purchase price at one time. A special type of contract has been devised in which the buyer makes a down payment and agrees to make a specified number of payments in the future. Such a transaction is known as an **installment sale.**

TRANSFER OF TITLE

In all cases the seller transfers actual physical possession of the property to the buyer. What protection does the seller have to insure payment of the remainder of the purchase price? The answer is that he must retain some interest in the property transferred and this may be done in one of three ways:

1. The seller retains the title until the total amount due is paid. This is a sale made under a **conditional sales contract.**
2. The seller transfers title to a third party who retains title until the payments are completed, at which time it passes to the buyer. This is a sale made under a **trust deed.**
3. The seller transfers title to the buyer subject to a lien, called a **real property mortgage** (in the case of realty) or a **chattel mortgage** (in the case of personalty).

All of these methods of transferring title give the seller (or the trustee) an avenue for repossessing the goods if the buyer does not make the payments required by the contract.

At the time the sale is made and the down pay-ment is given by the buyer to the seller, the seller goes through some procedure to determine if the buyer is a good credit risk. The amount of the down payment should be great enough to cover loss in value of the article sold so that the seller will not incur a loss if he must repossess and re-sell the item. The length of the contract should be as short as possible so that changes in the buyer's situation will not affect his ability to pay. Payments should be made frequently, preferably each month. Each payment should be large enough to cover loss in value of the article since the last payment date. The seller must devise the terms and length of contract so that in the event of repossession he will not lose any money after the repossessed merchandise is sold.

Once the sale is made, the question of profit determination must be made. If the payments are received in more than one fiscal period, during which period should the profit be recorded? There are two basic methods: profits are recognized at the time of sale or they are recognized over the life of the contract.

RECOGNITION OF PROFIT IN PERIOD OF SALE

The department store sells on short-term credit and recognizes the profit at the time of sale. This procedure is followed because the payment period is short-term—one, two, or three months. The sale is recorded as follows:

Accounts Receivable	$100	
Sales		$100

and in the same period the cost of sales is deducted to determine the gross profit.

It is easy to extend this concept in installment sales but there is one difference—the time period for payment is longer, and the fact that a buyer might not pay will not be known at the time of sale or even during the fiscal period in which the sale is made. But one method of accounting for installment sales ignores the objections that arise because of the protracted payment schedule and records the sale and the profit in the year of sale. The entry in this case is:

```
Installment Contracts Receivable   $100
   Sales                                    $100
```

In the same period the cost of sales is deducted to determine the gross profit.

RECOGNITION OF PROFIT DURING CONTRACT TERM

Some accountants recognized that in the event of losses on installment contracts in future years there would be a lack of matching of revenues and expense and the financial situation would be distorted. Therefore, methods were devised to recognize the profit during the contract term. These methods are as follows:

1. The payments at the beginning of the contract term are considered to be recoveries of the cost price. After the cost price is recovered, the balance of the payments is profit. This is a conservative treatment and has the effect of putting all the profit at the end of the contract term.
2. The payments at the beginning of the contract term are considered to be profit. After the profit is recovered, the balance of the payments are considered to be recoveries of cost. This treatment is less conservative than accountants may like and has the effect of putting all the profit at the beginning of the contract term, even before the cost is recovered.
3. All payments to the seller are considered to be recovery of cost and profit in the same proportion that cost and profit are to the total sale price. This method is called the **installment method** and is explained in detail below.

INSTALLMENT METHOD

In the installment method of accounting for sales made in one period with collections made in the current and subsequent periods, it is necessary to record installment sales separately from regular sales and to record cost of installment sales separately from cost of regular sales. This is done by introducing three new accounts: Installment Contracts Receivable—[Year]; Installment Sales—[Year]; and Cost of Installment Sales—[Year].

Assume the seller has an article that cost him $180 and carries a sales price of $200. A customer wants to buy the article, agreeing to pay $75 down and the balance in ten monthly installments of $15 each (total amount of the sale is $225). The sales entry is recorded as follows:

```
Cash                                      $ 75
Installment Contract Receivable—Year A    150
   Installment Sales—Year A                      $225
```

The cost of sales entry (using the perpetual inventory method) is recorded as follows:

```
Cost of Installment Sales—Year A   $180
   Merchandise Inventory                   $180
```

The entry to close the operating accounts (if this were the only sale):

```
Installment Sales—Year A              $225
   Cost of Installment Sales—Year A        $180
   Gross Profit on Installment Sales—
      Year A                                   45
```

The total profit to be realized in the current and future periods is $45, or 20% of the total sales price. Therefore, 20% of the collections on this contract is profit in the period in which the collection is made.

Assume that in the year the contract was made the following payments were received:

```
Down payment                   $ 75
Four installments of $15 each     60
                               $135
```

We have seen above how the down payment was

recorded at the time of the sale. Let us now examine the recording of the subsequent payments.

Cash	$15	
Installment Contracts Receivable—		$15
Year A (for each payment received)		

At the end of the year the Installment Contracts Receivable—Year A account would appear as follows:

Installment Contracts Receivable—Year A

Sale Balance	$150	Payment	$15
		"	15
		"	15
		"	15
			$60
Balance	$ 90		

Of the total contract ($225), the company has collected $135. The amount of profit is 20% of the year's collections, or $27. The entry to record the profit earned this year is:

Gross Profit on Installment Sales—Year A	$27	
Installment Sales Gross Profits Realized		$27

The Gross Profit on Installment Sales—Year A account would appear as follows:

Gross Profit and Installment Sales—Year A

Realized	$27	Total	$45
		Balance	$18

The balance is correct because it is 20% of $90, the remaining balance in the Installment Contracts Receivable—Year A account.

TAX TREATMENT OF INSTALLMENT SALES

Installment sales will be used by businesses as one way to increase sales and, thereby, profitability. The Internal Revenue Service had allowed, prior to the Tax Reform Act of 1986, companies to use the installment plan for reporting sales on their income tax returns. Under the 1986 Act the use of reporting sales on the installment basis was severely limited.

This is an example of a company being able to use an accounting method for its own internal reporting but being denied that method for tax reporting.

STATEMENT PRESENTATION

On the Balance Sheet are found the accounts Installment Contracts Receivable—[Year] and Gross Profit on Installment Sales—[Year]. The receivable account is shown by year and in total as follows:

Cash			$ 10,000
Accounts Receivable		$150,000	
Installment Contracts Receivable			
Year (A-2)	$ 20,000		
Year (A-1)	80,000		
Year A	160,000	260,000	410,000
	etc.		

or the yearly details may be shown on a separate exhibit.

The unearned gross profit may be shown in one of three ways:

1. As a current liability, like any other unearned income.
2. As a part of the equity accounts, on the proposition that only collection is needed to realize profit to the owners.
3. As a contra-asset or valuation account to be subtracted from the receivable account, on the proposition that there may be some accounts which will not be collected.

On the Income Statement the total sales may be shown or the regular sales may be shown, and the amount of profit earned on installment sales may be shown. If all sales are shown, the Income Statement appears as follows:

| | Sales | | |
	Regular	Installment	Total
Sales	$200,000	$300,000	$500,000
Cost of Sales (detailed)	140,000	180,000	320,000
Gross Profit	$ 60,000	$120,000	$180,000
Less unrealized gross profit on Year A sales		64,000	64,000
	$ 60,000	$ 56,000	$116,000
Profit realized on previous installment sales (detailed)			66,600
etc.			etc.

If only the regular sales are shown, the income statement appears as follows:

Regular Sales	$200,000
Cost of Regular Sales	140,000
Gross Profit on Regular Sales	$ 60,000
Profit realized on Installment Sales (detailed)	122,600
	$182,000
	$182,600
etc.	etc.

The details would show:

Year (A-2) Installment Sales Income (collections of $90,000 × 34%)		$ 30,600
Year (A-1) Installment Sales Income (collections of $100,000 × 36%)		36,000
Year A Installment Sales	$300,000	
Less Cost of Sales	180,000	
Gross Profit (40% of Sales)	$120,000	
(Collection of $140,000 × 40%)		56,000
		$122,600

TRADE-INS

Because installment sales are used for relatively high-priced items, it is not unusual to find the seller accepting a used piece of merchandise as a trade-in down payment. The amount given as a trade-in allowance may vary from customer to customer for an almost identical piece of used merchandise. How a particular trade-in value is arrived at for a particular prospect for a particular piece of used merchandise is unimportant to this discussion. What is important is the implication of the trade-in value. The trade-in may be priced so that it can be resold (after reconditioning) at a fair profit. Or it may be priced at a figure higher than one that would bring a fair profit on resale.

Let us assume that a piece of equipment is to be turned in as a down payment on a new piece of equipment. The used equipment could be sold for $1,000 (assuming a 25% markup on cost). It should then be carried on the books at $800 when reconditioned. The estimated cost of reconditioning should be subtracted from $800 to obtain the value of the trade-in. So long as the amount allowed is less than the figure thus obtained, the trade-in is properly priced. The trade-in, cash, and receivable from the customer are debited and Installment Sales is credited.

Example: A customer desires to purchase a new machine and offers a used machine in trade. The dealer shows a new machine priced at $10,000 to the customer and offers a trade-in value of $1,000 for the used machine with $9,000 cash. The normal markup is 25% on the selling price. It will take $400 to repair and recondition the used machine, which can then be sold for $2,000.

The following schedule may be used to determine whether the value for the trade-in is correct:

Sale price of used equipment	$2,000
Less profit on sale (25%)	500
	$1,500
Less reconditioning cost	400
Value of the trade-in	$1,100

The trade-in allowed is less than $1,100; therefore, the $1,000 is used as the value of the trade-in. The entry is:

Used Machinery Inventory	$1,000	
Cash	9,000	
Sales		$10,000

Let us now assume that the piece of used equipment is given a trade-in value higher than the sale price of the reconditioned equipment, less markup, less reconditioning costs. In this case the trade-in is to be written down and the installment sale is to be reduced a like amount.

Example: A customer desires to purchase a new machine and offers a used machine in trade. The dealer shows a new machine priced at $20,000 to the customer and offers a trade-in value of $2,500 for the used machine, with $17,500 in cash. The normal markup on used equipment is 20% on the selling price. It will take $1,000 to repair and recondition the used machine, which can then be sold for $4,000.

The following schedule may be used to determine whether the value for the trade-in is correct:

Sale price of used equipment	$4,000
Less profit on sale (20%)	800
	$3,200
Less reconditioning costs	1,000
Value of the trade-in	$2,200

The trade-in value allowed is greater than the $2,200 calculated above; therefore, the $2,500 is not recorded as the value of the trade-in. The entry is:

Used Machinery Inventory	$ 2,200	
Cash	17,500	
Sales		$19,700

or another entry showing sales as $20,000 (the amount on the contract) would be:

Used Machinery Inventory	$ 2,200	
Cash	17,500	
Loss on Trade-ins	300	
Sales		$20,000

DEFAULTS AND REPOSSESSIONS

When the buyer of merchandise on an installment contract stops payment before the contract is completely paid off, it is said to be in **default** and the seller may be able to repossess the merchandise. When the goods are repossessed, the seller sets them up on the books at the sales price less markup and reconditioning costs. The remainder of the entry is the write-off of the receivable and the unrealized portion of income and the recognition of loss due to repossession.

Example: A customer owes $500 on an installment contract. The gross profit ratio is 20% of the selling price. The contract is defaulted due to cessation of payments by the buyer and the goods are repossessed by the seller. When reconditioned at a cost of $100, the goods can be sold for $550. The gross profit ratio for used equipment is 10% of the selling price.

The amount of unrealized income on the original sale is $100 ($500 × 20%). The value of the repossessed goods is:

Selling price	$550
Gross profit (10%)	55
	$495
Reconditioning cost	100
Value of the repossessed item	$395

The entry to record the repossession is:

Repossessed Goods Inventory	$395	
Gross Profit on Installment Sales	100	
Loss on Repossessions	5	
Installment Contracts Receivable		$500

INTEREST ON INSTALLMENT SALES

The seller recognizes in making installment sales that the buyer has use of the goods before full payment is made. The seller generally charges the buyer for extended credit terms, so that the total amount paid by the buyer will exceed the price if it had been paid in cash at the time of purchase. The difference is the **interest** or **carrying charge**. This additional amount may be added in various ways; two of the most popular are:

1. Equal payments for a specified number of terms covering both interest and principal.
2. Equal payments on the principal each term plus interest on the principal since the last payment.

The first is the type of loan one might secure from a bank or finance company. Suppose the purchaser buys a piece of equipment priced at $2,600 and pays $1,100 down in cash. The balance is $1,500 to be paid $70 per month for 24 months. This means there is $180 of interest and service charges. Each month part of the $180 is earned. The entry to record the sale would be:

Cash	$1,100	
Installment Contracts Receivable	1,680	
Installment Sales		$2,600
Deferred Carrying Charge Income		180

When a payment is made the entry to record the receipt of cash is:

Cash	$70	
Installment Contracts Receivable		$70

An adjusting entry might be made now (or prepared at the end of the period for all payments) as follows:

Deferred Carrying Charge Income	$XX	
Carrying Charge Income		$XX

The amount would probably be determined by a schedule from which the installment contract was prepared. The amount "Deferred Carrying Charge Income" may be titled differently to reflect properly the composition of the additional charge.

The second method is the type of financing one might secure from a department store. Suppose a purchaser buys furniture priced at $2,600, paying $1,100 down in cash. The balance is to be paid at $70 per month and the seller will charge 1½% on the unpaid balance per month. The entry to record the sale is:

Cash	$1,100	
Installment Contracts Receivable	1,500	
Installment Sales		$2,600

The payment of $70 is made by the purchaser and is recorded as follows:

Cash	$70	
Installment Contracts Receivable		$70

An entry is made to record the interest earned as follows:

Installment Contracts Receivable	$22.50	
Interest Income (1½% × $1,500)		$22.50

In the following month the interest is $21.68 (1½% × $1,430). The amount of interest is computed each month and reduces by 1½% of the amount made the last payment on the principal balance.

The type of financing used for installment sales varies with the nature of the seller, the type of merchandise being sold, credit practices in the industry, and so on.

Government regulations now require that the buyer be informed of the contract terms. So in current contracts one sees APR (Annual Percentage Rate), which is the adjusted rate of interest for the contract.

EXERCISES

Exercise No. 75. Sales of $5,000 are made on charge accounts (terms net 30 days). Prepare the entry.

Exercise No. 76. The goods sold in Exercise No. 75 cost $3,500. The books are kept on a perpetual inventory basis. Prepare the entry.

Exercise No. 77. The customers who purchased the goods in Exercise No. 75 pay their bills. Prepare the entry.

Exercise No. 78. Goods costing $300,000 are sold for $500,000 on installment contracts in Year C. Prepare the required entry (entries).

Exercise No. 79. In Year C, collections on the installment contracts received for the merchandise sold in Exercise No. 78 amounted to $70,000. Prepare the required entry (entries).

Exercise No. 80. In Year D, collections on the installment contracts received for the merchandise sold in Exercise No. 78 amounted to $180,000. Prepare the required entry (entries).

Exercise No. 81. At the beginning of Year D there are credit balances in the accounts:

Gross Profit on Installment Sales—Year A $ 20,000
Gross Profit on Installment Sales—Year B   160,000
Gross Profit on Installment Sales—Year C   500,000

The gross profit margins in these years were:

Year A	32%
Year B	37%
Year C	35%

The balances in the accounts at the end of Year D are:

Gross Profit on Installment Sales—Year A $ —
Gross Profit on Installment Sales—Year B   30,000
Gross Profit on Installment Sales—Year C   220,000

What were the collections on the Year A, Year B, and Year C installment contracts? Carry out to the nearest dollar only.

Exercise No. 82. A customer wants to trade in a used machine on a new one priced at $15,000 that cost $13,000. The salesman allows $3,000 on the used machine and accepts an installment contract for $12,500. The used machine can be sold for $4,500 after spending $800 to recondition it. The markup for used equipment is 20% of the selling price.

a. Prepare a schedule showing the value of the trade-in merchandise.
b. Prepare the entry (entries) for the sale.

Exercise No. 83. A machine selling for $10,000 (costing $7,000) is sold on the installment basis in Year A. The customer pays $1,000 down and gives an installment note of $9,720. After making $2,160 in payments, the customer defaults and the merchandise is repossessed. It would cost $1,000 to recondition the machine, which could then be sold for $8,000. The normal gross profit ratio on used machine sales is 15% of sales price.

a. Prepare the entry (entries) for the sale.
b. Prepare the entry (entries) for the payments received (assume that interest earnings are prorated).
c. Compute the inventory value of the machine when repossessed.
d. Prepare the entry to record the repossession.

Chapter 11

COST ACCOUNTING

Cost accounting is the branch of accounting that has as its purpose the determination of per-unit cost of products manufactured. In a merchandising business, the per-unit cost of an article sold can be determined by the invoice (perhaps with an adjustment for freight or returned items). But in a manufacturing plant, values are added as a result of productive effort which cannot be found on a vendor's invoice; it must be determined from the accounting records.

FUNCTION OF COST ACCOUNTING

The collection of data concerning factory costs is the function of cost accounting. It requires an understanding of the production process, components of manufacturing cost, the establishment of a cost-gathering system, and the determination of total and per-unit cost.

The various production processes are too many to describe in detail here, but some general concepts of processes can be described. There are the chemical analytic processes (breaking down of water into hydrogen and oxygen) and synthesis processes (making nylon). There are the mechanical processes of drilling (drill press), turning (lathe), cutting (saw, planer, mill, or shear), and fastening (riveting, welding). There are annealing and tempering processes. There are sanding, painting, enameling, and other finishing processes. There is the assembly process. Although these are but a few, a knowledge of them and their place in the production to be costed is necessary if good cost figures are to be developed.

The components of manufacturing cost are direct labor, direct material, and factory overhead. These terms can be defined as follows:

Direct labor, the labor actually expended in producing the product. If we were to examine a chair, direct labor would include wages paid to the saw operator who cut the lumber to size, the assembler who glued and screwed the pieces of lumber together, the assembler who attached the springs, and the upholsterer who fit the padding and covered the chair with fabric.

Direct materials, those materials of which the product is made. If we examine the chair again, this category would include the wood, for the legs, rails, seat, and arms; glue, for the joints; nails and screws, for fastening the pieces together; the fabric, for covering; springs, for support; padding, for comfort; thread, for sewing; etc. For purposes of convenience in accounting, some of these items might not be considered (for example, the glue, nails, screws, and thread) because their costs may be minimal in relation to the total cost and the expense to account for these costs may well not be cost-effective.

Factory overhead, the cost of operating the factory other than the cost of direct labor and direct materials. Factory overhead includes indirect labor (supervisors' salaries, salaries of stockroom and receiving clerks, etc.), indirect materials (repair and maintenance supplies, janitorial supplies, factory office supplies, etc.), rent, taxes (real property, personal property, payroll, etc.), depreciation, utilities (other than those used directly in the manufacturing process, like gas and electricity for ovens), water, heat, lights, etc.

LABOR—DIRECT AND INDIRECT

The factory secures labor service from the local area on an individual basis and so each individual must be paid. The total amount of money earned by an individual is called his **gross pay.** This is computed by attendance or by work performance (number of pieces produced, etc.). In almost all cases attendance records are kept for other reasons than payroll computation purposes, such as wage and hour legislation, control of workers and production, to assist in determination of missing persons in event of catastrophe, etc. The payroll consideration in this discussion is of paramount interest, and the other aspects of attendance recording will be ignored.

Time. When time is used as the basis for pay, the payroll department takes the time of attendance and multiplies it by the rate of pay to get gross wages. In the case of monthly or weekly employees, the gross pay is generally the same, period after period (except where a rate is increased), even though the employee may have been absent for a day or two. In the case of hourly employees, the number of hours shown on the time card is multiplied by the rate to get gross wages, and an employee must be in attendance to be paid (except for legal holidays, contractual paid days off, etc.). The question of overtime pay is one that is confusing because state legislation, union rules, and factory policy vary from one situation to another and the definitions of overtime vary as well. Laws vary as to how long and under what conditions an employee may work. The union contract may establish the time to be classified as overtime (for example, all hours over forty in a week, or over eight in one day, etc.). The company may have established policies regarding overtime compensation. With respect to salaried employees, executive and supervisory personnel are generally not paid overtime while the nonadministrative salaried employees may be paid overtime or be given compensatory time off. Regarding hourly employees, there is generally an established work

week of a stated number of hours and any time worked over the stated limit is paid for at premium rates. In some situations the employee may be paid a premium for any time over eight hours in one day, even though he may not work the stated hours in one week.

This gross wage is distributed to the direct labor or indirect labor accounts. Each of these accounts can be subdivided into more meaningful categories, and the following schema might be developed:

Direct Labor:

Department 1		Job No. 1
Department 2	or	Job No. 2
etc.		etc.

Indirect Labor:

Department F1		Supervision
Department F2	or	Inspection
etc.		etc.

These amounts become the debits for the payroll entry. The credits are for taxes deducted from the gross wages (Social Security and Medicare, federal and state [if any] income tax, disability insurance, etc. as required by statute), union dues (where applicable), pension plan, health or life insurance or bond deductions (or similar deductions), and the net wage payable. The preparation of wages and salaries for a factory is the same as for a merchandising company in all respects, except that the debits are classified as needed by factory accounting.

Production. When productive output is used as the basis for pay, it is necessary to relate the production to the time necessary to complete the task so that an equitable rate per piece completed can be established. The relationship can be established by having an operator complete the task and by measuring the units produced per hour. The pieces completed per hour are related to the suggested wage rate per hour and determine the price rate per hour. For example, an employee works eight hours producing 400 units. His wage rate is $6 per hour. To determine the piecework rate for that particular employee or job, the following formulas are used:

$$\frac{400 \text{ units}}{8 \text{ hrs.}} = 50 \text{ units/hr.}$$

$$\frac{\$6/hr.}{50 \text{ units/hr.}} = \$0.12/\text{piece}$$

A more scientific method used for determining the number of pieces per time period is a systematic analysis of the production process, sometimes called a **time and motion study.** In the early days of time and motion study, the engineer was accused of wanting to get continually greater production at no increase in cost, and these were days of physical violence against the industrial engineer. Today the time and motion studies are more acceptable and the engineer can save money through the elimination of needless steps in the process, combining steps, etc. There is still cause for resentment when the piece-rate-per-hour standards are set too tightly (so few can complete the tasks in the time allowed) or too loosely (so the goal is easily achievable and the task becomes a "plum" to be given to favored employees).

Many systems have been devised using production as a basis for pay, but the details of each system will not be discussed here; it would be better to discuss the principles upon which the systems depend. One important principle is that the worker should be guaranteed a minimum wage regardless of the quantity produced. He has put in the time and is available for work and should be paid. The reasons why he cannot produce the quota may be that he is a new employee and is still in training; the machine might break down; goods delivered to the employee for his task might be defective. When the employee is guaranteed a wage he will perform better because the anxiety of not earning a living wage is removed. If an employee continually fails to earn the minimum salary, then management must analyze the reasons and take corrective action. This corrective action may involve transfer to a different job, additional training, or, in extreme cases, separation.

Another important principle is that production in excess of the established goal reduces per-unit cost. Since the total cost of production is direct material, direct labor, and factory overhead, the major source of total production cost increase is direct material and direct labor. Factory overhead is relatively constant. Therefore, when production rises, the per-unit cost falls, and the company encourages the employee to produce more than the expected quantity per hour.

Another important principle is that employees will increase production over the expected amount if they are paid more. Therefore, pay incentive systems recognize the value of the additional units in reducing cost per unit. These systems may have a built-in sliding scale of incentive. This can be illustrated as follows:

For:	Employee is paid:
0–100 pieces	$0.060 per piece (or guarantee of $5 per hour)
101–110 pieces	0.062 per piece
111 and over	0.066 per piece

Thus, a worker can achieve the guaranteed wage of $5 per hour by producing 83⅓ pieces per hour or less. If he produces 100 pieces per hour he earns $6 per hour; 110 pieces, $6.82 per hour; and 120 pieces, $7.92 per hour. To prevent careless work on the part of the worker, some notion of acceptable quality is tied to the production measurement.

Payroll Entry. After the gross pay is determined by the measure of production (or a guarantee, when it is operative), the debit and credit distributions are made as before. A proforma of that entry might look as follows:

Work in Process—Department 1	$XX	
Work in Process—Department 2	XX	
etc.		
Factory Overhead—Department F1	XX	
Factory Overhead—Department F2	XX	
etc.		
F.I.C.A Taxes Payable		
(for Social Security and Medicare)		$XX
Federal (and State [if any])		
Income Taxes Withheld		XX
Other Statutory Taxes Withheld		
Payable		
(state disability insurance, etc.— itemized by account)		XX
Other Amounts Withheld		
Owing to Contractual Agreements (medical insurance premium, life insurance premium, savings bond deduction, etc. —itemized by account)		XX
Salaries and Wages Payable		XX

Notice that the debits may be made in total to Work in Process and to Factory Overhead and the details may be shown in subsidiary ledgers or account analyses. The Work in Process debits may also be shown to Job or Process Orders as well as to Departments. The credits reflect the statutory and contractual deductions from the employee's pay and the net amount due the employee.

Nonpayroll Labor Costs. The total cost of labor to an employer is not the total of the gross pay earned by employees during a period. Rather, it is the total of the gross pay earned by employees during a period *plus* all other costs the employer pays out for employees. These additional costs might be required by statute, by a union contract, or by an agreement between the employer and employee. The payroll taxes levied against an employer are Social Security and Medicare and federal and state unemployment (although there are exceptions). The employer may be required by the union to make payments to a pension or welfare fund based on wages, hours worked, or production. The employer may institute a fringe-benefit program under which he pays all or part of the employee's life insurance or health insurance premiums (to certain limits) or contributes to a pension plan, or matches employee's savings for stock purchases, etc. Only when these additional items are considered, does the employer know his total labor cost. These nonpayroll labor costs may be charged to factory overhead, or an attempt may be made to allocate them to productive effort. In some studies made these "fringe benefit" costs can be as high or higher than one third of the employee's gross pay although he may be completely unaware of the expense of the employer for his benefit.

MATERIAL—DIRECT AND INDIRECT

The question of what should be produced is decided by the company before production begins. There is an assumption that materials will be received in a particular stage of completion to be combined with other materials and formed into a new product after going through some industrial process.

The factory secures materials from the market in whatever stage of completion production requires—iron may be purchased in ore form (by a steel mill) or in rolls of sheet steel (by a tin-can manufacturer).

The problems of purchasing in an industrial situation are the same as in a merchandising situation; that is, to get the proper amount of suitable material delivered when needed at the lowest cost per unit. The purchasing agent shops the vendor market to obtain the material.

After the material is ordered and the vendor delivers it, a materials handling and storage system is involved. The material is received and, if necessary, tested for quality. It is then stored until needed in production. At this stage it might be well for the company to ask itself whether a centralized storeroom or a number of decentralized storerooms should be used. There are arguments for and against each method, but the ultimate decision is in the hands of management.

As the material is required by a worker for his task, he prepares a storeroom requisition (Fig. 23) and presents it to the storekeeper. The storekeeper locates the material, reduces the inventory as shown on the bin card, and gives the material to the worker.

In the accounting department, each item is priced out by LIFO, FIFO, average, or some other method discussed previously. The requisitions are recorded in a Material Journal, which shows the date, requisition number, and job or department to be charged.

When the journal is footed an entry is made debiting the jobs or departments and crediting materials as follows:

Work in Process—Job No. 1	$XX	
Job No. 2	XX	
etc.		
Factory Overhead—Department F1	XX	
Department F2	XX	
etc.		
Materials (Inventory)		$Total

Inventory Security. Inventory is often composed of low-volume, high-value items, or items with high personal utility, or some that may be crucial to the smooth flow of manufactured goods. When these types of items are included in

QUANTITY	ARTICLES	STOCK NO.	PRICE	AMOUNT
	STOREROOM REQUISITION Req. No. *1-063-A*			
	Storekeeper: Please furnish bearer with the following. Date *January 15, Year A*			
	Charge Acct. No. *625-93* Dept. *7-assembly* Dept. No. ____			
10	SHANK	351	1.97	19 70
10	SPINDLE	338	2.15	21 50
10	SHANK BUSHING	413	3.27	32 70
20	SPINDLE WASHERS	341	0.02	40
				74 30
CHARGE JOB NO. **93**	ENTERED ON STOCK LEDGER *QD* ENTERED ON RECAP *M* Signed *C. W. Leary*			

Figure 23. Storeroom Requisition.

the inventory, it is essential that there be a system of control. This will vary from minimum control over the coal pile (because one can see if there is enough coal, and the value of coal stolen by employees and others is negligible) to maximum control over gold and jewels in a watch manufacturing plant.

It is important to remember that not all items in inventory must be under the same degree of control. Each item must be reviewed to determine the degree of control that must be placed over the material. Remember that control costs money and the cost of control must be measured against the savings resulting from the use of the controls.

Economic Order Quantity. In order to reduce the cost of material to the lowest possible price at point and time of use, a study should be made of the usage of inventory, the cost of ordering merchandise, and the costs of storing and holding merchandise. Ideally, a company would like each unit of material to arrive just before it is needed so that no storage costs are incurred, and it would like to be able to issue one purchase order for the requirements of materials for long periods of time. In practical terms, these two goals are opposed, and neither is absolutely attainable. The business must store materials, and purchase orders have to be processed to purchase

new material. The problem then resolves itself into finding out how much to order and how often.

The total cost of material at point and time of use is invoice price per unit plus ordering cost per unit plus storage cost per unit. The invoice cost is easily calculated. The ordering cost per *order* can be determined by ascertaining the number of purchase orders processed and dividing that number into the total purchasing department expense for a period, adding the total receiving department expense for the same period, and dividing by the number of shipments received. A similar analysis is performed for all elements of the expenses of ordering materials.

Let us assume that the order cost equals $60 per order. The larger the quantity ordered, the lower the cost per unit. This is shown in Fig. 24.

Let us assume that a company orders 1,000 units, at a cost of $2 per unit, four times a year, and that the materials are used equally over the year and there are no days off. A graph of the usage pattern would show fluctuations in inventory size as in Fig. 25.

The average inventory would be 500 units (1,000 units × ½) at $1,000 (500 units × $2/unit). There is storage space required for these 1,000 units as well as custody costs (storekeepers' salaries), fire insurance, interest on the investment in inventory, and the possibility of deterioration, destruction, or theft. Collectively, these are called **holding costs.**

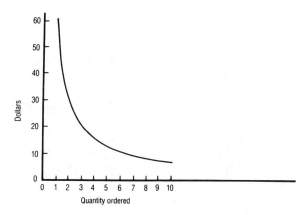

Figure 24. Ordering Cost Curve.

If, however, the company ordered 500 units per order, eight orders per year would be required. The graph of usage would appear as in Fig. 26. The average inventory would be 250 units (500 units × ½) at $500 (250 units × $2/ unit). The storage space required for the item, fire insurance, and interest on investment in inventory is cut in half. There is a reduction (although not necessarily by half) of custody costs and deterioration, destruction, and theft losses.

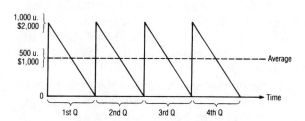

Figure 25. Fluctuations in Inventory Size.

Plotting the holding cost against number of units ordered would produce a graph similar to Fig. 27.

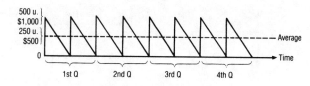

Figure 26. Graph of Usage.

Superimposing the ordering cost curve (Fig. 24) on the holding cost curve (Fig. 27) would produce a graph showing the two curves and a curve of total cost (Fig. 28).

Point Q would be the most economic quantity to order. To produce a graph for each item may prove to be quite a time-consuming job, so formulas have been developed to allow a more rapid calculation of the economic lot quantity size. One such formula is as follows:

$$Q = \sqrt{\frac{2 \times R \times P}{C \times I}}$$

where Q is the economic order quantity
  R is the annual requirement of the item in units
  P is the cost of placing one order
  C is the invoice price of one unit of the item
  I is the holding cost of inventory expressed as a percentage of the average inventory.

To use the formula P and I must be determined for the company.

$$P = \frac{\text{total cost of ordering}}{\text{number of orders placed per year}}$$

and $I = \dfrac{\text{total cost of holding inventory}}{\text{average inventory}}$

Assume that the cost of processing an order (writing the purchase order, purchasing department salaries and expenses, receiving depart-

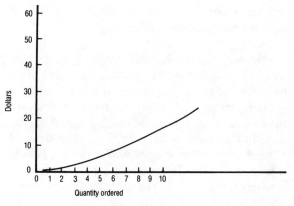

Figure 27. Holding Cost Curve.

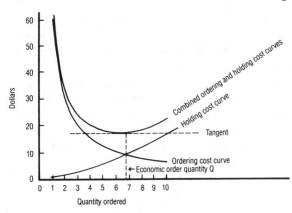

Figure 28. Combined Ordering and Holding Cost Curves.

ment salaries and expenses, and all other costs relative to purchasing) is $80,000 per year and 4,000 purchase orders are written. Then $P = $ $20. Assume that holding costs (storeroom salaries and expenses, inventory insurance, personal property taxes on inventory, obsolescence, deterioration, inventory loss) are $100,000, and the average inventory is $400,000. Then $I = 25\%$.

If a company uses 2,000 units per quarter ($R = 8,000$) and material costs $3 per unit ($C = 3), the economic order quantity is:

$$Q = \sqrt{\frac{2 \times 8,000 \times 20}{3.00 \times .25}} = \sqrt{\frac{320,000}{.75}}$$
$$= \sqrt{426,667}$$
$$= 653.2 \text{ units}$$

If each order were for 653 units it would require 8000/653.2 or 12.25 orders per year. Since the units or orders must be in whole numbers the economic lot quantity would be 653 (or 700 if the items are packed 100 to the box, or 660 if they are packed by the dozen).

Minimum Stock. Because it takes time for material to be delivered, the purchasing agent must order before stock is depleted so that production is uninterrupted. A study is made of delivery time of each item, and the quantity used during this time is computed to establish the time of reorder in terms of quantity of material. This is shown in Fig. 29. The economic lot quantity size is determined to be 800 units ordered every eight weeks (a usage of 100 per week). It takes two weeks between the time an order is placed and

the time it is delivered. Therefore, the order is placed two weeks prior to the time the inventory will be depleted or when the quantity level is 200 units (2 weeks $\times$ 100 units/week). When the stock arrives, two weeks after it is ordered, the inventory is just reaching the depletion point. The time between the order date and the receiving date is called "lead time."

Safety Stock. For critical items the minimum quantity may be increased by some amount to insure that there never is a **stock-out** (that is, a time when there is no material). This quantity is called the **safety stock.** For example, if it is decided that, to ensure against stock-out, an additional 150 units is needed, the minimum quantity in the immediately preceding example would be raised from 200 to 350 units.

DEFECTIVE WORK

When some of the goods produced are inspected and found to be defective, the production department assesses whether the items are to be reworked into acceptable items or scrapped.

Reworking. If the defective items are to be reworked, they are separated from the acceptable items and moved along whatever line is necessary to turn them into acceptable units. The item may be disassembled or reworked, new parts may be added for defective ones, etc., until it is ready for sale.

These defective items are segregated from an accounting standpoint as well. The entry is easy enough to prepare except for the valuation of the defective items. Three approaches to the prob-

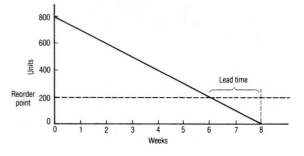

Figure 29. Lead Time Illustrated.

lem can be taken. The first is to assume that up to the point of separation all items in the group cost the same per unit. The second is to value the defective items at their present worth but increase the per-unit cost of the nondefective ones. The third is to value the defective items at their present worth but not increase the per-unit cost of the nondefective items. The results of these different treatments will be discussed.

1. All units up to point of separation cost the same. Under this assumption it is an easy matter to determine the cost of the group of items and the number of items produced (good and defective) and obtain a per-unit cost. The entry made to separate the defective items from the acceptable ones is:

W.I.P.— Defective Goods $280
     W.I.P. (7 units @ $40) $280
(W.I.P. = Work in Process)

As the nondefective goods continue to completion, additional costs are normally collected. The cost per unit of these completed goods will be approximately what it would have been if there were no defective goods and the entire batch had been completed as acceptable.

As the defective goods continue to completion, additional costs are normally collected. The cost per unit of these defective goods brought to completion will be higher than if there had been no deficiencies. The entries to record cost of direct labor and direct material to defective goods is:

W.I.P.—Defective Goods   Debit
                 Debits
W.I.P.—Defective Goods $XX Credits
     Material Inventory $XX

The objection to using this method is that the per-unit cost of finished goods is greater for the defective goods than for the nondefective ones.

2. Defective items are valued at their present worth, but the per-unit cost of the nondefective items will increase. Under this assumption an analysis is made of how much, per unit, it would cost to complete the defective goods. Let us assume this cost is $65. Assume the unit cost to point of separation is $40, as used in the example before, and the expected completion cost of a

unit is $90. Then the present value must be $25 ($90 − $65), and the entry is:

W.I.P.—Defective Goods $175
     W.I.P. (7 × $25) $175

The objection to this treatment is that by only removing the present value of the defective goods the *total* cost of nondefective goods rose by $105, and the per-unit cost rose accordingly. The third approach overcomes this objection.

3. Defective items are valued at their present worth, but the per-unit cost of the nondefective items will not increase. Under this assumption an analysis is made of how much, per unit, it would cost to complete the nondefective goods (say $50). An analysis is also made of how much, per unit, it would cost to complete the defective goods (say $65, as used in the example before). If the per-unit cost to point of separation was $40 (as above), the expected completion cost per nondefective unit is $90, but the reworked defective items would cost $105 per unit. To equalize the per-unit cost of the defective and nondefective goods *at the end* of the productive effort, the defective goods are reduced in value now by the following entry:

W.I.P.—Defective Goods
   (7 × $25) $175
Factory Overhead—Defective Goods
   (7 × $15)   105
   Work in Process $280

As the nondefective and defective goods continue to completion, the cost per unit of these completed goods will be approximately what it would have been if there were no defective goods and the entire batch of goods had been completed as acceptable.

Scrapping. If the defective items are not to be reworked, but instead are scrapped, they are separated from the acceptable items and put into bins or elsewhere for disposal.

The accountant should remove these defective items from the remainder of the batch, just as the goods were physically removed. Three methods can be used to calculate the value of the defective items. The first is to assume that up to the point of separation all items in the group cost the same per unit. The second is to value the scrap at its present market value and to increase the per-unit cost of the nondefective items. The third is to value scrap at its present market value and to maintain the per-unit cost of the nondefective items. These different treatments are discussed below.

1. All units up to the separation cost the same. As explained before, a per-unit cost to point of separation is determined. The entry made to separate the scrap from the acceptable units is:

Scrap Inventory $280
   W.I.P. (7 units @ $40) $280

The treatment for the nondefective goods is the same as explained in the section on "Reworking"—they collect additional costs and at completion the unit cost approximates what it would have been had there been no scrap and the whole batch of goods had been completed as acceptable.

When the scrap is sold, an entry is made as follows:

Cash (or Accounts Receivable) $XX
Loss or Gain on Sales of Scrap
   (or Factory Overhead)   XX or $XX
    Scrap Inventory   280

The objection to this treatment is that in many cases the market value of the scrap may not be as great as the per-unit cost up to the point of separation. This method overstates scrap inventory, although the per-unit cost of the units remaining in production is equitable.

2. Scrap is valued at its present marked value and the per-unit cost of the nondefective items is increased. Under this method the market value of the scrap is obtained. The Scrap Inventory account is set up at this value, while Work in Process in reduced by the same amount as follows:

Scrap Inventory $75
   W.I.P. $75

When the scrap is sold, the entry is as follows:

Cash (or Accounts Receivable) $XX
Loss or Gain on Sale of Scrap
   (or Factory Overhead)   XX or $XX
    Scrap Inventory   75

The objection to this treatment is that the per-unit cost of the nondefective goods up to point

of separation is increased. The way to overcome this objection is to use the third approach.

3. Scrap is valued at its present market value but the per-unit cost of the nondefective items remains the same. Under this assumption the market value of scrap is determined, and Scrap and Inventory is debited by this amount, but Work in Process is credited with the per-unit cost to the point of separation. The difference in these two values is absorbed by Factory Overhead as follows:

Scrap Inventory $ 75
Factory Overhead—Scrap   205
   Work in Process (7 × $40) $280

When the scrap is sold, the entry prepared for the second treatment is used. You can see that this treatment establishes scrap at its conservative value and preserves the per-unit cost up to point of separation.

One of the purposes of the account records is to present facts on which management can act. The method to be used for recording the value of defective goods or scrap, and the per-unit cost of work in process at point of separation, should be chosen keeping in mind the use to be made by management of the additional information and the cost of collection versus the potential savings.

FACTORY OVERHEAD

Factory overhead is the cost, other than direct labor and direct materials, of operating the factory. The costs of the factory may come from goods and services purchased from outsiders and goods and services previously purchased but now used up. The entries for these types of transaction are:

Factory Overhead—Indirect Labor $XXX
(or Factory Overhead—Dept. F1)
   etc.
Remainder of payroll   XXX
   Payroll credits $XXX
    To record the payroll for the
    period. (This entry is
    prepared from the payroll
    summary. At the end of the
    period the normal payroll
    accrual entry is made.)

Factory Overhead—Materials (or Factory Overhead—Dept. F1) etc.	XXX	
Remainder of material debits	XXX	
Inventory		XXX

To record the material usage for the period. (This entry is prepared from the Material Journal.)

Factory Overhead—Telephone	XXX	
Factory Overhead—Utilities	XXX	
Factory Overhead—Rent etc.	XXX	
Vouchers (Accounts) Payable		XXX

To record invoices received for goods or services purchased for use. (At the end of the period the normal accrual entry is made.)

Factory Overhead—Insurance	XXX	
Factory Overhead—Supplies etc.	XXX	
Various Prepaid Assets		XXX

To record the expired cost of the prepaid assets.

Factory Overhead—Depreciation of Factory Equipment	XXX	
Factory Overhead—Depreciation of Factory Building, etc.	XXX	
Accumulated Depreciation—		
Factory Equipment		XXX
Factory Building, etc.		XXX

To record depreciation expense determined by the depreciation schedules.

If these charges were posted to the Factory Overhead account, it would appear as follows:

Factory Overhead

Indirect Labor
Indirect Material
Charges from the voucher register
Expired cost of prepaid assets
Depreciation expense

Factory Overhead is one account, and the balance of this account is a cost applicable to all production during the period. To calculate total per-unit cost, the debit balance in this account must be allocated to the production of the period. The total in the account is not known until the end of the period.

CHARGES TO PRODUCTION— BURDEN RATE

How can this debit balance be charged to production during the year when the total is not known until the end of the period? Cost accounting has developed a principle of overhead allocation. In manufacturing a product, direct labor and direct materials are used. In many cases there is a relationship between the productive output and direct labor hours, direct labor dollars, direct material dollars, or some other measurable factor. When this relationship exists, a way can be devised to allocate the factory overhead.

First, the total factory overhead must be estimated. This estimate can be determined by an analysis of last year's expense and productive process and the changes in costs since last year. Second, the **distribution basis** that can be measured and used for allocation is selected, and the portion of this basis to be used in the next period is estimated. This estimate can be obtained by use of the figures from the prior year and by an analysis of the changes in the productive situation. (More than one basis may be used, but for purposes of illustration only one will be discussed now.) Third, the estimated factory overhead in dollars is divided by the estimated number of units produced to get the factory **burden rate**. The burden rate is expressed in either of two ways:

1. Where the basis is expressed in dollars the burden rate is expressed as some figure multiplied by the distribution basis (1.2 times direct labor dollars, for example) or by a percentage of the distribution basis (as, 120% of direct labor dollars).

2. Where the basis is expressed in units other than dollars the burden rate is expressed as some dollar figure times the distribution basis (for example, $2.50 per direct labor hour).

Once the burden rate is determined, the distribution basis is measured as production progresses. When the company is ready to add overhead to work in process (as when a job is completed or at the end of a fiscal period), the distribution basis for the production is multiplied by the burden rate to obtain the total amount of the overhead charge to production.

Example of the Burden Rate Calculation and Use:

It is estimated that the factory overhead for Year A will be $180,000, that direct labor hours best measure the productive effort, and that in Year A 120,000 direct labor hours will be used. The burden rate is calculated as follows:

$$\text{Burden rate} = \frac{\text{Estimated factory overhead}}{\text{Estimated number of distribution units to be used}}$$

$$= \frac{\$180,000}{120,000 \text{ hours}}$$

$$= \$1.50/\text{direct labor hour (DLH)}$$

During January, Year A, direct labor was used as follows:

On Product A—	2,000 direct labor hours
On Product B—	6,000 direct labor hours
On Product C—	2,500 direct labor hours
	10,500 direct labor hours

The amount of factory overhead to be allocated to each product would be:

Product A—$3,000 (2,000 DLH × $1.50/DLH)
Product B— 9,000 (6,000 DLH × 1.50/DLH)
Product C— 3,750 (2,500 DLH × 1.50/DLH)

and the entry would be:

Work in Process—Product A	$3,000	
Work in Process—Product B	9,000	
Work in Process—Product C	3,750	
Factory Overhead		$15,750

(In some instances an account called Factory Overhead Applied is used as the credit. At the end of the period the Factory Overhead and Factory Overhead Applied accounts are merged to give the same results as the entry above would give.)

Use of Different Bases for the Distribution of Factory Overhead. In some manufacturing situations the use of a single base might not give intelligent results. For example, consider a situation in which all effort in one department is by machine (mechanized spray painting booth) and all labor in the next is by hand (hand rubbing of the finish). To use direct labor hours would put all the overhead in the second department. To use material dollars (the cost of the paint and the rubbing compound) would put most of the overhead in the first department. Either result does not reflect the facts—both departments probably contribute some relatively equal value to the finished product.

Therefore, to find a measurable factor to relate to productive effort, it might very well be that the use of two or more bases will result in a better and more plausible distribution of the factory overhead. The total overhead is then allocated on some basis, and a series of burden rates is determined, one for each distribution basis, so that the factory overhead can be distributed according to the analysis of productive effort.

Direct Department Charges. Where the factory is large and there are many possible bases for the burden rate allocation, a system is sometimes used of departmentalizing all factory expense. Wherever possible, the individual charges for goods or services are broken down by department (on some basis such as, for telephone expense, the number of telephones in the department, etc.). Then the expense of the nonproductive departments is allocated to the production department (on a basis such as heating requirement to keep the space at proper working temperature) until all factory overhead is allocated. A burden rate is determined for each production department and is used to allocate the departments' factory overhead to its productive effort.

In the area of overhead analysis the computer has become a valuable tool. With the use of spread sheet analysis programming it is possible to build a large matrix of figures that might well be used to accumulate overhead costs by department and type of expenditure and distribution basis data. Then it is a relatively easy matter to determine overhead distribution bases and to make the overhead allocations.

A word of caution is necessary. Because of various pressures on the accountant by operating personnel, he might be led to make judgmental errors in expense allocation that might benefit one department over another. By carefully establishing the premises of expense distribution beforehand he can minimize, if not eliminate, errors of this type. If these premises and distribution formulae are written in a procedure manual (with review and revision requirements), the tendency of some operations personnel to propose allocations favorable to themselves may be largely reduced.

Variance Analysis. At the end of the period, after the actual expenses are posted and the distribution of overhead is made, the Factory Overhead account appears as follows:

Factory Overhead

Indirect Labor	Allocation of overhead
Indirect Material	to production (using
Charges from the voucher	burden rate[s])
register	
Expired cost of prepaid	
assets	
Depreciation expense	

There will almost always be a difference between the total debits and the total credits, although it may be relatively small. In such an event, the accountant prepares an entry to close the account to Cost of Goods Sold as follows:

1. If the balance in the account is a debit:

  Cost of Goods Sold $XX
      Factory Overhead $XX

This increases the Cost of Goods Sold by the balance in the Factory Overhead account.
2. If the balance in the account is a credit:

  Factory Overhead $XX
      Cost of Goods Sold $XX

This decreases the Cost of Goods Sold.
Even though the difference is relatively small, there may be some areas of trouble or improvement, and the difference, called "factory overhead variance," should always be analyzed. Let us consider again the components of the Factory Overhead account. The debits were actual costs.

The credits were the charges to Work in Process obtained by multiplying the distribution basis by the burden rate. The burden rate was the estimated factory overhead divided by the estimated number of distribution units. Implied in the estimated number of distribution units is the assumption that the firm operates at some percentage of capacity, because the distribution units will be greater or lesser as the capacity is greater or lesser.

In the analysis we can examine the following variances:

1. *Budget variance.* This is the difference between the estimated factory overhead and the actual factory overhead. A comparison of each item in the total may reveal significant areas.
2. *Volume (or capacity) variance.* This is the difference between what the overhead is at the actual production capacity and what the estimated overhead was with the implied production capacity.
3. *Efficiency variance.* This is the difference between the actual factory overhead at the actual production capacity, and the estimated factory overhead at the actual production capacity, assuming normal rate of efficiency.

These three variances individually may be great but may combine in such a fashion that the net variance is relatively small. Therefore, the relative size of the total variance cannot be relied on exclusively. The analysis will tell more.

Assume that a plant plans to operate at 80% capacity. At this capacity, it is expected that there will be $96,000 of factory overhead expense and 40,000 direct labor hours which will be used as the distribution base. The burden rate is set at $2.40 per direct labor hour. If the plant operates at 86% capacity using 44,000 direct labor hours in production, and the total actual expense is $102,000, the Factory Overhead account is as follows:

Factory Overhead

Actual $102,000	Applied
	44,000 DLH ×
	$2.40/DLH = $105,600

The total variance is $3,600. In analyzing this variance, however, we find some interesting data:

Budget variance: It was planned to spend $96,000 for overhead, but actually $102,000 was spent, an actual expenditure of $6,000 more than was planned.

Volume variance: It was planned to operate at 80% of capacity, using 40,000 direct labor hours (500 direct labor hours per 1% of capacity), but actually the capacity was 86% (which would have been 43,000 direct labor hours) or an actual expense of $7,200 more than was planned [(43,000 − 40,000) × $2.40].

Efficiency variance: Had the ratio of 500 direct labor hours per 1% of capacity held constant, there would have been only 43,000 direct labor hours, but actually there were 44,000, or an additional 1,000, direct labor hours charged at $2.40 per direct labor hour, or $2,400 more applied factory overhead.

Now management is in a position to ask questions such as:

1. Were the budgeted figures correct for 80% capacity?
2. Using the same data and methods as in the original budget, what would the budgeted figures for 86% capacity have been?
3. Does the direct labor usage vary directly with percentage capacity, or is there some other relationship?
4. Why is there a lowering of efficiency between 80% and 86% of capacity?
5. Can figures be developed so that budgets can be amended during the operating cycle?

By analyzing the variances intelligently, management can often discover areas for improvement. As these areas are reviewed and changes are made, the business becomes more profitable (because per-unit cost decreases) and we find that operating personnel start questioning areas of operation *before* the cost appears in the accounting records. An attitude of awareness and care becomes more prevalent, and the business improves its competitive position.

EXERCISES

Exercise No. 84. The time analysis for Department 1 is:

	Mon.	Tue.	Wed.	Thurs.	Fri.
Jones	8	8	8	8	8
Smith	7	9	8	8	8
McCarthy	8	8	7	7	9
Shea	8	9	9	6	10
Catalli	3	11	8	6	10

The hourly rates of pay are as follows:

Jones	$ 7.25
Smith	10.50
McCarthy	10.25
Shea	9.75
Catalli	7.60

Compute the gross pay, assuming:

　a. Overtime of 50% is paid for all hours over 40 worked in one week.

　b. Overtime of 50% is paid for all hours over 8 worked in one day.

Exercise No. 85. The piecework rate for Part 632 is:

First 100 pieces	$0.70 each
Next 50 pieces	0.72 each
All over 150 pieces	0.76 each

Jones produces 70 pieces; Smith, 110 pieces; and Blue, 180 pieces. Compute the day's wages for each worker.

Exercise No. 86. Would any of the answers to Exercise No. 85 have been different if the minimum daily rate were $90?

Exercise No. 87. What would the day's wages be if the piece rate in Exercise No. 85 had read:

0–100 pieces	$0.70 each
0–150 pieces	0.72 each
over 150 pieces	0.76 each

Exercise No. 88. The sheet used by the Payroll department for weekly computation shows:

Gross Pay	$12,300
F.I.C.A. taxable pay	$ 2,200
Unemployment taxable pay (federal and state)	$ 1,500
F.I.C.A. taxes withheld	$ 310
Income taxes withheld	2,091
Bond deductions	210
United Crusade deductions	100
Transferred to payroll account	???

Labor was used as follows:

In Department 1 (Lathes)	$2,000
Department 2 (Presses)	1,200
Department 3 (Assembly)	4,100
Department 4 (Shipping)	650
Department 5 (Power Plant)	550
Department 6 (Maintenance)	400
Plant Office	3,400

a. Prepare the payroll entry.

b. Prepare the employer's payroll tax entry. (Assume 14.1% total for F.I.C.A. [Social Security and Medicare]; 0.8% for federal unemployment; and 1.2% for state unemployment. Round off to the nearest dollar. Assume further that the limit for state disability insurance has been reached for all employees and that income taxes include both federal and state [if any]).

Exercise No. 89. In analyzing storeroom requisitions, the following is found:

Storeroom Requisition Number	Total	Job 16	Job 19	Job 22	Dept. A	Dept. B
615	$ 19.20	$19.20				
616	42.50		$20.50	$12.00		$10.00
617	53.15				$53.15	
618	109.30	19.00	80.00	10.30		
619	41.70					41.70

Prepare an entry to record the above data. (Assume that the departments mentioned are service departments.)

Exercise No. 90. Using the formula given in the chapter, determine the economic order quantity for Item 335, given:

Annual requirement	2,000 units
Cost per unit	$6.40
Inventory holding cost	30%
Ordering cost per order	$14.00

Exercise No. 91. Assuming 250 working days a year, how often must Item 335 (Exercise No. 90) be ordered?

Exercise No. 92. Determine the minimum stock for Item XB-222, given the following:

Daily usage	30 units
Lead time	2 calendar weeks

The plant is on a five-day-per-week schedule.

Exercise No. 93. A batch of 700 units in production is inspected. Twenty units are found to be defective. The cost sheet up to the point of inspection shows:

Labor	$2,114
Material	$4,228
Overhead	$1,057

How much is the cost of defective items, assuming:

a. Defective goods and accepted goods should be valued the same at point of separation?

b. Defective goods are valued present worth (assume completed value to be $18.00; it costs $9.75 to complete) with all costs chargeable to Work in Process?

c. Defective goods priced at present worth and accepted goods priced at cost to point of inspection?

Exercise No. 94. Prepare entries for parts a., b., and c., of Exercise No. 93.

Exercise No. 95. To the Factory Overhead account post data from the following facts:

a. An analysis of the payroll summary shows Work in Process $18,629; Factory Overhead $2,302; Sales Salaries $5,621; Office Salaries $8,897.

b. An analysis of the Material Requisition shows:

Work in Process	$42,915
Plant Maintenance	297
Equipment Repair Orders	623
Factory Office Supplies	105

c. The Voucher Register shows purchases as follows:

Materials	$62,336	
Telephone	128	50% sales 30% office 20% factory
Utilities	215	10% sales 10% office 80% factory
Rent	1,450	5% sales 5% office 90% factory

d. An analysis of the prepaid accounts shows:

	Beginning Balance	Additions	Ending Balance
Insurance expense	$3,900	$9,000	$3,600
Factory supplies	$4,200	5,000	4,800

Seventy percent of insurance expenses are chargeable to the factory.

e. The depreciation expense is computed to be $15,320.

Exercise No. 96. The Year A factory overhead is $152,310. It is estimated that in Year B this will increase 10%. Determine the various burden rates:

a. per direct labor hours (assuming 16,750 direct labor hours in Year B).

b. per direct labor dollars (assuming an average of $5/hour).

Exercise No. 97. In Year A it is determined that Year B plant production would involve 42,700 direct labor hours, that factory overhead would be $623,950, and that the plant would operate at 80% of capacity. However, the plant operated at 85% capacity, using 45,000 direct labor hours. The actual factory overhead was $651,259. Determine the total variance.

Exercise No. 98. Analyze the variance determined in Exercies No. 97 as to:

a. budget variance.
b. volume variance.
c. efficiency variance.

Chapter 12

COSTING METHODS

There are two basic methods for collecting most accounting data. The first is based on the **method of production** (job-order vs. process costing). The second is based on the **cost price of labor and material** (historical costing vs. standard costing). These methods can be combined as follows:

		Based on Method of Production	
		Job-Order	Process
Based on Price of Labor and Materials	Historical	Historical Job-Order	Historical Process
	Standard	Standard Job-Order	Standard Process

It is important to see the relationships of these methods, because the organization of many cost accounting texts has led readers to believe that there are three costing methods: job-order, process, and standard.

JOB-ORDER VERSUS PROCESS METHODS

Much has been written in accounting literature about job-order and process cost accounting. Homer Black and James Edwards in *The Managerial and Cost Accountant's Handbook* say: "In JOB-ORDER shops, costs are accumulated by individual jobs, and unit costs are determined by dividing the number of units into the total costs assigned to the job. Cost centers or time periods may be employed to accumulate cost to be allocated. . . . Job order costing is generally used where the products or services are expected to be unique or dissimilar. . . . PROCESS COSTING collects costs incurred within a given cost center for a certain period of time. Unit costs are computed by dividing the total costs by the units passing through the cost center during the time period. . . . Process costing procedures are more frequently found in organizations where product or services are homogeneous."*

There is no basic difference in the accounting treatment; the difference is in the processing. In both productive situations the elements of cost are direct labor, direct materials, and factory overhead. In both cases a productive operation is set in motion and then terminates at some future time. If the work project is separable from all other work projects in the factory, or if the completion time is relatively short, we might call the project a **job-order project** and use the job-order method of accounting. If the work project could be defined as Matz *et al.* define it, we might call the project a **process project** and use the process method of accounting.

Job-Order Costing. If a job-order project is started and completed in the same fiscal period, the total cost of the job consists of direct labor, direct material, and factory overhead. The per-unit cost is the total cost divided by the actual number of units produced.

Assume that a job started in January and was completed in June in a company that has a calendar-year fiscal period. The direct labor charged

* Dow Jones–Irwin, Homewood, Ill., 1979.

to Work in Process is $50,000; direct material, $30,000; factory overhead, $20,000 (40% of direct labor). The total is $100,000. If 50 units are produced, the per-unit cost is $2,000.

But what happens if a job-order project is started in one year and completed in the next? You can see that a problem of valuation of year-end inventory arises, even though when the job is completed the total cost is the same.

Assume a job started in October, Year A, and was completed in April, Year B, in a company that operates on a calendar-year fiscal period. The direct labor charges to Work in Process are $50,000 ($20,000 in Year A and $30,000 in Year B); direct material, $30,000 ($7,000 in Year A and $23,000 in Year B); factory overhead, $20,000 (40% of direct labor, or $8,000 in Year A and $12,000 in Year B). The total is $100,000. At December 31, Year A, the Work in Process inventory is valued at $35,000 (charges in Year A of direct labor of $20,000; direct materials, $7,000; and factory overhead, $8,000). In Year B the additional $65,000 is spent to complete the job.

Process Costing. If a process project is started and completed in the same period, the total cost of the process consists of direct labor, direct material, and factory overhead. The per-unit cost is the total cost divided by the actual number of units produced. You can see that this is the same definition used for job-order costing when the project is started and completed in the same accounting period.

If, however, a process project is started in one period and is not completed by the end of the period, the situation is different from the job-order project started in one year and completed in the next. In the latter *none* of the project is completed, while in the process project some units may be completed. To illustrate, if a continuous process takes 60 days from start to completion, the item completed at the end of the period was begun 60 days before, but in the process line there are goods 59 days complete, 58 days complete, etc., down to items one day complete. And each day the unit begun 60 days ago is completed. The stage of completion is not the same throughout the process. The ending inventory comprises the total cost of the uncompleted product, and the remaining cost of production

for the period is established as completed inventory.

Thus the original charges are to Work in Process as described in Chapter 11 for direct labor, direct material, and factory overhead. At the end of the period the total charges must be separated into those applicable to Finished Goods and those still remaining in Work in Process. Total costs charged to production ("T.P.C." below) during the period equal the cost of goods finished ("F.G.") during the period plus cost of goods unfinished at the end of the period:

$$\text{T.P.C.} = \text{F.G.} + \text{Ending W.I.P.}$$

If there had been a beginning Work in Process inventory (production uncompleted at the previous year end) the formula is changed to:

Beginning W.I.P. + T.P.C.
$$= \text{F.G.} + \text{Ending W.I.P.}$$

The problem of valuing the ending Work in Process inventory can be solved by calculating what has been done on the ending Work in Process inventory and pricing out the production thus far. Subtracting that figure from the beginning inventory and total costs charged to production during the period gives the finished goods.

Assume at December 31, Year A, the Work in Process inventory is valued at $55,250 (direct labor, $29,250; direct materials, $16,250; and factory overhead, $9,750) and contains 325 units of salable merchandise only partially complete. In Year B the 325 units are completed and an additional 540 units are started, of which 400 are completed. The effort made by the business in Year B can be summarized as follows:

1. Effort needed to complete the 325 units, *plus*
2. Effort needed to begin and complete 400 units, *plus*
3. Effort needed to begin and bring 140 units up to their present stage of completion.

In any well-organized productive effort the amount of direct labor, direct materials, and factory overhead needed to complete a project is fairly well known. Therefore one could say, with a high degree of accuracy, that the Work in Process is a certain percentage of direct labor costs, another percentage of direct materials, and a third percentage of factory overhead. The production can then be analyzed in terms of equivalent full units of production.

In the illustration above, determining the amount of completion for the beginning and ending inventories might produce a chart similar to the following:

	Labor	Material	Overhead
Beginning Inventory	30%	10%	10%
To complete the beginning inventory	70	90	90
	100%	100%	100%
Completion of the ending inventory	20%	25%	15%

To determine how many completed items the direct labor effort would have produced the computation is as follows:

To complete beginning inventory (70% × 325)	227.5 equivalent units (e.u.)
To begin and complete new production	400.0
To begin and bring 140 units up to present completion (20% × 140)	28.0
Equivalent units of direct labor	655.5 e.u.

The total cost of direct labor used in the production of this item might be divided as follows:

$$\frac{227.5}{655.5} \text{ (or 34.7%)}; \frac{400.0}{655.5} \text{ (or 61.0%)}; \frac{28.0}{655.5} \text{ (or 4.3%)}$$

The same type of computation would be made for direct materials as follows:

To complete beginning inventory (90% × 325)	292.5 e.u.
To begin and complete new production	400.0
To begin and bring 140 units up to present completion (25% × 140)	35.0
Equivalent production of direct materials	727.5 e.u.

The total cost of direct material used in the production of this item might be divided as follows:

$$\frac{292.5}{727.5} \text{ (or 40.2%)}; \frac{400.0}{727.5} \text{ (or 55.0%)}; \frac{35.0}{727.5} \text{ (or 4.8%)}$$

The same type of computation would be made for factory overhead as follows:

To complete beginning inventory (90% × 325)	292.5 e.u.
To begin and complete new production	400.0 e.u.
To begin and bring 140 units up to present completion (15% × 140)	21.0
Equivalent production of factory overhead	713.5 e.u.

The total cost of factory overhead used in the production of this item might be divided as follows:

$$\frac{292.5}{713.5} \text{ (or 41.0%)}; \frac{400.0}{713.5} \text{ (or 56.1%)}; \frac{21.0}{713.5} \text{ (or 2.9%)}$$

During Year B the following charges were made to Work in Process for this item:

Direct Labor	$1,900,950
Direct Material	3,710,250
Factory Overhead	2,069,150

It is now possible to determine the cost of production and the ending inventory as follows:

	Direct Labor	Direct Material	Factory Overhead	Total
Beginning Inventory	$ 29,250	$ 16,250	$ 9,750	$ 55,250
Charges during year	1,900,950	3,710,250	2,069,150	7,680,350
Total Cost	$1,930,200	$3,726,500	$2,078,900	$7,735,600

Cost per unit is as follows:

$$\text{Direct labor/equivalent unit} = \frac{\$1,900,950}{655.5}$$
$$= \$290/\text{e.u.}$$
$$\text{Ending inventory} = 28.0 \text{ e.u.} \times \$290/\text{e.u.}$$
$$= \$8,120$$
$$\text{Direct material/equivalent unit} = \frac{\$3,710,250}{727.5}$$
$$= \$510/\text{e.u.}$$

Ending inventory = 35.0 e.u. $\times$ \$510/e.u.

= \$17,850

$$\text{Factory overhead/equivalent unit} = \frac{\$2,069,150}{713.5}$$

= \$290/e.u.

Ending inventory = 21.0 e.u. $\times$ \$290/e.u.

= \$6,090

The transfer of finished goods inventory and the ending inventory is as follows:

Transferred to finished goods		\$7,703,540
Ending inventory (December 31, Year B)		
Direct labor	\$ 8,120	
Direct material	17,850	
Factory overhead	6,090	32,060
Total charges to production		\$7,735,600

Where the product of one process becomes the material of the next process, it is only a matter of making an analysis similar to the one above for each successive process through which an item in production passes. There may be a beginning Work in Process inventory in each process and an ending Work in Process inventory in each process, but the effort within the process in the period under study can be broken down into equivalent units of direct labor, direct materials, and factory overhead. Once the cost per equivalent unit of the production factors is determined, it is relatively simple to compute the value of the ending inventory and the material transferred to the next department.

COST ALLOCATION

When two different products, or perhaps a main product and a by-product, are produced as the result of a single operation, the cost of the goods transferred out of the process (determined as shown above) must then be allocated between the products. Definitions of joint products and by-products may help in understanding the following discussion. If two or more products are produced together and each bears a significant value relationship to the other, the products are called **joint products.** If two or more products are produced together and one of them bears an insignificant value relationship to the others, that one is called a **by-product.** Because of the differ-

ence in relative significance, the accounting treatment varies somewhat.

Joint Product Treatment. The problem of cost allocation is one of giving to each product an equitable share of the cost up to the point of cost division (which may occur at the end of any process where the physical processing is separated). There are several methods that can be discussed here.

1. Market value of the end product. In this method the total sales value of the various products is determined, and the joint costs are divided between the joint products in like proportion. To illustrate:

Product	No. of Units Produced	Sale Value	Percentage	Joint Cost
A	2000	\$32,000	66⅔%	\$20,000
B	3000	16,000	33⅓%	10,000
		\$48,000	100 %	\$30,000

2. Market value of the end product less further conversion costs. In this method the total sales price of the various products is determined, the cost to complete the product is determined and subtracted, and the joint costs are divided between the joint products in like proportion. To illustrate:

Product	No. of Units Produced	Sale Value	Further Conversion Cost	Allocable Cost
C	7000	\$ 70,000	\$25,000	\$45,000
D	6000	30,000	15,000	15,000
		\$100,000	\$40,000	\$60,000

Then:

Allocable Cost	Percentage	Joint Cost at Separation
\$45,000	75%	\$37,500
15,000	25%	12,500
\$60,000	100%	\$50,000

3. Quantitative unit allocation. At the point of separation, the products are measured in units which are used to allocate the costs. In pouring concrete into decorative molds, for example, the allocation of cost can be made on the basis of weight of the decorative item.

4. Equivalent unit allocation. If, at the point of separation, the units of measurement vary from product to product, it may be possible to assign relative weights to the end products so that an allocation can be made.

There are other methods for cost allocation of joint product cost. The object here is not to exhaust them all but rather to give you an idea of some of the prevalent methods. If you are confronted with a joint-cost pricing situation at least you will be able to recognize it.

By-product Treatment. The problem that this treatment attempts to solve is the allocation of cost to the by-product which leaves the main product with an equitable share of the total production cost to date. The treatment is different than in joint product costs because of the relative insignificance in value of the by-product with respect to the main product.

1. Sales price of the by-product is treated as income. Where the by-product is sold, the sales price can be added to the sales price of the main product or it can be shown at the bottom of the Income Statement as Other Income.

Sales (main product)	$40,000
Sales (by-product)	2,000
TOTAL SALES	$42,000
Cost of Sales (main product only because no cost is assigned to the by-product)	$30,000
GROSS PROFIT	12,000
Selling and General Expenses	8,000
OPERATING PROFIT	$ 4,000

An alternative form of presentation is:

Sales (main product)	$40,000
Cost of sales	30,000
GROSS PROFIT	10,000
Selling and General Expenses	8,000
OPERATING PROFIT	2,000
Other Income (by-product sales)	2,000
NET INCOME	$ 4,000

2. Sales price of the by-product is treated as income but the costs or product completion, sales, and administration are allocated to the by-product. When this treatment is used, the selling and general expenses are allocated between the main product and the by-product, and the costs necessary to complete the by-product are collected.

Using the facts above, the Income Statement might look as follows:

	Main Product	By-product	Total
Sales	$40,000	$2,000	$42,000
Cost of Sales	29,500	500	30,000
GROSS PROFIT	$10,500	$1,500	$12,000
Selling and General Expenses	7,400	600	8,000
OPERATING PROFIT	$ 3,100	$ 900	$ 4,000

Remember that the cost of sales by the by-product includes only the costs applicable to the by-product after separation from the main product.

3. Sales price of the by-product is deducted from the cost of sales of the main product.

Sales (main product)		$40,000
Cost of Sales	$30,000	
Less by-product sales	2,000	28,000
GROSS PROFIT		$12,000
Selling and General Expenses		8,000
OPERATING PROFIT		$ 4,000

4. Sale price of the by-product is deducted from factory overhead. Since the by-product is an unwanted result of the production of the main product, it can be treated as scrap (see Chapter 11): credit Factory Overhead with the income from by-product sales. The Income Statement would not show the income from by-product sales as a separate item, but the Cost of Goods Manufactured Schedule would have a lower overhead cost than would be the case in the above examples.

5. By-product used in production is valued at its replacement cost. When a by-product is separated from a main product somewhere in the productive process and then later used in the productive process, the company may assign to the by-product the value it would have had to pay to purchase it from an outside vendor. If the by-product is available, the problem of costing is simplified. The by-product is set up in inventory, and the costs of the main product in process are reduced a like amount.

6. By-product is assigned a cost that will yield an estimated rate of gross profit return. In this method the value of the finished by-product, the gross profit ratio, and the cost of completing the by-product are estimated. The value of the by-product is then the amount which when added to the completion cost and the estimated gross profit will equal sales.

Assume 1,000 units of a by-product can be sold for $5 each upon completion; it would take $2.75 to complete each item; and the gross profit ratio is estimated to be 20%. The computation to determine the value of the by-product is as follows:

Sales (1,000 × $5)	$5,000
Gross Profit (20%)	1,000
Cost of Sales	4,000
Completion costs (1,000 × $2.75)	2,750
Value of by-product	$1,250

HISTORICAL VERSUS STANDARD COSTING

It was pointed out earlier in the chapter that one of the costing alternatives is concerned with determining the prices that will be used, actual or standard. Regardless of which method is used, the actual costs must ultimately be charged to production. At this point we might recall that there are different methods of pricing inventory, devised because of price fluctuations of the items in inventory. The use of one method or another may yield different profits in any one year, but in the total life of the business the total profits must be the same.

Historical Costs. Historical costs are the costs of production which can be traced to an actual invoice or other document and which are used to establish price based on the actual expenditure. In this method, direct and indirect labor costs are determined from the Payroll voucher, and the exact amount of the credits in the Payroll entry are charged to Work in Process or Factory Overhead. Raw materials costs are determined from invoices, and the exact amount of the credits to Cash or Accounts Payable are charged to Raw Materials Inventory. When the materials are used they are priced out at actual cost (using LIFO, FIFO, average, or some other inventory pricing system).

The historical method might produce varied costs of goods manufactured, depending on the wage rate and skill of an individual performing a task, the pricing system used in charging inventory to production, and the quantity of material used. The increase of wage rates with increase of skills would tend to minimize the cost differences attributable to the use of different persons for performing a given task. Fluctuation in price levels would create some problems in costing materials, but we have already seen that methods have been devised to handle the problem.

If production costs can vary from year to year or period to period, management might like to know why. A superimposed analytic method might prove very costly; thus the standard cost method was devised.

Standard Cost. In the standard cost system, an assumption is made that a given volume of production requires definite units of direct labor and direct material and that the prices of the direct labor and direct material can be determined. This is sometimes called a "budget of direct costs."

How can the quantities and prices of direct labor and direct materials be determined? One method is to analyze what happened in the past; another method is to study analytically the production process and the present price structure; a third is to study analytically the production process and the changes that might be made; a fourth is to study the present price structure and possible price changes.

Once the hours of direct labor needed to complete a project and the wage rate per hour are determined, and once the quantities and costs of direct materials needed to complete a project are calculated, the direct costs of production can be determined. Any difference in expenditure between the standard and the "actual" cost can be measured more quickly because the accounting system provides special accounts for variance measurement.

Assume the production of 100 units of Tomred requires 40 hours of direct labor and two ingredients: 100 lbs. of A and 200 lbs. of B. It is estimated that labor costs $8 per hour, A costs $3/lb., and B costs $1/lb. The estimated total cost of 100 units of Tomred would be:

Direct Labor (40 hrs. × $8/hr.)		$320
Direct Material (100 lbs. of A × $3/lb.)	$300	
(200 lbs. of B × $1/lb.)	200	500
Total Direct Costs		$820

The entries to Work in Process are as follows:

Work in Process	$320	
Labor Summary		$320
To record direct labor used in production.		

Work in Process	$500	
Materials		$500
To record direct materials used in production.		

If, however, the number of hours spent on the project, or the wage rate per hour, varied from the estimate, there might be a variance in total labor costs.

Assume that it took 41 hours at $8 per hour to complete the project. There are $328 of actual labor charges. The entry for this would be:

Work in Process (40 hrs. × $8/hr.)	$320	
Labor Hours Variance (1 hr. × $8/hr.)	8	
Labor Summary (actual wage)		$328
To record direct labor used in production.		

This variance, being a debit, is an **unfavorable variance.** Assume that it took 40 hours at $7.90 to complete the project. There are $316 of actual direct labor charges. The entry for this would be:

Work in Process (40 hrs. × $8/hr.)	$320	
Labor Summary		$316
Wage Rate Variance (40 hrs. × $0.10/hr.)		4
To record direct labor used in production.		

This variance, being a credit, is a **favorable variance.**

Thus, actual hours worked can be greater than, equal to, or less than those estimated; and the wage rate can be greater than, equal to, or less than what was estimated. There are nine conditions, then, for direct labor, shown graphically in Fig. 30.

If the actual hours are *less* than standard and the actual wage rate is *less* than standard, the hour and wage rate variances are always favorable: the hour and wage rate lines cross in area A. If the actual hours are *more* than standard and the actual wage rate is *more* than standard, the hour and wage rate variances are always unfavorable; the hour and wage rate lines cross in area B. If the actual hours are *less* than standard but the actual wage rate is *more* than standard, the hour and wage rate lines cross in area C; the wage rate variance is unfavorable, but the hours variance is favorable. If the actual hours are *more* than standard but the actual wage rate is *less* than standard, the hour and wage rate is less than standard. The hour and wage rate lines cross in area D; the wage rate variance is favorable, but the hours variance is unfavorable. When the hour and wage rate lines cross in areas C or D, the total direct labor costs may be less than, equal to, or greater than the estimates, depending upon whether the favorable variance is more than, equal to, or less than the unfavorable variance.

A similar analysis can be made of materials when standard costs are used to determine the cost of work in process.

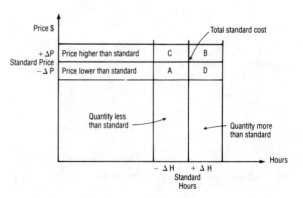

Figure 30. Relationship of Prices, Quantities, and Variances.

ABSORPTION VERSUS DIRECT COSTING

Further refinements in the incidence of cost have been made possible by the introduction of overhead allocation called **direct costing.** Direct costing breaks down overhead costs into fixed and variable overhead, and a greater emphasis on revenue-producing activity rather than production. Previously in this chapter we have been discussing what is called **absorption costing.**

It is argued that fixed costs are not related to production and therefore should be charged as an expense in the period in which they were incurred. Thus, depreciation on buildings and equipment, realty taxes, factory administrative salaries, etc., are to be considered period costs.

The variable costs (direct labor, direct materials, and variable overhead) are production-related costs and should be included in inventories and Cost of Goods Sold.

Much has been written in accounting literature about direct costing. The direct costing system has merit because it concentrates attention on variable costs where management's cost reduction efforts can be effective, and eliminates from the cost reduction consideration those costs that are allocations of expenditures of past years (depreciation), costs determined by outside agencies (taxes), or costs determined by considerations of maintaining administrative continuity (salaries and wages).

Direct costing can be used with either job-order or process cost accounting or with either historic or standard costing methods. Direct costing has gained much acceptance in the past decade, and it is likely that it will be used by more and more firms in the future.

EXERCISES

Exercise No. 99. Part of the debit side of the Payroll entry for November, Year A, is:

Work in Process—Job 16	$7,387
Job 17	7,622
Job 20	9,468
Job 21	763

Part of the debit side of the Payroll entry for December, Year A, is:

Work in Process—Job 17	$7,341
Job 20	2,901
Job 21	2,538
Job 22	806

Part of the debit side of the Payroll entry for January, Year B, is:

Work in Process—Job 20	$ 203
Job 21	4,742
Job 23	1,542

Part of the debit side of the Materials Requisition analysis entry for November, Year A, is:

Work in Process—Job 16	$6,802
Job 17	2,121
Job 20	2,253
Job 21	968

Part of the debit side of the Materials Requisition analysis entry for December, Year A, is:

Work in Process—Job 17	$8,591
Job 20	905
Job 21	6,437
Job 22	8,807

Part of the debit side of the Materials Requisition analysis entry for January, Year B, is:

Work in Process—Job 20	$ 347
Job 21	8,642
Job 23	3,763

The overhead rate is computed anew each month based on the performance of the two previous months:

November:	47% of direct labor dollars
December:	44% of direct labor dollars
January:	46% of direct labor dollars

Job 20 is completed in January, Year B. What is the value of Job 20 on:

a. November 30, Year A?
b. December 31, Year A?
c. January 31, Year B (before transfer to Finished Goods Inventory)?

Exercise No. 100. In a situation where process cost accounting is used, the following facts are determined:

3,000 lbs. of Material A and 2,000 lbs. of Material B have been put into production at the beginning of the job. Material A costs $3/lb.; B costs $15/lb. Direct labor expended in processing this material is $18,400. Overhead burden is 1.4 times direct labor. No shrinkage of material is involved in the process. At the end of the month 4,000 lbs. of the end product are completely finished and 1,000 lbs. are 60% complete as to direct labor (100% complete as to material).

Determine the value of:

a. Completed production.
b. Work in Process at the end of the month.

Exercise No. 101. In a process situation there is beginning inventory whose cost for completion to the present stage is:

Direct labor	$ 6,000
Direct material	14,000
Overhead	12,000

To complete this inventory would take $9,000 of direct labor. (The overhead is expressed as a percentage of labor, and this percentage has not changed.) How much will the completed inventory cost?

Exercise No. 102. In Department 6 there is both beginning and ending inventory for January, Year B. Details concerning the status of production in the department are as follows:

	Units	Percentage Completion Direct Labor and Overhead	Direct Material
Beginning inventory	300	50%	75%
Started in production	2,000		
Ending inventory	500	60%	100%

Determine the equivalent units of production for labor, material, and overhead. (Check your answer before answering Exercise No. 103.)

Exercise No. 103. The value of the beginning inventory in Exercise No. 102 is as follows:

Direct labor	$1,050
Direct material	2,250
Overhead	2,100

The value of additions to production during the month is as follows:

Direct labor	$13,845
Direct materials	20,542
Overhead	27,495

Determine the value of the equivalent units of production.

Exercise No. 104. In a joint product situation, it costs $40,000 to produce Products A and B to point of separation. When completed, the sales value of A and B will be $60,000 and $40,000 respectively. It will cost $10,000 and $20,000 respectively to complete A and B. Determine the valuation of A and B at point of separation, using:

a. Market value of the end product.
b. Market value of the end product less further conversion.

Exercise No. 105. In a company using a standard costing system, the following facts are found:

The standard labor rate for drilling is $8 per hour.

The standard labor time required to complete 100 units of Part X34B is 7 hours.

The actual time it took to complete 100 units of Part X34B was 7.1 hours and the pay rate of the operator was $8.40 per hour.

a. How much was the actual cost of direct labor to produce the 100 units of Part X34B?

b. How much was the standard cost of direct labor to produce the 100 units of Part X34B?

c. Analyze any variance.

Chapter 13

INCOME TAXES OF A BUSINESS

Benjamin Franklin said, before our country was founded, "In this world nothing is certain but death and taxes." The Sixteenth Amendment, adopted in 1913, is short but pithy and its effect is felt by most Americans: "The Congress shall have the power to lay and collect taxes on incomes, from whatever source derived, without apportionment among the several States, and without regard to any census or enumeration." On every payday the employer and employee are reminded of the income tax—the employer because he deducts the required amount from the employee's check, and the employee because the amount is deducted. In this chapter we shall discuss the effects of the tax laws on business organizations, the forms to be filed, and regulations affecting the accounting methods acceptable to the Treasury Department. Because of the diversity of state tax laws, only the federal income tax will be discussed here.

PROPRIETORSHIP

The proprietorship is not taxed as a business; rather, the proprietor includes in his personal tax return (Form 1040—U.S. Individual Income Tax Return) Schedule C—Profit or (Loss) From Business or Profession, which shows the income from the proprietor's business computed by the federal rules of income taxation. The proprietor also files Schedule SE—Computation of Social Security Self-Employment Tax, and if any tax is due for Social Security purposes it is added to the income tax due.

At various times the Internal Revenue Service has allowed certain business activity as credits against the tax. This is an example of using the income tax as a way of moving individuals in some socially good direction. These credits have included: (1) investment credit for the purchase of business property to stimulate production in other industries; (2) targeted job credits for employers who hire individuals from certain targeted unemployed groups; (3) business tax credits; and other credits, some of which might also have been available to nonproprietorship taxpayers. It is important to check with your accountant or tax preparer to see which credits are available to you as a proprietor and/or as an individual according to the current tax rules.

In addition to the regular way of computing the income tax some additional methods have been included at various times. These methods are: (1) Income Averaging; (2) Minimum Tax; and (3) Alternative Minimum Tax. Here again can be seen the attempt to make the income tax "more equitable" as a social good.

Tax laws change. During the process of writing this book the Tax Reform Act of 1986 was enacted into law. This book reflects the changes that came about because of that act. None of the new law has been tested by any administrative or legal process. You can only be cautioned again—BECOME CONVERSANT WITH THE TAX LAW—BUT ENGAGE AN ACCOUNTANT OR OTHER TAX PREPARER WITH WHOM TO DISCUSS YOUR TAX SITUATION.

PARTNERSHIP

The partnership is not taxed as an entity either; rather, it files Form 1065—U.S. Partnership Return of Income. This return is filed separately from the tax returns of the partners and is called an **information return;** no tax is assessed on it against the partnership for its income. Rather, the partners complete Schedule K—Partners' Shares of Income, Credits, and Deductions, which details information that the partners must include in their personal returns (Form 1040). Partners fill out Schedule SE as part of their personal return to determine the amount of Social Security tax that is due and that will be added to the income tax.

The partnership return is also used for syndicates, pools, joint ventures, etc.

CORPORATIONS

As an entity the corporation is taxed in its own right. Under the Tax Reform Act of 1986 the rates were established as follows:

Not over $50,000	15%
Over $50,000 but not over $75,000	25%
Over $75,000	34%

On income over $100,000 an additional tax of 5% is levied up to $335,000 of income. This provision phases out the corporate graduated tax rate for high-earning companies.

As with the proprietor, there are some credits against the corporate tax.

The form used by a corporation in reporting its taxable income and federal income tax is Form 1120—U.S. Corporation Income Tax Return. The income is computed according to the rules of federal income taxation and the liability becomes a liability of the corporation. Note that after the corporation records its income tax liability it may declare dividends from the undistributed profits. These dividends are distributed to the stockholders, who then may have to declare them on their own individual tax returns, on which the profits are again taxed. This is the origin of the phrase "double taxation."

There is a special type of corporation called a Subchapter S corporation. This files a return on Form 1120S. A Subchapter S corporation is one that has elected, by unanimous consent of its shareholders, not to pay any corporate tax on its income (with certain exceptions) and, instead, to have the shareholders pay tax on it, even though such income is not distributed. An S corporation

and its shareholders are treated, in effect, like a partnership and its partners.

ACCOUNTING PERIODS AND METHODS

Accounting Periods. The Internal Revenue Code defines a "taxable year" as:

1. The taxpayer's annual accounting period, if it is a calender year or a fiscal year;
2. The calendar year if:
   a. the taxpayer keeps no books;
   b. the taxpayer does not have an annual accounting period; or
   c. the taxpayer has an annual accounting period but it does not qualify as a fiscal year.

There are special rules for years consisting of 52–53 weeks.

A taxpayer may change his annual accounting period, but it will not become his "taxable year" until approved by the Internal Revenue Service.

The Tax Code and regulations discuss circumstances under which returns for less than twelve months may be prepared, and the computation of the tax, and the exceptions and adjustments.

Accounting Methods. The Internal Revenue Code states that "taxable income shall be computed under the method of accounting on the basis of which the taxpayer regularly computes his income in keeping his books; except, if no method of accounting has been regularly used by the taxpayer, or if the method used does not clearly reflect income, the computation of taxable income shall be made under such a method as, in the opinion of the Secretary or his delegate, does clearly reflect income."

Under the Tax Reform Act of 1986 the following cannot use the cash method of reporting income:

1. C corporations,
2. Partnerships that have one or more C corporations as partner or partners,
3. Tax shelters, and
4. Trusts that are subject to the tax on unrelated income, but only with respect to that income.

The following may use the cash method of reporting income:

1. Small businesses with average annual gross receipts of $5 million or less over the past five years,
2. Farmers, and
3. Personal service corporations.

Adjustments. A separate section of the Internal Revenue Code deals with adjustments necessitated by changes in accounting method. It has application only for those taxpayers who have changed or contemplate a change of accounting method.

INCOME TAX ADVICE

The Internal Revenue Code is a document that affects almost all citizens of the United States. It has in it much material that would benefit taxpayers if they only knew about it. For the person whose only income is from salary, with perhaps some interest or dividends, and from other sources where no alternatives are available and the taxable income is relatively small, preparation of the tax return by the taxpayer himself may yield satisfactory results. But if the taxable income can be computed by alternative methods, or if alternative sources of income are available, it may well be that the advice of an accountant, lawyer, or other tax expert will save the taxpayer money by reducing taxable income. It goes without saying that the taxpayer should get advice that is good and that will reduce his tax. It would be prudent not to get advice from the personnel at an Internal Revenue Service office. The position of the Internal Revenue Service has always been that taxpayers must pay every cent due the government *but not a penny more than necessary.*

The Internal Revenue Code is a revenue-raising document, but it is more than that: it is a document of social legislation. Through it economic activities are encouraged by preferential tax treatment, and other activities are discouraged by disadvantageous tax treatment. Any document that attempts to collect taxes on income, encourages some economic activities, and discourages others is bound to have the effect of benefiting some taxpayers at the expense of others. Considering the number of people required to pay taxes and the amount of taxes collected, the inequities are relatively few. Of course there are loopholes and methods of reducing taxable income. But by and large there is a willingness to pay income tax by a vast majority of the public—even though there is much complaining each year in early April.

STATE INCOME TAXES

Obviously, it is impossible to cover the subject of income taxation by the state governments in all the states where this book may be read. So the advice here is to suggest that if the tax return to be filed with the Internal Revenue Service is such that special help is required, it would probably be wise to let the person preparing the federal return papers prepare the state returns as well.

TAX PLANNING

In many instances the accountant, lawyer, or other professional cannot do much about the recording of transactions that have already occurred. A conference between the taxpayer and his adviser held before the beginning of the new year (or similar fiscal period) to discuss alternative methods of reporting income or deductions might result in a substantial saving of income tax in future years. Such a conference will bring to the taxpayer's situation a fresh perspective—that of someone knowledgeable in tax matters who can leave the taxpayer in a better position than he was before.

The author, having been a tax preparer for over 25 years, has seen many changes in the income tax laws. The Tax Reform Act of 1986 is not to be considered the final tax act in America. Major changes were made in the taxing structure. But other changes, major and minor, will be made. Get to know your accountant or tax preparer well. He can guide you through the intricacies of the current tax situation.

Chapter 14

TAXES ON PAYROLLS

The gross amount of pay which is debited to the appropriate expense accounts is the amount of pay earned by the employee. However, the employee does not receive all the money he has earned, as we have already seen. The employer is obligated to withhold from the employee's earned wages Social Security and Medicare and federal income taxes and such other deductions as are required by the local jurisdictions (state or city income taxes, disability tax, etc.). Besides the taxes on gross earnings paid by the employee, the employer pays certain taxes on his employees' earnings as well (under certain conditions and up to specified amounts). In this chapter only federal taxation will be discussed, because local legislation varies from state to state and it would be too cumbersome in a volume of this nature to cover all the tax legislation in each state.

The total amount of wage expense for the employer includes (but is not limited to) the following items:

Gross earnings of employees;
Federal Insurance Contribution Act payments on the taxable wages of employees (Social Security and Medicare);
Federal Unemployment Insurance taxes on the taxable wages of employees;
State Unemployment Insurance taxes on the taxable wages of employees.

Federal Insurance Contribution Act. Each employer pays a tax on wages earned by employees up to $43,800 (in 1987). That amount will automatically be increased in the future to keep pace with current average wage levels. The total amount paid by the employee deduction from wages will be $3,131.70 (the rate is 7.15%); this will be matched by an equal amount by the employer. The self-employed person will pay $5,387.40 on wages up to a maximum of $43,800 (the rate is 12.3%). As retired people are living longer, inflation continues, and the older population becomes a larger percentage of the total population, the rates for Social Security/Medicare will go up and the amount of wages taxed will go up.

Here again a word of caution: Do not use the above rates. When an employer fills out the form on which he reports Social Security/Medicare amounts withheld by him from employee wages and reports the amount of the employee contribution, be sure to use the then current rates on the eligible wages up to the proper limit in effect at that time.

The terms "wages," "employment," "employee," etc., are defined in detail by the Internal Revenue Code; these definitions are too specialized to be detailed here. The Code specifies computation of wages in the special cases of household service, service in the armed forces, service in the Peace Corps, etc. The Code also discusses the services of persons in transportation systems. Some services are covered while others are not. There is also discussion of certain organizations that are exempt from the tax but that may want to waive this exemption so that their employees can become part of the Social Security system. There are also agreements that can be made by American companies that employ American citizens in foreign subsidiaries.

Federal Unemployment Tax Act. This tax is levied against employers so that the federal government can recover some of the cost of assisting unemployed persons to secure employment. The federal government set up a Federal Employment Service that was to serve as a coordinating agency which would perform job placement functions if the states did not. The states were enabled to establish employment offices and collect taxes from the employers to support the effort to help the unemployed find work. If the state met the requirements laid down by the federal government, the tax paid by the employer to the state (up to certain limitations) could be claimed as a credit on the federal tax.

At present (1987) the federal tax rate for unemployment insurance is 6.2% on the first $7,000 of each employee's earnings, less certain credits based upon payments to the state(s) unemployment funds, with a maximum deduction of 5.4%.

Form 940 explains the current rates, making it easy to file the amount due for federal unemployment.

As in the F.I.C.A. discussion earlier, many terms are defined in the regulations for federal unemployment tax purposes. But terms are not necessarily defined in the same way throughout the Code. Therefore, it is important that the definitions be read carefully to ascertain if a particular business is required to pay taxes or not.

State Unemployment Tax. It is not the purpose of this book to discuss all the unemployment tax requirements of all the states, but it must be mentioned that states generally follow the requirements set down by the Federal Unemployment Tax Act.

The business files a return with the appropriate state agency (or a designated representative). The rate is based on the federal rate, subject to reduction due to "good" experience by the employer in keeping his employees employed. This rate reduction places on the employer the obligation to use employment practices which would tend to prevent arbitrary dismissal, seasonal peaks, discriminatory practices, and the like. It does not prevent or hinder an employer from, or penalize him for, discharging an employee for good cause, such as excessive tardiness, insubordination, or other habits not conducive to good discipline or morale or to sound operation of his business.

When an employer first starts in business, he pays the maximum unemployment tax rate (federal and state combined). As the employer demonstrates "good" employment practices the state rate goes down and may eventually become zero. The federal taxation rate remains the same because of the continuing coordination function performed by the federal government that benefits all states, all employers, and all employees. The employer's credit for state payments remains at the state maximum so as not to penalize the employer for having a reduced (even a zero) state tax rate.

Chapter 15

AUDITING

We have seen that an important result of maintaining business records is that of having facts upon which management can act. The summarized figures are only as good as the framework of organization—basically the schema of the chart of accounts—and the accuracy with which the transactions are recorded. To insure that the transactions recorded are properly recorded, that no transactions are unrecorded, and that there are no recordings of transactions that did not occur, **auditing** of the records by persons other than those recording the transactions may be performed.

INTERNAL CONTROL

In the course of this book the author has described techniques to check the work while the recording process is going on. In discussing vouchers, for example, we saw that approvals for the voucher preparation and voucher distribution must be secured before the voucher is entered in the Voucher Register. When the voucher is given to the person who writes the check it is examined to see if the approver's signature is there and that the voucher has been recorded. If this is in order, a check is prepared. The person who signs the check reviews the transaction before signing. Any system in which the operating job or recording job can be broken down into elements that are done by different people, each checking the work of the others, is called in accounting **internal control.** Other examples of internal control are the cashier-wrapper system and separation of the cash receipts function from the posting of accounts receivable. The business

should use as many internal control devices as it can install and still continue at a relatively efficient level. There are choices for management to make—which internal control devices *must* be installed and which ones *can* be installed versus the cost of installing and maintaining the systems.

INTERNAL AUDITING

Auditing, or the review of the records by persons other than the record-keepers, is another method by which management can determine the completeness and accuracy of the accounting records. There are two types of auditing: **internal auditing** and **auditing by independent accountants.**

Internal auditing is performed by auditors who work as employees of the business. These auditors review operating procedures and accounting records with the view of reporting to management the present state of operating technique, any deviation from established operating procedure, suggestions for improvement, and the completeness and correctness of the accounting records. In more progressive companies, the role of the internal auditor is geared more toward increasing the effectiveness of the management's efforts than determining the completeness and accuracy of the accounting records. A deficiency in internal audit effectiveness is that the report, if unfavorable, for various reasons may not be brought to the attention of the person (department head, etc.) who could correct the situation.

This is not meant to imply that the internal auditor is not a useful person on the management team. But if management does not properly use the internal auditor and the contribution that he can make, the business may be lulled into the false security that things "must be right because we have an internal audit setup." An intelligent management will examine the business to determine the place of the internal audit function and will foster an attitude that more can be gained by facing unpleasant facts and correcting the situations exposed than by sweeping them under the rug and ignoring them.

INDEPENDENT AUDITING

Auditing by independent accountants is another way in which businesses can determine the completeness and accuracy of the accounting records. Independent accountants are professionals who examine the accounting records of clients and express an opinion concerning these records. The independent accountant is not an employee of the firm audited, and he is generally a Certified Public Accountant. The clients of the independent accountant are usually the owners of the business or their representatives, the Board of Directors.

The Scope Paragraph. Perhaps it might be well to show here the document sent by the independent accountant to the client after the audit examination. This document consists of the letter addressed to the client and contains **scope and opinion paragraphs.** A form of the letter might read:

To the Board of Directors
South Shore Groceries, Inc.

We have examined the balance sheet of the South Shore Groceries, Inc., as of December 31, Year B [and if a two-year presentation is made, Year A], and the related statement of operations and retained income for the year then ended. Our examination was made in accordance with generally accepted auditing standards, and accordingly included such tests of the accounting records and such other auditing procedures as we considered necessary in the circumstances.

In our opinion, the accompanying balance sheet and statements of operation and retained income present fairly the financial position of South Shore Groceries, Inc., at December 31, Year B [and if a two-year presentation is made, Year A], and the results of its operations for the year(s) then ended, in conformity with generally accepted accounting principles applied on a basis consistent with that of the preceding year(s).

February 14, Year B   Jones, Smith, and Brown
                         Certified Public Accountants

The scope paragraph tells what the accountant examined:

1. The Balance Sheet for December 31, Year B (and perhaps Year A).
2. The Statement of Operations for the year ended December 31, Year B (and perhaps Year A).
3. The Statement of Retained Earnings for the year ended December 31, Year B (and perhaps Year A).

This is known as a **complete examination** since it includes all acounts in the General Ledger. In a proprietorship, you recall, the Equity Statement was called the Statement of Proprietor's Capital and included all changes to the owner's equity accounts from whatever sources. In a corporation the Statement of Retained Income is limited to the retained income portion of equity because the changes in the other equity accounts are few and can be explained by footnote perhaps better than by schedules or statements. There are certain times when comparative statements are required. These may be set forth in SEC regulations and are modified from time to time to meet better reporting presentations.

The auditing standards spoken of in the scope paragraph derive from standards developed in the accounting profession and put forth by the Committee on Auditing Standards of the American Institute of Certified Public Accountants:

General Standards:

1. The examination is to be performed by a person or persons having adequate technical training and proficiency as an auditor.

2. In all matters relating to the assignment an independence in mental attitude is to be maintained by the auditor or auditors.

3. Due professional care is to be exercised in the performance of the examination and the preparation of the report.

Standards of Field Work:

1. The work is to be adequately planned, and assistants, if any, are to be properly supervised.

2. There is to be a proper study and evaluation of the existing internal control as a basis for reliance thereon and for the determination of the resultant extent of the tests to which auditing procedures are to be restricted.

3. Sufficient competent evidential matter is to be obtained through inspection, observation, inquiries, and confirmations to afford a reasonable basis for an opinion regarding the financial statements under examination.

Standards of Reporting:

1. The report shall state whether the financial statements are presented in accordance with generally accepted principles of accounting.

2. The report shall state whether such principles have been consistently observed in the current period in relation to the preceding period.

3. Informative disclosures in the financial statements are to be regarded as reasonably adequate unless otherwise stated in the report.

4. The report shall either contain an expression of opinion regarding the financial statements, taken as a whole, or an assertion to the effect that an opinion cannot be expressed. When an over-all opinion cannot be expressed, the reasons therefore should be stated. In all cases where an auditor's name is associated with the financial statements the report should contain a clear-cut indication of the character of the auditor's examination, if any, and the degree of responsibility he is taking.

The General Standards require training and proficiency as an auditor. These standards are presumed by the public when a person holds a C.P.A. certificate because he has passed a Uniform C.P.A. Examination and has met (in most states) some form of experience requirement. The General Standards require an independent attitude in the sense that the auditor will be able to make objective evaluation and reporting of the findings of the examination. The General Standards also require due professional care of the same kind that might be found with any professional person who is working in his professional capacity.

The Standards of Field Work require the auditor to properly plan the work and supervise assistants.

The scope paragraph states that tests of the accounting records are included in the examination and the Standards of Field Work state that a study and evaluation of internal control be made to determine how much testing shall be done. So the auditor not only reviews the accounting records but also reviews systems and procedures, internal checks, organization and policy, and other areas of the business as part of the audit examination. The testing is greater if his reliance on these areas is not great; it is lesser if his reliance on these areas is great. The accountant does what he deems necessary in the circumstances in his review—leaving to his professional judgment what must be done to perform the audit properly.

The Opinion Paragraph. The accountant examines sufficient evidential matter so as to afford a reasonable basis for the expression of an opinion regarding the financial statements. This may include physical examination (by himself or by other experts), documentary evidence (both internally and externally generated), discussions with and observations of personnel in their operating situations, review of operating procedures, any other kinds of tests that might give the auditor facts, comparison of one year's figures with those of the previous periods, percentage figures of sales, etc., and ratios of various kinds.

The opinion paragraph tells the auditor's opinion of the statements and is closely allied to the Standards of Reporting. The language is important—the auditor does not *certify*, but he states that the statements are *presented fairly.* His opinions relate to the statements which he said, in the scope paragraph, that he examined.

The accountant says that the statements are presented in conformity with generally accepted accounting principles. If this is not so, he enumerates the variances. The reason for this is so the reader can better interpret the statements. "Cash" cannot mean one thing on one set of statements and an entirely different thing on the next set of statements. Certain transactions are handled in a particular fashion in all businesses. Other transactions that are peculiar to a special business may be handled in a special way, but that is the generally accepted method for this particular transaction within that industry.

The requirement that the statements be consistent from one year to another insures that they can be compared year to year and that an alternative generally accepted method of accounting is not used to distort the operations of any one period. This does not mean that there can be no change in accounting treatment of certain transactions. It only means that the accountant must disclose this fact so the reader is aware of the change.

The statements in normal presentation may not say all that is necessary for an intelligent reading of the record. The auditor then includes notes and other explanatory data that may help the reader. These must include matter for the year under audit and the significant events up to the date of the report.

The opinions that an auditor may express in the report are:

1. *Unqualified:* The auditor has no reservations concerning the financial statements. Also called a *positive, clean,* or *good opinion.*

2. *Qualified:* The auditor takes exception to certain current-period accounting applications or is unable to establish the potential outcome of a material uncertainty. Also called a *partially good opinion.*

3. *Disclaimer of opinion:* The auditor has been so restricted that an opinion cannot be rendered, if statements are issued without audit, or if there are major uncertainties which are not susceptible to audit. Reasons for disclaiming an opinion must be set forth. Also called *no opinion.*

4. *Adverse:* The auditor believes the statements are misleading or do not reflect the proper application of generally accepted accounting principles, and qualification is not considered strong enough. Also called an *unfavorable opinion.*

WHY AN AUDIT?

In the author's opinion every business should be audited unless the owner keeps the books himself and knows he is doing a conscientious job. The manager's job includes making decisions, and good decisions require good facts. The auditor can help the business set up the books so that facts are more readily available in a form that is easy for management to use.

The auditor's services are professional; like any other professional service they cost money. But one does not choose a physician or dentist or lawyer on the basis of the cheapest fee. It is the quality of service that one is after, and the fee (within reason) is secondary. The auditor is the business's "doctor." He can suggest preventive measures that can keep the business healthy. By his presence alone the auditor often makes the owner and manager think about the business. Often the neglect of the business that brings business illness can be changed into the care that brings business growth and prosperity.

There are further considerations for an audit—the social role of the auditor. Those who operate businesses of relatively large scope must report the activities to outsiders (except for privately held businesses)—owners, governmental agencies, financial analysts, etc. The outsiders who rely on these statements should be assured that these statements have been examined by professionals who are independent of the management and that the statements are presented in the proper manner. Many persons outside the firm will use the data to make or recommend important resource allocation decisions: Should we buy or sell this security? What effect will a pay raise demand, if granted, have on the enterprise? Should management explore new sources of income? Should a division be sold off to enhance the company's position in the remaining enterprise? etc. All these and many more questions can be effectively answered if the facts are reflected fairly and are as neutral as the auditor can make them.

ANSWERS

Exercise No. 1

Golden Gate Landscaping Company
Balance Sheet
December 31, Year A

ASSETS

Current Assets
Cash	$ 562	
Accounts Receivable	2,116	
Garden Supplies	402	
Prepaid Insurance	109	
Total Current Assets		$3,189

Plant Assets
Truck	$2,100		
Less Accumulated Depreciation	560	$1,540	
Gardening Tools		317	
Total Plant Assets			$1,857
TOTAL ASSETS			$5,046

LIABILITIES AND OWNER'S EQUITY

Current Liabilities
Accounts Payable	$ 107	
Contracts Payable	660	
Total Liabilities		$ 767
Mr. Wilkinson, Capital		4,279
TOTAL LIABILITIES AND OWNER'S EQUITY		$5,046

Golden Gate Landscaping Company
Statement of Proprietor's Capital
Year Ended December 31, Year A

Capital, January 1, Year A	$3,500
Investment in May	1,000
	4,500
Add Profit for Year A	3,379
	7,879
Less Withdrawals During Year A	3,600
CAPITAL, DECEMBER 31, YEAR A	$4,279

Golden Gate Landscaping Company
Profit and Loss Statement
Year Ended December 31, Year A

Sales		$7,350
Expenses:		
Gardening Supplies	$2,516	
Depreciation Expense—Truck	560	
Gas and Oil Expense	373	
Telephone Expense	50	
Office Supplies Expense	27	
Insurance Expense	207	
Miscellaneous Expense	238	
Total Expenses		3,971
NET PROFIT		$3,379

Exercise No. 2

LIABILITIES AND OWNER'S EQUITY

Current Liabilities:
Accounts Payable	$ 107	
Contracts Payable	660	
TOTAL LIABILITIES		$ 767

Mr. Wilkinson, Capital:
Balance, January 1, Year A	3,500	
Investment in May	1,000	
	4,500	
Add Profit for Year A	3,379	
	7,879	
Less Withdrawals During Year A	3,600	
CAPITAL, DECEMBER 31, YEAR A		4,279
TOTAL LIABILITIES AND OWNER'S EQUITY		$5,046

Exercise No. 3

Santini & Casey, Insurance Brokers
Balance Sheet
December 31, Year A

ASSETS

Current Assets
Cash	$4,015	
Accounts Receivable	700	
Commissions Receivable	5,603	
Office Supplies	1,210	
Prepaid Insurance	570	
Prepaid Rent	600	
Total Current Assets		$12,698

Plant Assets
Office Furniture	$9,315		
Less Accumulated Depreciation	3,702	5,613	
Automobiles	$7,600		
Less Accumulated Depreciation	3,300	4,300	
Total Plant Assets			9,913
TOTAL ASSETS			$22,611

LIABILITIES AND PARTNERS' EQUITY

Current Liabilities
Premiums Payable	$2,950	
Accounts Payable	111	
TOTAL LIABILITIES		3,061

Partners' Capital:

	M. Santini	W. Casey	
Balance 1/1/Year A	$ 8,000	$10,000	
Investment 3/3/Year A	2,000	—	
	$10,000	$10,000	
Add Profit for Year A	4,975	4,975	
	$14,975	$14,975	
Less Withdrawals for Year A	5,200	5,200	
TOTAL CAPITAL, DECEMBER 31, YEAR A	$ 9,775	$ 9,775	19,550
TOTAL LIABILITIES AND PARTNERS' CAPITAL			$22,611

Santini & Casey, Insurance Brokers
Income Statement
Year Ended December 31, Year A

Commissions Income		$29,585
Expenses:		
Wages	$9,050	
Rent	2,400	
Automobile	2,300	
Telephone	1,100	
Office Supplies	560	
Insurance	210	
Depreciation—Office Equipment	955	
Depreciation—Automobiles	2,010	
Miscellaneous	1,050	
Total Expenses		19,635
PROFIT FOR YEAR A		$9,950

Profit Distribution	
M. Santini	$4,975
W. Casey	4,975
TOTAL PROFIT FOR YEAR A	$9,950

Exercise No. 4

Santini & Casey, Insurance Brokers
Income Statement
Year Ended December 31, Year A

	M. Santini	W. Casey	Total
Balance 1/1/Year A	$ 8,000	$10,000	$18,000
Investment 3/3/Year A	2,000	—	2,000
	$10,000	$10,000	$20,000
Add Profit for Year A	4,975	4,975	9,950
	$14,975	$14,975	$29,950
Less Withdrawals for Year A	5,200	5,200	10,400
TOTAL CAPITAL, DECEMBER 31, YEAR A	$ 9,775	$ 9,775	$19,550

LIABILITIES AND PARTNERS' EQUITY

Current Liabilities:

Premiums Payable	$2,950	
Accounts Payable	111	
Total Liabilities		$ 3,061

Partners' Capital:

M. Santini	9,775	
W. Casey	9,775	
Total Partners' Equity		19,550
TOTAL LIABILITIES AND PARTNERS' CAPITAL		$22,611

Exercise No. 5

CAPITAL

Common Stock $10 Par Value (5,000 shares authorized; 4,500 shares issued)[1]	$45,000
Retained Earnings, December 31, Year A	19,350
TOTAL CAPITAL	$64,350

Note 1. 4,000 shares issued as of January 1, Year A. An additional 500 shares issued April 15, Year A.

SZALAY, INC.
Retained Earnings Statement
Year Ending December 31, Year A

Balance, January 1, Year A		$17,000
Add Profit for Year Before Taxes	$8,000	
Less Estimated Income Taxes	3,900	4,100
		$21,100

Less Dividends Declared

March 31 4,000 shares @ .10/share	400	
June 30 4,500 shares @ .10/share	450	
Sept. 30 4,500 shares @ .10/share	450	
Dec. 31 4,500 shares @ .10/share	450	1,750
BALANCE, DECEMBER 31, YEAR A		$19,350

Exercise No. 6

LLURIA IMPORTERS
Income Statement
Year Ending January 31, Year B

Sales		$437,103
Cost of Goods Sold:		
Inventory, February 1, Year A	$ 39,060	
Merchandise Purchases	321,322	
Purchase Freight and Insurance	7,512	
	$367,894	
Less Inventory, January 31 Year B	36,202	
Cost of Goods Sold		331,692
Gross Profit on Sales		$105,411

Expenses:			
Selling Expenses:			
Sales Salaries	$29,227		
Store Supplies	11,050		
Depreciation Expense— Store Equipment	2,051	42,328	
Administrative Expenses:			
Office Salaries	5,602		
Communications Expense	706		
Insurance Expense	409		
Depreciation Expense— Office Equipment	527	7,244	
Total Expenses			49,572
NET PROFIT FOR FISCAL YEAR ENDING JANUARY 31, YEAR B			$55,839

Exercise No. 7

		Dr.	Cr.
a.	CASH	300—	
	SALES		300—
	TO RECORD CASH SALES OF $300.		
b.	CASH	400—	
	ACCTS. RECEIVABLE - Jonathan Jones		400—
	TO RECORD CASH RECEIVED ON ACCT.		
c.	CASH	200—	
	CAPITAL, SMYTH		200—
	TO RECORD INVESTMENT BY MR. SMYTH		
d.	CASH	10000—	
	NOTES PAYABLE		10000—
	TO RECORD PROCEEDS FROM NOTE		
e.	CASH	940—	
	PREPAID INTEREST (or Interest Expense)	60—	
	NOTES PAYABLE		1000—
	TO RECORD PROCEEDS FROM DISCOUNT NOTE		

Exercise No. 8

		Dr.	Cr.
a.	RENT EXPENSE	325—	
	CASH		325—
	TO RECORD MONTH'S RENT		
b.	MERCHANDISE INVENTORY (or PURCHASES)	700—	
	CASH		686—
	PURCHASE DISCOUNTS		14—
	TO RECORD PURCHASE OF MERCHANDISE		
	LESS 2% CASH DISCOUNT		
c.	DRAWING, CORUM	500—	
	CASH		500—
	TO RECORD DISINVESTMENT		
	by MR. CORUM		

Exercise No. 9.

DEPOSIT			
Pegboard Systems, Inc.	CURRENCY	287	00
	COIN	157	87
301 GRAND AVENUE, SUITE 2-D	C H E C K S 60-132	117	62
SOUTH SAN FRANCISCO, CALIFORNIA 94080	11-198	73	15
(415) 873-1710	19-37	215	00
	TOTAL FROM OTHER SIDE	—	
DATE	SUB TOTAL	850	64
	LESS CASH RECEIVED (–)		
SIGN HERE FOR CASH RECEIVED	TOTAL DEPOSIT	850	64

9996

000
─────
0000

USE OTHER SIDE FOR ADDITIONAL LISTINGS
IMPORTANT NOTICE
A HOLD FOR UNCOLLECTED FUNDS MAY BE PLACED ON FUNDS DEPOSITED BY CHECK OR SIMILAR INSTRUMENTS. THIS COULD DELAY YOUR ABILITY TO WITH DRAW SUCH FUNDS. THE DELAY IF ANY WOULD NOT EXCEED THE PERIOD OF TIME PERMITTED BY APPLICABLE LAW

BANK BRANCH
NAME OF BANK
ADDRESS
CITY, STATE ZIP

⑈"000 10 1"⑈ ⑆:000000000:0000 000000"⑈

Exercise No. 10.

a.	Pegboard Systems Inc.			
	Bank Reconciliation			
	Sept. 30, Year A			
	Bank Balance, Sept. 30, Year A			6416 34
	Add Deposits in Transit Sept 30			395 10
				6807 44
	Less Outstanding Checks Sept. 30 #119		201 03	
	#191		206 37	
	#155		122 16	
	#176		197 35	
	#180		92 06	818 97
				5988 47
	Balance Per General Ledger Sept. 30 Year A			5809 20
	Add Bank Credits - Collection Non Interest-bearing Notes			200 00
				6009 20
	Less Bank Debits - Returned Checks		10 73	
	Service Charge on Returned Checks		5 00	
	Note Collection Fee		5 00	20 73
				5988 47
b.	Adjusting Entries			
Oct. 3	Cash		200 00	
	Notes Receivable			200 00
	To record collection of non-interest-bearing note by the bank			
Oct. 3	Bad Debt Expense (OR ALLOWANCE FOR DOUBTFUL ACCOUNTS)		15 73	
	Bank Charges		5 00	
	Cash			20 73
	To record returned checks and related charge and note collection fee. (It is assumed the check is uncollectable. If it is collectable and the maker agrees to pay the service charge, the 15.73 would be debited to A/Rec)			

Exercise No. 11

Pegboard Systems, Inc.
301 GRAND AVENUE, SUITE 2-D
SOUTH SAN FRANCISCO, CALIFORNIA 94080
(415) 873-1710

BANK BRANCH
NAME OF BANK
ADDRESS
CITY, STATE ZIP

000
0000

101

PAY *EIGHTY-FOUR and thirteen /100* ———————— DOLLARS

TO THE ORDER OF *PETTY CASH*

DATE	CHECK NO	AMOUNT	
		DOLLARS	CENTS
8/31/ year A	101	84	13

Pegboard Systems, Inc.

SAMPLE

⑈000000000⑈0000 000000⑊

Exercise No. 12

REMCO INC.
ANALYSIS OF PROPOSED
CREDIT CARD PLAN

		PRESENT (ACTUAL)	% OF SALES	PROPOSED	AT PRESENT BASIS	CREDIT CARD BASIS
SALES		200000 —	100%			
25% INCREASE IN SALES				250000 —		
LOSS OF 20% OF CURRENT CASH					160000 —	
SALES INCREASE + 20% OF OLD BASIS						90000 —
COST OF GOODS SOLD		170000 —	85%	212500 —		
GROSS PROFIT		30000 —	15%	37500 —		
OPERATION EXPENSES		12000 —				
+ 5% OF NEW SALES	2500 —					
+ 6% OF CREDIT SALES	5400 —			19900 —		
NET PROFIT		18000 —		17600 —		

The analysis indicates that increasing sales by $50,000 will result in a loss of profit of $400 and on that basis the proposed plan should be rejected. But since there is such a small dollar drop in profit, it might be well to re-examine some of the assumptions:

a. Will operating expenses increase at the rate of 5% for new sales? If they only increase 4%, the proposed plan would increase profits by $100 and should be adopted.

b. Will 20% of the present customers convert to credit card buying? If only 15% convert, the proposed plan would increase profits by $200 and should be adopted.

It seems advisable, therefore, to study the proposed plan again for the purpose of getting another chance to review the fact-gathering assumptions and methods.

Exercise No. 13

a. Ability and willingness to repay obligation; borrower's income vs. outgo (not more than 30% of net income should be necessary to amortize the loan); willingness is determined by means of a credit report; recorded deed of trust so property can be taken over if payments are not made. (Source: George L. Clark, Vice President, Citizens Federal Savings and Loan Assn., San Francisco, Calif.)

b. Sufficient down payment (different for new and used cars); steady employment (two years); two years' residence in the area; "good credit" (Retail Credit Association check); evidence of coverage of fire, theft, comprehensive, and collision insurance; bank takes title to car until the obligation is paid. (Source: William J. Thompson, Assistant Vice President, Hibernia Bank, San Francisco, Calif.)

c. Stability in employment and home address; good credit background (calls to the stores where accounts are now open); bank references. (Source: Joseph Kelly, Assistant Credit Manager, Sears Roebuck & Co., San Francisco, Calif.)

d. Length of time employed; type of job; other credit accounts; bank accounts; own or rent home; credit rating (Retail Credit Association check). (Source: Mrs. Sylvia Ribiero, Credit Analyst, Macy's of California, San Francisco, Calif.)

Exercise No. 14

DERINI Products
Computation of Balance in
Allowance for Uncollectible Accounts

a.

Age of Account	Amount	Loss Ratio	Estimated Allowance
31–60 days	$80,000	2%	$1,600
61–90 days	40,000	5%	2,000
over 90 days	30,000	10%	3,000
			$6,600

b. Bad Debt Expense $4,400
  Allowance for
  Uncollectible
  Accounts $4,400
    To increase
    allowance from
    $2,200 to $6,600.

Exercise No. 15

Cash $192,000
Financing Expense   8,000
  Accounts Receivable $200,000
    To record sale of
    $200,000 of accounts
    receivable for
    $192,000.

Exercise No. 16

a. Accounts Receivable—
Pledged $150,000
    Accounts Receivable $150,000
       To separate
       pledged accounts
       receivable from
       regular accounts
       receivable.

Cash $100,000
    Notes Payable $100,000
       To record receipt
       of cash
       from the note
       payable under
       the pledging
       contract.

b. Cash $ 20,000
    Accounts Receiv-
    able—Pledged $ 20,000
       To record receipt
       of cash in
       February on
       accounts
       receivable pledged.

Notes Payable $ 20,000
Interest Expense
  ($100,000 × 5% ÷
  12) 416.67
    Cash $ 24,167
       To record payment
       on loan plus
       interest on
       $100,000 for
       February.

c. Cash $ 50,000
    Accounts Receiv-
    able—Pledged $ 50,000
       To record receipt
       of cash in March
       on accounts
       receivable pledged.

Notes Payable $ 50,000
Interest Expense
  (80,000 × 5% ÷
  12) 333
    Cash $ 53,333
       To record payment
       on loan plus
       interest on $80,000
       for March.

d. Cash $ 30,000
    Accounts Receiv-
    able—Pledged $ 30,000
       To record receipt
       of cash in April on
       accounts
       receivable pledged.

Notes Payable $ 30,000
Interest Expense
  ($30,000 × 5% ÷
  12) 125
    Cash $ 31,250
       To record payment
       on loan plus
       interest on $30,000
       for April.

Accounts Receivable $ 50,000
    Accounts Receiv-
    able—Pledged $ 50,000
       To return
       pledged accounts
       receivable to the
       regular accounts
       receivable now
       that the loan is
       paid.

Exercise No. 17

a. Advantages: 1. Inexpensive because no detailed inventory cards must be kept. 2. Cost of Goods Sold can be determined by formula.

b. Disadvantages: 1. Lack of control because the quantity on hand cannot be determined readily. 2. Counting must be done when the plant is shut down or at night or on weekends.

Exercise No. 18

PLEV YAK CO.
Cost of Goods Sold Statement
Fiscal Year Ended March 31, Year A

Beginning Inventory, April 1, Year (A-1)			$ 130,000
Purchases		$1,600,000	
Less: Purchase Returns and Allowances	$30,000		
Purchase Discounts	31,000	61,000	
		$1,539,000	
Plus Freight in		12,000	1,551,000
			$1,681,000
Less Inventory, March 31, Year A			150,000
Cost of Goods Sold			$1,531,000

Exercise No. 19

				ITEM
OUT	OUT			

DESCRIPTION: **6290**

ROCKER ARM

6290 ROCKER ARM

	ANNUAL USAGE	STOCK LOCATION	STANDARD PACKAGE	MAXIMUM QUANTITY	MINIMUM QUANTITY
			DOZ.		

DATE	REFERENCE/COMMENTS		IN	OUT	BALANCE ON HAND
1/1 A					500
1/19	*Received*	60 doz.	720		1,220
2/3	*Used*			125	1,095
2/10	*Received*	20 doz.	240		1,335
2/11	*Returned to Vendor*			9	1,326
2/17	*Used*			75	1,251

Exercise No. 20

Inventory (10 units @ $1.25 each)	$12.50	
Inventory Over and Short		$12.50
To record overage of material.		

Exercise No. 21

a. Cash	$400	
Sales		$400
To record sale of 200 units @ $2 each.		

b. In the periodic inventory method no Cost of Goods Sold entry is made when the goods are sold.

Exercise No. 22

Inventory Over and Short	$44.80	
Inventory (28 units @ $1.60 each)		$44.80
To record shortage of material.		

Exercise No. 23

a. Advantages: 1. Affords greater control over inventory quantity of low volume–high value items (diamonds and watches); in items of great personal utility (hand tools and whiskey); in situations of operating complexity (manufacturing of automobiles); in items of changing consumer demand (women's fashions or fad items). 2. Affords an immediate costing of sales.

b. Disadvantages: 1. Requires an investment in filing equipment and cards. 2. Maintaining current records is expensive.

Exercise No. 24

a. Cash	$1,500	
Sales		$1,500
To record sale of 300 units @ $5 each.		

b. Cost of Sales	$1,200	
Inventory		$1,200
To record reduction in inventory due to sale (300 units @ $4 each).		

Exercise No. 25

		LIFO	AVERAGE	FIFO
SALES 3000 @ 7.40 ea.	22200 —			
1500 @ 8.00 ea.	12000 —			
4,500		34200 —	34200 —	34200 —
COST OF GOODS SOLD				
LIFO 2000 @ 6.600 ea.	13200 —			
2000 @ 6.400 ea.	12800 —			
500 @ 6.200 ea.	3100 —	29100 —		
4500				
AVERAGE: 1000 @ 5.700 ea.	5700 —			
2000 @ 6.200 ea.	12400 —			
2000 @ 6.400 ea.	12800 —			
2000 @ 6.600 ea.	13200 —			
7000	44100 —			
44,100 = 6.300 ea.				
7000				
4500 @ 6.300 ea.			28350 —	
FIFO 1000 @ 5.700 ea.	5700 —			
2000 @ 6.200 ea.	12400 —			
1500 @ 6.400 ea.	9600 —			27700 —
4,500				
GROSS PROFIT		5100 —	5850 —	6500 —
INVENTORY, MAY 31				
LIFO 1500 @ 6.200 ea.	9300 —			
1000 @ 5.700 ea.	5700 —	15000 —		
2500				
AVERAGE: 2500 @ 6.300 ea			15750 —	
FIFO 500 @ 6.400 ea.	3200 —			
2000 @ 6.600 ea.	13200 —			16400 —
2500				
PROOF				
COST OF GOODS SOLD 4500		29100 —	28350 —	27700 —
INVENTORY 2500		15000 —	15750 —	16400 —
TOTAL GOODS 7000		44100 —	44100 —	44100 —

Exercise No. 26

ITEM	No. of UNITS	COST	MARKET	INVENTORY VALUE
A1	100	✓ 60	67	6000
A2	120	120	✓ 110	13200
A3	600	210	✓ 200	120000
A4	210	300	✓ 290	60900
B1	430	✓ 400	410	172000
B2	10	75	✓ 72	720
B3	25	450	✓ 430	10750
C1	900	✓ 790	810	711000
C2	42	575	✓ 560	23520
C3	150	815	✓ 804	120600
C4	200	✓ 615	627	123000
				1361690

Exercise No. 27

Selling Price	$5.00
Cost	4.00
Gross Profit	$1.00

Gross Profit as a percentage of sales:

$$\frac{\$1.00}{\$5.00} = 20\%$$

Gross Profit as a percentage of cost:

$$\frac{\$1.00}{\$4.00} = 25\%$$

Notice that as the base changes, the percentage changes.

Exercise No. 28

Land	$47,507.00	
Prepaid Taxes	27.95	
Cash		$47,534.95

Exercise No. 29

a. Cash	$5,200	
Land		$5,200
b. Land	$3,700	
Cash		$3,700

Exercise No. 30

Cash	$ 99,059.00
Mortgage Payable—Bank	360,000.00
Mortgage Payable—Galli	40,000.00
Rental Deposits	3,742.00
Rental Income	2,108.50
	504,909.50
Less Interest Expense	1,800.00
Taxes Expense	16,801.50
Cost of Land and Building	$486,308.00

a. Land $486,308 $\times \dfrac{\$125,000}{\$500,000} = \$121,577.00$

b. Building $486,308 $\times \dfrac{\$375,000}{\$500,000} = \underline{\$364,731.00}$

$\$486,308.00$

Land	$121,577.00	
Building	364,731.00	
Interest Expense	1,800.00	
Taxes Expense	16,801.50	
Cash		$ 99,059.00
Mortgage Payable— Bank		360,000.00
Mortgage Payable— Galli		40,000.00
Rental Deposits		3,742.00
Rental Income		2,108.50

To record the
purchase of land
and building at
6259 Geary
Drive, San
Francisco, Calif.
(appraisal
valuation used
for allocation).

a. Land $\quad$ \$486,308.00 $\times \dfrac{\$10,000}{\$70,000}$ = \$ 69,472.57

b. Building \$486,308.00 $\times \dfrac{\$60,000}{\$70,000}$ = \$416,835.43

$\qquad\qquad\qquad\qquad\qquad$ \$486,308.00

Land	\$ 69,472.57	
Building	416,835.43	
Interest Expense	1,800.00	
Taxes Expense	16,801.50	
Cash		\$ 99,059.00
Mortgage Payable— Bank		360,000.00
Mortgage Payable— Galli		40,000.00
Rental Deposits		3,742.00
Rental Income		2,108.50

To record purchase
of land and
building at 6259
Geary Drive, San
Francisco, Calif.
(assessment
valuation used for
allocation).

Exercise No. 31

a. Building $\qquad$ \$25,600

$\quad$ Accounts Payable $\qquad$ \$25,600

$\qquad$ To record remodeling
$\qquad$ cost.

b. The total cost of the building is \$139,432 (\$113,832 + \$25,600).

Exercise No. 32

a. Building $\qquad$ \$16,000

$\quad$ Repairs and Maintenance $\quad$ 2,600

$\quad$ Accounts Payable $\qquad$ \$18,600

$\qquad$ To record costs of
$\qquad$ remodeling and
$\qquad$ repairing building.

b. Yes. Although in both cases the exterior is painted, in Exercise 31 the painting was done as part of the work necessary to prepare the building for occupancy. In Exercise 32 the painting is unrelated to the interior remodeling and is therefore in the nature of repairs.

Exercise No. 33

Machine	\$5,000
Freight	105
Insurance in Transit	75
Installation Cost	200
Total Cost	\$5,380

Exercise No. 34

Machinery	\$10,600	
Deferred Interest	1,000	
Cash		\$2,000
Contracts Payable		9,600

To record purchase of machine
under an installment contract.

Exercise No. 35

$$\frac{\$9,800 - \$200}{8 \text{ years}} = \frac{\$9,600}{8 \text{ years}} = \$1,200/\text{year}$$

Exercise No. 36

a. $\dfrac{\$15,000 - \$1,000}{2,000 \text{ hours}} = \dfrac{\$14,000}{2,000 \text{ hours}} = \$7/\text{hour}$

b. Year A: 175 hours × \$7/hr. = \$1,225
$\quad$ Year B: $\;$ 62 hours × \$7/hr. = \$ $\;$ 434

Exercise No. 37

$$\frac{\$14,300 - \$300}{20,000 \text{ units}} = \frac{\$14,000}{20,000 \text{ units}} = \$0.70/\text{unit}$$

Exercise No. 38

Year A: 7,000 units × $0.70/unit = $4,900
Year B: 5,000 units × $0.70/unit = $3,500
Year C: 6,500 units × $0.70/unit = $5,550

Exercise No. 39

Allowance for Depreciation—		
Dies and Tools	$12,950	
Cash	200	
Loss on Disposal of Plant Assets—	1,150	
Dies and Tools		$14,300
To record sale of dies and tools.		

Exercise No. 40

Explanation	Depreciation Expense for the Year	Allowance for Depreciation Dec. 31, 19—	Book Value
Purchase			$20,000.00
1st Year	$4,000.00	$ 4,000.00	16,000.00
2nd Year	3,200.00	7,200.00	12,800.00
3rd Year	2,560.00	9,760.00	10,240.00
4th Year	2,048.00	11,808.00	8,192.00
5th Year	1,638.40	13,446.40	6,553.60
6th Year	1,310.72	14,757.12	5,242.88
7th Year	1,048.76	15,805.88	4,194.12
8th Year	838.82	16,644.70	3,357.08
9th Year	671.42	17,316.12	2,685.38
10th Year	537.13	17,853.24	2,148.30

Exercise No. 41

$8 + 7 + 6 + 5 + 4 + 3 + 2 + 1 = 36$
To determine $\frac{1}{36}$th:

$$\frac{\$40,000 - \$400}{36} = \frac{\$39,600}{36} = \$1,100.$$

Depreciation:				
	1st Year	$\frac{8}{36}$ ×	$1,100 =	$ 8,800
	2nd Year	$\frac{7}{36}$ ×	1,100 =	7,700
	3rd Year	$\frac{6}{36}$ ×	1,100 =	6,600
	4th Year	$\frac{5}{36}$ ×	1,100 =	5,500
	5th Year	$\frac{4}{36}$ ×	1,100 =	4,400
	6th Year	$\frac{3}{36}$ ×	1,100 =	3,300
	7th Year	$\frac{2}{36}$ ×	1,100 =	2,200
	8th Year	$\frac{1}{36}$ ×	1,100 =	1,100
		$\frac{36}{36}$		$39,600

Exercise No. 42

a. Depreciation Expense—Plant Machinery	$ 900	
Allowance for Depreciation—Plant Machinery		$ 900
To record 9 months' depreciation ($\frac{9}{12}$ × $1,200 = $900).		
Cash	$4,000	
Allowance for Depreciation—Plant Machinery	3,900	
Plant Machinery		$7,500
Gain on Sale of Plant Assets		400
To record sale of asset.		
b. Depreciation Expense—Plant Machinery	$ 900	
Allowance for Depreciation—Plant Machinery		$ 900
To record 9 months' depreciation ($\frac{9}{12}$ × $1,200 = $900).		
Cash	$3,000	
Allowance for Depreciation—Plant Machinery	3,900	
Loss on Sale of Plant Assets	600	
Plant Machinery		$7,500
To record sale of asset.		

Exercise No. 43

Allowance for Depreciation—		
Truck	$17,000	
Truck (new)	14,460	
Cash ($23,400 − $2,540)		$20,860
Truck (old)		20,600
To record trade of old truck for new truck. (Note: "New" and "old" are used here to distinguish between the asset acquired and the one traded. This would not be found in a General Ledger account.)		

Exercise No. 44

a. $\dfrac{\$25,200 - \$1,200}{10 \text{ years}} = \dfrac{\$24,000}{10 \text{ years}} = \$2,400/\text{year}$

9 months' depreciation = $\frac{9}{12} \times \$2,400 = \$1,800$.

Depreciation Expense— Machinery	$1,800	
Allowance for Depreciation— Machinery		$1,800
To record 9 months' depreciation.		

b. Allowance for Depreciation— Machinery ($18,000 + $1,800)	$19,800	
Machinery (new)	32,600	
Cash ($30,000 − $2,800)		$27,200
Machinery (old)		25,200
To record trade of old machinery for new machinery.		

c. $\dfrac{\$32,600 - \$2,600}{8 \text{ years}} = \dfrac{\$30,000}{8 \text{ years}} = \$3,750/\text{year}$

3 months' depreciation = $\frac{3}{12} \times \$3,750 = \$937.50$

Depreciation Expense— Machinery	$937.50	
Allowance for Depreciation— Machinery		$937.50
To record 3 months' depreciation.		

Exercise No. 45

a. Amount to be received from the insurance company:

1. Face amount of the policy		**$12,000**
2. Formula:		
$\dfrac{\$12,000}{\$15,000 \times 75\%} \times \$15,000$		$16,000
3. Amount of loss		$15,000

(Note: Because premiums on only $11,250 were required under the 75% co-insurance clause there may also be a premium refund.)

b. Allowance for Depreciation—Machinery ($9,900 + $450)	$10,350	
Loss Due to Fire	7,950	
Machinery		$18,300
To close out asset and accumulated depreciation accounts.		

c. Cash	$12,000	
Loss Due to Fire		$12,000
To record receipt of cash from the insurance company.		

d.

Loss Due to Fire			
(b)	$7,950	(c)	$12,000

e. Loss Due to Fire		$4,050
Expense and Revenue Summary		$4,050
To close out Loss Due to Fire account.		

f. Loss Due to Fire is shown at the bottom of the Income Statement with Other Expense. (It is an extraordinary item after the Net Operating Profit.)

Exercise No. 46

Amount to be received from the insurance company:

1. Face amount of the policy		$400,000
2. Formula:		
$\dfrac{\$400,000}{\$500,000 \times 80\%} \times \$36,000$		$ 36,000
3. Amount of loss		$ 36,000

$36,000 will be received from the insurance company.

Exercise No. 47

1. Face amount of the policy $400,000
2. Formula:

$$\frac{\$400,000}{\$500,000 \times 80\%} \times \$440,000 \quad \$440,000$$

3. Amount of loss $440,000

$400,000 will be received from the insurance company.

Exercise No. 48

1. Face amount of the policy $450,000
2. Formula:

$$\frac{\$450,000}{\$600,000 \times 80\%} \times \$480,000 \quad \$450,000$$

3. Amount of loss $480,000

$450,000 will be received from the insurance company.

Exercise No. 49

1. Face amount of the policy $450,000
2. Formula:

$$\frac{\$450,000}{\$600,000 \times 80\%} \times \$96,000 \quad \$\,90,000$$

3. Amount of loss $\,96,000

$90,000 will be received from the insurance company.

Exercise No. 50

Franchise Amortization		
Expense	$4,000	
Franchise		$4,000
To record annual franchise		
amortization expense.		

Exercise No. 51

Increase in Asset Value	$186,000	
Overstreet, Capital		$186,000
To record increase in value		
of building to reflect current		
market value:		

Current value	$250,000
Book value	64,000
	$186,000

Exercise No. 52

a. Merchandise Purchases	$7,000	
Accounts (or Vouchers)		
Payable		$7,000
To record purchases		
of merchandise for		
sale.		
b. Accounts (or Vouchers)		
Payable	$7,000	
Cash		$6,860
Purchase Discounts		140
To record payments		
during discount		
period.		
c. Accounts (or Vouchers)		
Payable	$7,000	
Cash		$7,000
To record payments		
after discount		
period.		

Exercise No. 53

a. Merchandise Purchases	$5,880	
Accounts (or Vouchers)		
Payable		$5,880
To record purchases		
of merchandise for		
sale.		
b. Accounts (or Vouchers)		
Payable	$5,880	
Cash		$5,880
To record invoices		
paid during discount		
period.		
c. Accounts (or Vouchers)		
Payable	$5,880	
Discounts Lost	120	
Cash		$6,000
To record invoices		
paid after discount		
period.		

Exercise No. 54

a. Cash	$7,000.00	
Notes Payable		$7,000.00
To record loan from bank (60-day 12% note).		
b. Notes Payable	$7,000.00	
Interest Expense	140.00	
Cash		$7,140.00
To record payment of $7,000 60-day 12% note.		

Exercise No. 55

a. Cash	$8,000.00	
Notes Payable		$8,000.00
To record loan from bank (90-day 13% note).		
b. Interest Expense	$ 130.00	
Accrued Interest Payable		$ 130.00
To record accrued interest for 45 days ($8,000 × 13% × $^{45}/_{360}$).		
c. 1. Accrued Interest Payable	$ 130.00	
Interest Expense		$ 130.00
To Reverse.		
2. Notes Payable	$8,000.00	
Interest Expense	260.00	
Cash		$8,260.00
To record payment of note and interest.		
d. Interest Expense	$ 130.00	
Accrued Interest Payable	130.00	
Notes Payable	8,000.00	
Cash		$8,260.00
To record payment of note and interest.		

Exercise No. 56

Cash	$10,000.00	
Prepaid Interest	3,600.00	
Notes Payable		$13,600.00
To record loan from bank, prepaying interest.		

Exercise No. 57

	Ay	Bee
a. Money each receives	$1,000.00	$870.00
b. Dollars paid for money used	130.00	130.00
c. Effective interest rate	13.0%	14.9%

Exercise No. 58

Sales Salaries Expense ($5,000 × ⅚ × 110%)	$3,300.00	
Office Salaries Expense ($2,000 × ⅚ × 105%)	1,260.00	
Accrued Salaries Payable		$4,560.00
To record accrued salaries.		

Exercise No. 59

a. Merchandise Purchases (or Merchandise Inventory)	$8,200	
Accounts Payable		$8,200
To record merchandise purchased in Year A.		

b. No entry is required because goods were shipped F.O.B. destination and they did not arrive until January 5, Year B.

Exercise No. 60

Month Factor	1-year Subscriptions		2-year Subscriptions		5-year Subscriptions	
	Number	Total Months	Number	Total Months	Number	Total Months
12	100	1,200	175	2,100	130	1,560
11	75	825	162	1,782	205	2,255
10	83	830	181	1,810	197	1,970
9	97	873	135	1,215	188	1,692
8	105	840	166	1,328	142	1,136
7	82	574	175	1,225	155	1,085
6	56	336	185	1,110	187	1,122
5	71	355	119	595	193	965
4	89	356	122	488	167	668
3	43	129	163	489	152	456
2	52	104	180	360	193	386
1	60	60	205	205	215	215
TOTAL	913	6,482	1,968	12,707	2,124	13,510

$\dfrac{\$9.00}{} = \$0.75/$ month $\dfrac{\$17.00}{} = \$0.708/$ month $\dfrac{\$34.00}{} = \$0.567/$ month

	1-year	2-year	5-year
a. Year A income	$4,861.50	$ 8,996.56	$ 7,660.17
b. Unearned at 12/31/Year A	$3,355.50	$24,459.44	$64,555.83

c. Prepaid Subscriptions Received in Year A

	$21,517.23
Subscription Income	$21,517.23

To record subscriptions earned in Year A.

1-year =	$ 4,861.50
2-year =	8,996.56
5-year =	7,660.17
	$21,517.23

d. Subscriptions received in Year A and earned in Year B (assuming no cancellations):

1-year	$ 3,355.50
2-year (1,968 × 12 mos. × $0.708/mo.)	16,720.13
5-year (2,124 × 12 mos. × $0.567/mo.)	14,451.70
	$34,537.33

Exercise No. 61

a. $25,000 at 12% for 25 years requires $263.31/ month payments (.010532241 × 25,000 vs. 10.54 × 25 or 263.50). $263.31/mo. × 12 × 25 years = $78,991.50.

b. $25,000 at 12% for 24 years requires $265.10/ month payments (.010603819 × 25,000). $265.10/ mo. × 12 × 24 years = 76,348.80.

c. $25,000 at 11¾% for 25 years requires $258.70/ month payments (.010347982 × 25,000). $258.70/ mo. × 12 × 25 years = $77,610.00.

d. $25,000 at 12¼% for 24 years requires $269.68/ month payments (.010787168 × 25,000). $269.68/ mo. × 12 × 24 years = $77,667.12.

Loan b has the smallest *total* payments, or $76,348.80. However, Loan c has the smallest monthly payments ($258.70/mo.). The question "Which is the best loan?" really rests with the circumstances of the borrower. What might be good for Borrower X might not be what satisfies Borrower Y. (The answers above may be off a few dollars from your answers depending on what tables you used.)

Exercise No. 62

Cash	$490,000	
Deferred Bond Discount	10,000	
Bonds Payable		$500,000

To record sale of
bonds on issue date
per commission
agreement with
investment banker.

Exercise No. 63

Interest on bonds per year = $1,000,000 \times 12\%$ =
$120,000.
How much money at 12.2% will yield $120,000? *Answer: 983,606.55.*

Exercise No. 64

Cash	$390,000	
Deferred Bond Discount	10,000	
Bonds Payable		$400,000

To record sale of
bonds to investment
banker on issue date at
97.5.

Exercise No. 65

Cash	$612,500	
Notes Payable		$600,000
Interest Expense		12,500

To record the sale of
bonds dated April 1,
Year A, sold on June 1,
Year A (2 months;
12.5% interest).

Deferred Bond Discount	$ 18,000	
Cash		$ 18,000

To record commission
on sale of bonds.

Exercise No. 66

Estimated Real Property Taxes	$3,572,862
Estimated Personal Property Taxes	385,140
Estimated Sales Taxes	468,438
Estimated Business Licenses Income	111,386
Estimated Fines Income	91,851

Unappropriated Surplus	$4,629,677

To record estimated
revenues.

Exercise No. 67

Unappropriated Surplus	$4,519,816	
Appropriation for Administration		$330,180
Appropriation for Legislation		86,082
Appropriation for Judicial		869,635
Appropriation for Education Dept.		379,784
Appropriation for Health Dept.		171,656
Appropriation for Police Dept.		198,018
Appropriation for Fire Dept.		125,344
Appropriation for Correction Dept.		169,274
Appropriation for Welfare Dept.		834,791
Appropriation for Street Dept.		594,467
Appropriation for Recreation Dept.		433,558
Appropriation for Office and Building Repairs		33,094
Appropriation for Elections		134,534
Appropriation for Publications, Advertising, etc.		159,399

To record
appropriations.

Exercise No. 68

Real Property Taxes Receivable	$3,572,862	
Real Property Taxes Income		$3,572,862

To record real
property tax schedule.

Exercise No. 69

Cash	$4,440,175	
Real Property Taxes Receivable		$3,368,518
Personal Property Taxes Income		383,273
Sales Taxes Income		485,683
Business Licenses Income		109,776
Fines Income		92,925
To record cash receipts.		

Exercise No. 70

Administrative	$329,110	
Legislative	85,877	
Judicial	806,906	
Education Dept.	379,653	
Health Dept.	170,356	
Police Dept.	197,172	
Fire Dept.	122,882	
Correction Dept.	168,940	
Welfare Dept.	834,615	
Street Dept.	581,687	
Recreation Dept.	377,432	
Office and Building Repairs	30,444	
Elections	133,482	
Publications, Advertising	158,775	
Vouchers Payable		$4,377,331
To record vouchers processed.		

Exercise No. 71

Vouchers Payable	$4,377,331	
Cash		$4,377,331
To record payment of vouchers.		

Exercise No. 72

	Actual Year A		Budget Year B	
Sales		$200,000		$240,000
Cost of Goods Sold				
Labor	$80,000		$92,000	
Material	46,000		55,200	
Overhead	14,000		16,800	
		140,000		164,000
Gross Profit		$ 60,000		$ 76,000
Selling Expenses	25,000		28,750	
Administrative Expenses	20,000		22,000	
		45,000		50,750
Net Profit		$ 15,000		$ 25,250

Exercise No. 73

	Department 1		Department 2		Department 3		Department 4		Total	
Total Sales	$85,000	100.0%	$72,000	100.0%	$93,000	100.0%	$110,000	100.0%	$360,000	100.0%
Beginning Inventory	7,000		6,000		7,000		11,000		31,000	
Net Purchases	74,000		68,000		81,000		99,000		322,000	
	$81,000		$74,000		$88,000		$110,000		$353,000	
Ending Inventory	6,000		7,000		8,000		10,000		31,000	
	$75,000	88.2%	$67,000	93.1%	$80,000	86.0%	$100,000	90.9%	$322,000	89.5%
Gross Profit on Sales	$10,000	11.8%	$ 5,000	6.9%	$13,000	14.0%	$10,000	9.1%	$38,000	10.5%
Selling Expenses	7,000	8.3	4,000	5.5	6,000	6.5	4,000	3.6	21,000	5.8
Departmental Income	$ 3,000	3.5%	$ 1,000	1.4%	$7,000	7.5%	$ 6,000	5.5%	$17,000	4.7%
Administrative Expenses									8,000	2.2
Net Operating Profit									$ 9,000	2.5%

Exercise No. 74

Items	Expected Sales		Actual Sales		Increase or (Decrease) Actual over Expected	
	Dollars	Percentage	Dollars	Percentage	Dollars	Percentage
Groceries	1,710.00	45.0	1,960.24	50.0	250.24	14.6
Taxable	570.00	15.0	482.16	12.3	(87.84)	(15.4)
Drugs	190.00	5.0	203.84	5.2	13.84	7.3
Meats	475.00	12.5	454.72	11.6	(20.28)	(4.3)
Produce	285.00	7.5	301.84	7.7	16.84	5.9
Liquor	570.00	15.0	517.44	13.2	(52.56)	(9.2)
Totals	3,800.00	100.0	3,920.24	100.0	120.24	3.2

Exercise No. 75

Accounts Receivable	$5,000	
Sales		$5,000
Charge sales.		

Exercise No. 76

Cost of Goods Sold	$3,500	
Inventory		$3,500
Cost of Goods Sold.		

Exercise No. 77

Cash	$5,000	
Accounts Receivable		$5,000
Received payment on account.		

Exercise No. 78

Installment Contracts Receivable	$500,000	
Installment Sales		$500,000
Sales on installment.		
Cost of Installment Sales	$300,000	
Inventory		$300,000
Cost of installment sales.		
Installment Sales	$500,000	
Cost of Installment Sales		$300,000
Unrealized Gross Profit on Installment Sales—Year C		200,000
Close out Installment Sales and Cost of Installment Sales accounts and set up deferred profit. (Gross profit is 40%.)		

Exercise No. 79

Gross Profit on Installment Sales—Year C	$28,000	
Installment Sales Gross Profits Realized		$28,000
Record gross profits realized on Year C installment sales collected. ($70,000 × 40%.)		
Gross Profit on Installment Sales—Year C	$72,000	
Installment Sales Gross Profits Realized		$72,000
Record gross profits realized on Year C installment sales collected. ($180,000 × 40%.)		

Exercise No. 80

Cash	$180,000	
Installment Contracts Receivable		$180,000
Received moneys on installment sales contracts.		
Gross Profit on Installment Sales—Year C	$72,000	
Installment Sales Gross Profit Realized		$72,000
Record gross profits realized on year C installment contract collections. ($180,000 × 40%.)		

Exercise No. 81

Year A: $\dfrac{\$20,000}{.32} = \$62,500$

Year B: $\dfrac{\$160,000 - \$30,000}{.37} = \dfrac{\$130,000}{.37} = \$351,351$

Year C: $\dfrac{\$500,000 - \$220,000}{.35} = \dfrac{\$280,000}{.35} = \$800,000$

Exercise No. 82

a. Selling price of used machine	$ 4,500	
Markup on selling price (20%)	900	
	$ 3,600	
Less reconditioning cost	800	
	$ 2,800	
b. Trade-in Inventory	$ 2,800	
Installment Contracts Receivable	12,500	
Installment Sales		$14,800
Unearned Interest Income [12,500 − (15,000 − 3,000)]		500
Sale on installment. Customer traded in used machine.		
Cost of Installment Sales	$13,000	
Inventory		$13,000
Cost of installment sales.		
Installment Sales	$14,800	
Cost of Installment Sales		$13,000
Unrealized Gross Profit on Installment Sales—Year A		1,800
Close out Installment Sales and Cost of Installment Sales accounts, and set up deferred profit. (Gross profit ratio is 12.2%.)		

Exercise No. 83

a.

Installment Contracts		
Receivable	$ 9,720	
Cash	1,000	
Installment Sales		$10,000
Unearned Interest		
Income		720

    Sale of goods on an
    installment contract
    with $720 interest
    and carrying charges.

Cost of Installment Sales	$ 7,000	
Inventory		$ 7,000

    Cost of goods sold on
    installment.

Installment Sales	$10,000	
Cost of Installment		
Sales		$ 7,000
Unrealized Gross Profit		
on Installment		
Sales—Year A		3,000

    Close out Installment
    Sales and Cost of
    Installment Sales
    accounts and set up
    gross profit deferred.
    (Gross profit ratio is
    30%.)

b.

Cash	$ 2,160	
Installment Contracts		
Receivable		$ 2,160

    Receipts of cash on
    installments
    receivable.

Unrealized Gross Profit		
on Installment		
Sales—Year A	$ 900	
Gross Profit on		
Installment Sales		
Realized		$ 900

    Record realized
    portion of profit on
    receipts of
    installment sales
    payments.

		Original Contract	Paid on Contract
Sale	100%	$9,000	$2,000
Charges	8%	720	160
Total	108%	$9,720	$2,160

($1,000 down payment + $2,000 payments × 30%
= $900)

Unearned Interest Income	$160	
Interest Income		$160

    Record interest earned (%
    × $720 = $160). See
    schedule above.

(This is not asked for in the exercise but is shown to
explain the answers to c. and d. which follow.)

Installment Contracts Receivable

$9,720	$2,160
7,560 Bal.	

Unrealized Gross Profit on Installment Sales—Year A

$900	$3,000
	Bal. 2,100

Unearned Interest Income

$160	$720
	Bal. 560

c.

$5,000 × 1.15	= $5,750
Less reconditioning =	1,000
	$4,750

d.

Repossessed Inventory	$4,750	
Unrealized Gross Profit		
on Installment Sales—		
Year A	2,100	
Unearned Interest Income	560	
Loss on Repossessions	150	
Installment Contracts		
Receivable		$7,560

    Record termination
    of installment
    contract due to
    default on payments
    and set up
    repossessed inventory
    and recognize loss on
    repossessions.

Balance Due

108%	$7,560	
100%	7,000 × 30%	= $2,100
8%	560	

Exercise No. 84

		Regular Hours	Overtime Hours	Total Hours	Rate Per Hour	Gross Pay
a.	Jones	40	—	40	$1.75	$70.00
	Smith	40	—	40	2.10	84.00
	McCarthy	39	—	39	2.05	79.95
	Shea	40	2	42	1.95	83.85
	Catalli	38	—	38	1.52	57.76
b.	Jones	40	—	40	1.75	70.00
	Smith	39	1	40	2.10	85.05
	McCarthy	38	1	39	2.05	80.98
	Shea	38	4	42	1.95	85.80
	Catalli	33	5	38	1.52	61.56

Exercise No. 85

Jones:	70 × $0.70 each =		$ 49.00
Smith:	100 × $0.70 each =	$70.00	
	10 × $0.72 each =	7.20	77.20
Blue:	100 × $0.70 each =	$70.00	
	50 × $0.72 each =	36.00	
	30 × $0.76 each =	22.80	128.80

Exercise No. 86

Yes. Jones would have earned $75.

Exercise No. 87

Jones:	70 × $0.70 =	$ 49.00
Smith:	110 × $0.72 =	79.20
Blue:	180 × $0.76 =	136.80

Exercise No. 88

	Details	Debits	Credits
a. Work in Process—Dept. 1	$2,000		
Work in Process—Dept. 2	1,200		
Work in Process—Dept. 3	4,000	$7,300	
Factory Overhead—Plant Office	3,400		
Factory Overhead—Power Plant	550		
Factory Overhead—Maintenance	400	4,350	
Selling Expenses—Shipping		650	
F.I.C.A. Taxes Payable			$ 155
Income Taxes Withheld			2,091
Bond Deductions Payable			210
United Crusade Payable			100
Cash (OR Salaries Payable)			9,744
Record labor entry.			
b. Payroll Tax Expense		$185	
F.I.C.A. Taxes Payable			
($2,200 × 0.0705)			$155
Federal Unemployment Tax Payable			
($1,500 × 0.008)			12
State Unemployment Tax Payable			18
($1,500 × 0.012)			
Record employer's tax.			

Exercise No. 89

	Detail	Debits	Credits
Work in Process— Job 16	$ 38.20		
Work in Process— Job 19	100.50		
Work in Process— Job 22	22.30	$161.00	
Factory Overhead— Dept. A	53.15		
Factory Overhead— Dept. B	51.70	104.85	
Inventory			$265.85

Record use of materials requisitioned from storeroom.

Exercise No. 90

$$Q = \sqrt{\frac{2 \times R \times P}{C \times I}}$$

$$= \sqrt{\frac{2 \times 2,000 \times \$14.00}{\$6.40 \times .30}}$$

$$= 171$$

Exercise No. 91

$$\frac{2,000}{171} = 11.8 \text{ orders/year}$$

$$\frac{250}{11.8} = 21.2$$

Order must be placed every 20 and 21 days alternately.

Exercise No. 92

2 calendar weeks = 10 days
30 units per day usage × 10 days = 300 units minimum stock.

Exercise No. 93

a. Total cost = $7,399.00

Average cost = $\frac{\$7,399.00}{700}$ = $10.57 each.

b. $18.00 − $9.75 = $8.25 each.

c. $8.25 each.

Exercise No. 94

a.
Work in Process— Defective Goods	$211.40	
Work in Process		$211.40

Record cost of defective units @ $10.57 each.

b.
Work in Process— Defective Goods	165.00	
Work in Process		165.00

Record cost of defective units @ $8.25 each.

c.
Work in Process— Defective Goods	165.00	
Factory Overhead— Defective Goods	46.40	
Work in Process		211.40

Record cost of defective units @ $8.25 each but relieve Work in Process for 20 units @ $10.57 each.

Exercise No. 95

Factory Overhead

Payroll Summary	$ 2,302,00
Materials Requisition	1,025.00
Voucher Register	1,347.80
Insurance Expense	6,510.00
Factory Supplies	4,400.00
Depreciation Expense	15,320.00

Exercise No. 96

$$\$152,310 \times 1.10 = \$167,541$$

a. $\frac{\$167,541}{16,750 \text{ DLH}}$ = $10/direct labor hour.

b. $\frac{\$10/\text{DLH}}{\$5/\text{hour}}$ = $2/DLD (direct labor dollar).

Exercise No. 97

Factory Overhead

Actual $651,259	Applied $657,540
	(45,000 DLH ×
	$14.612/DLH)

Computations: $\dfrac{\$623,950}{42,700 \text{ DLH}} = \$14.612/\text{DLH}$

Total Variance: $651,259 − $657,540 = ($6,281)

Exercise No. 98

Budget Variance: $623,950 − $651,259
$$= \$27,309 \text{ Unfavorable}$$

Volume Variance:
$\dfrac{42,700 \text{ DLH}}{80\%} = 5,337.5 \text{ DLH/1\% capacity}$

85% × 5,337.5 = 45,368.75 DLH
(45,368.75 − 42,700) DLH × $14.612/DLH
$$= \$38,996 \quad \text{Favorable}$$

Efficiency Variance:
(45,368.75 − 45,000) DLH × $14.612/DLH
$$= \$ 5,388 \text{ Unfavorable}$$

$$\underline{\$ 6,299 \text{ Favorable}}$$

(The difference between the answer to Exercise No. 97 [$6,281] and the answer to this exercise is due to rounding.)

Exercise No. 99

Work in Process—Job 20

11/30/Year A	Labor	$ 9,468
	Material	2,253
	Overhead	4,450
	Balance	16,171
12/31/Year A	Labor	2,901
	Material	905
	Overhead	1,276
	Balance	21,253
1/31/Year B	Labor	203
	Material	347
	Overhead	93
	Balance	$21,896

Exercise No. 100

CALCULATIONS:

Material:
3,000# A @ $3.00/lb.	$ 9,000
2,000# B @ $15.00/lb.	30,000
5,000# Total Material	$39,000
4,000# completed (80%)	$31,200
1,000# in process (20%)	7,800
5,000#	$39,000

Labor:
4,000# (of end product) × 100%	4,000 e.u.	$16,000
1,000# (of end product) × 60%	600 e.u.	2,400
	4,600 e.u.	$18,400

Overhead:
$16,000 × 1.4	$22,400
$2,400 × 1.4	3,360
	$25,760

ANSWERS:

	Part a.	Part b.	Total
Material	$31,200	$7,800	$39,000
Labor	16,000	2,400	18,400
Overhead	22,400	3,360	25,760
Total	$69,600	$13,560	$83,160

Exercise No. 101

	Cost to Date	Cost to Complete	Total
Direct labor	$ 6,000	$ 9,000	$15,000
Direct material	14,000	—	14,000
Overhead	12,000	18,000	30,000
Total	$32,000	$27,000	$59,000

Exercise No. 102

Direct labor:	300 × 50%	=	150	
	1,500 × 100%	=	1,500	
	500 × 60%	=	300	1,950 e.u.
Direct material:	300 × 25%	=	75	
	1,500 × 100%	=	1,500	
	500 × 100%	=	500	2,075 e.u.
Overhead:	300 × 50%	=	150	
	1,500 × 100%	=	1,500	
	500 × 60%	=	300	1,950 e.u.

Exercise No. 103

Direct labor: $\dfrac{\$13,845}{1,950 \text{ e.u.}} = \$ 7.10/\text{e.u.}$

Direct material: $\dfrac{\$20,542}{2,075 \text{ e.u.}} = \$ 9.90/\text{e.u.}$

Overhead: $\dfrac{\$27,495}{1,950 \text{ e.u.}} = \$14.10/\text{e.u.}$

Exercise No. 104

	Sales Price	Percentages	Cost to Separation
a. Product A	$ 60,000	60%	$24,000
Product B	40,000	40	16,000
	$100,000	100%	$40,000

	Sales Price Less Added Conversion	Percentages	Cost to Separation
b. Product A	$50,000	83.33%	$33,333
Product B	10,000	16.67	6,667
	$60,000	100.00%	$40,000

Exercise No. 105

a.

7.1 hrs. × $8.40/hr.	= $ 59.64
7.0 hrs. × $8.00/hr.	= 56.00
Variance	= $ 3.64

b.

Excess time × standard wage rate (0.1 hrs.) × ($8.00/hr.)	= $ .80
Excess wage rate × actual time ($0.40/hr.) × (7.1 hrs.)	= 2.84
Variance	= $ 3.64

OR

Excess wage rate × standard time ($0.40/hr.) × (7.0 hrs.)	= $ 2.80
Excess time × actual wage rate (0.1 hr.) × ($8.40/hr.)	= .86
Variance	= $ 3.64

INDEX